LARRY MCMURTRY

Photo of Larry McMurtry by Diana Ossana. Courtesy of Larry McMurtry.

LARRY MCMURTRY

A Critical Companion

John M. Reilly

CRITICAL COMPANIONS TO POPULAR CONTEMPORARY WRITERS
Kathleen Gregory Klein, Series Editor

Greenwood Press
Westport, Connecticut • London

Library of Congress Cataloging-in-Publication Data

Reilly, John M. (John Marsden)
    Larry McMurtry : a critical companion / John M. Reilly.
      p. cm.—(Critical companions to popular contemporary writers, ISSN 1082–4979)
    Includes bibliographical references and index.
    ISBN 0–313–30300–2 (alk. paper)
    1. McMurtry, Larry—Criticism and interpretation. 2. McMurtry,
Larry—Examinations—Study guides. 3. Western stories—History and
criticism. I. Title. II. Series.
    PS3563.A319Z84   2000
    813'.54—dc21   99–049695

British Library Cataloguing in Publication Data is available.

Copyright © 2000 by John M. Reilly

All rights reserved. No portion of this book may be
reproduced, by any process or technique, without the
express written consent of the publisher.

Library of Congress Catalog Card Number: 99–049695
ISBN: 0–313–30300–2
ISSN: 1082–4979

First published in 2000

Greenwood Press, 88 Post Road West, Westport, CT 06881
An imprint of Greenwood Publishing Group, Inc.
www.greenwood.com

Printed in the United States of America

The paper used in this book complies with the
Permanent Paper Standard issued by the National
Information Standards Organization (Z39.48–1984).

10 9 8 7 6 5 4 3 2 1

For
Janet Louise Potter
Placet!

Contents

viii   Contents

Series Foreword

The authors who appear in the series Critical Companions to Popular Contemporary Writers are all best-selling writers. They do not simply have one successful novel, but a string of them. Fans, critics, and specialist readers eagerly anticipate their next book. For some, high cash advances and breakthrough sales figures are automatic; movie deals often follow. Some writers become household names, recognized by almost everyone.

But their novels are read one by one. Each reader chooses to start and, more importantly, to finish a book because of what she or he finds there. The real test of a novel is in the satisfaction its readers experience. This series acknowledges the extraordinary involvement of readers and writers in creating a best-seller.

The authors included in this series were chosen by an Advisory Board composed of high school English teachers and high school and public librarians. They ranked a list of best-selling writers according to their popularity among different groups of readers. For the first series, writers in the top-ranked group who had received no book-length, academic, literary analysis (or none in at least the past ten years) were chosen. Because of this selection method, Critical Companions to Popular Contemporary Writers meets a need that is being addressed nowhere else. The success of these volumes as reported by reviewers, librarians, and teachers led to an expansion of the series mandate to include some writers with wide critical attention—Toni Morrison, John Irving, and Maya Angelou, for example—to extend the usefulness of the series.

The volumes in the series are written by scholars with particular expertise in analyzing popular fiction. These specialists add an academic focus to the popular success that these writers already enjoy.

The series is designed to appeal to a wide range of readers. The general reading public will find explanations for the appeal of these well-known writers. Fans will find biographical and fictional questions answered. Students will find literary analysis, discussions of fictional genres, carefully organized introductions to new ways of reading the novels, and bibliographies for additional research. Whether browsing through the book for pleasure or using it for an assignment, readers will find that the most recent novels of the authors are included.

Each volume begins with a biographical chapter drawing on published information, autobiographies or memoirs, prior interviews, and, in some cases, interviews given especially for this series. A chapter on literary history and genres describes how the author's work fits into a larger literary context. The following chapters analyze the writer's most important, most popular, and most recent novels in detail. Each chapter focuses on one or more novels. This approach, suggested by the Advisory Board as the most useful to student research, allows for an in-depth analysis of the writer's fiction. Close and careful readings with numerous examples show readers exactly how the novels work. These chapters are organized around three central elements: plot development (how the story line moves forward), character development (what the reader knows of the important figures), and theme (the significant ideas of the novel). Chapters may also include sections on generic conventions (how the novel is similar to or different from others in its same category of science fiction, fantasy, thriller, etc.), narrative point of view (who tells the story and how), symbols and literary language, and historical or social context. Each chapter ends with an "alternative reading" of the novel. The volume concludes with a primary and secondary bibliography, including reviews.

The alternative readings are a unique feature of this series. By demonstrating a particular way of reading each novel, they provide a clear example of how a specific perspective can reveal important aspects of the book. In the alternative reading sections, one contemporary literary theory—way of reading, such as feminist criticism, Marxism, new historicism, deconstruction, or Jungian psychological critique—is defined in brief, easily comprehensible language. That definition is then applied to the novel to highlight specific features that might go unnoticed or be understood differently in a more general reading. Each volume defines two or three specific theories, making them part of the reader's understanding of how diverse meanings may be constructed from a single novel.

Taken collectively, the volumes in the Critical Companions to Popular Contemporary Writers series provide a wide-ranging investigation of the complexities of current best-selling fiction. By treating these novels seriously as both literary works and publishing successes, the series demonstrates the potential of popular literature in contemporary culture.

Kathleen Gregory Klein
Southern Connecticut State University

LARRY MCMURTRY

1

The Life of Larry McMurtry

Although Larry McMurtry can produce dialogue, character, and compelling story to compete with the best of American authors, for the audience that gives him its devotion by elevating his novels to best-sellers, shares the sentiment and nostalgia of their film adaptations, and avidly follows the adventures related in the television miniseries made from still others of his works, he will always be a voice of the Southwest. Most of this audience also counts him deservedly popular, because they take his stories to be not simply entertaining, and surely not glamorous in their portrayal of the Southwest, but authentic. His writing echoes in some ways the contrivances of cowboy westerns made familiar in inexpensive paperbacks, cheaper magazines, and Grade B movies. His characters include figures seemingly as stereotypical as any easterner could imagine a Texan to be. But when McMurtry does the Western, he seems to ring true for the most skeptical readers or viewers who might be lying in wait for the exaggerations and glorification of old-time myths.

Not surprisingly, then, McMurtry's audience has a natural interest in how he manages, most of the time at least, to get it right. His biography is not disappointing on that score. Larry (Jeff) McMurtry was born on June 3, 1936 in Wichita Falls, Texas, the son of rancher William Jefferson McMurtry, Jr. and his wife, Hazel Ruth (neé McIver) McMurtry. The elder McMurtry was one of nine sons born to the first William Jefferson McMurtry (1858–1940) and Louisa Frances McMurtry (1859–1946), who

came to Denton County, Texas in 1877 from Missouri. In an essay entitled "Take My Saddle from the Wall: A Valediction," Larry explains that
when his grandparents arrived in Denton County, sixty miles west of
Dallas, "the fearsome Comanche had been but recently subdued—in fact,
it was still too early to tell whether they *were* subdued," because there
were skirmishes as late as 1879 (*In a Narrow Grave*, 145). In 1889, though,
the couple moved farther west to Archer County, where they bought a
half-section of land located along an old military road used by cowboys
driving their cattle north. Here it was possible for the McMurtry boys
"to [just] step out their door to see their hero figures riding past" (*In a
Narrow Grave*, 146).

Since his grandfather died when Larry was four, he was known to the
boy only by a handful of stories, including one about his having been a
reformed drunk whose jug of whiskey hung untouched from a nail in
the saddle room for nineteen years. Larry's grandmother, who survived
(deaf and ailing) five years longer than her husband, took her place in
the boy's memory as a stern woman, spoken of by her children as "one
speaks of the Power" (*In a Narrow Grave*, 143–44). The offspring of William Jefferson and Louisa Frances McMurtry were quite another sort of
influence, for his uncles provided Larry vivid examples of the ways of
cowboys. Uncle Jim was a supreme rider of broncs, who was recorded
to have broken seventeen incorrigible horses in one day. Uncle Roy
rivaled Jim in riding bucking horses. Their brothers, Charley and John,
ran an operation in the Texas Panhandle "which at times involved as
many as 4,000 cattle" (*In a Narrow Grave*, 154). It seems that most of the
McMurtry boys about the age of seventeen left for the Panhandle, where
the town of Clarendon "was their Paris" (*In a Narrow Grave*, 155). Seven
of the boys and two of the girls stayed there for life, and young Larry
would join them in family reunions to listen to shared stories and learn
about the standards and values of people who had grown up in touch
with the grand doings of cattle raising in the Southwest.

Years after, when he was writing his valedictory essay, Larry Mc-
Murtry would devote more space to his Uncle Johnny than to any of the
other boys who went to Clarendon; perhaps because Johnny presented
the essence of the hard life of the plains. Johnny settled well outside of
town on such land that "I thought the first time I saw it that only a man
who considered himself forsaken of God would live in such country."
His bed had eleven quilts, "compensation, no doubt, for having wintered
on the baldies with one blanket." Like all the other McMurtrys, Johnny
was a "near-fanatic" worker, even after his movement was hindered by

arthritis and numerous broken bones. "For nostalgia's sake [Johnny] grazed a few [old] animals among them a large male elk and an aging buffalo bull" (*In a Narrow Grave*, 164–68). With this description of his uncle Johnny in mind, it is not hard to see where Larry McMurtry found inspiration for the detailed portrait of the old man Homer Bannon in *Horseman, Pass By*.

It was this intimate association with a family whose memories could reach back to the early settlement of Texas and whose character was formed by experiences as cowhands and ranchers that seems to have fixed Larry McMurtry's vision upon the historical changes unique to the Southwest. In the foreword to *In a Narrow Grave*, he describes his love of Texas by analogy to the scene in Shakespeare where the god abandons Marc Antony. In Shakespeare's play, the guards hear a strange music that marks the departure, and McMurtry can believe that he has heard such music himself "in Fort Worth, Houston, Dallas; by the Rio Grande and the Brazos; in the brush country and on the staked plains." Sometimes the god appears in the guise of Teddy Blue or Old Man Goodnight, two famous historical cowboys whom McMurtry imports into his fiction, "but the one thing that is sure is that he was a horseman, and a god of the country. His home was the frontier, and his mythos celebrates those masculine ideals appropriate to a frontier" (xii). This may be about all one needs to know to start to comprehend Larry McMurtry's inevitable literary subject. Possibly it contributes, too, some sense of the source of his authenticity.

There is more, though, some of it complicating the impression that Larry McMurtry works like a channel for the spiritualism of the West. For one thing McMurtry and his parents did not stay long on his grandfather's ranch. When he was six years old, they took a house in Archer City. This made him a witness to the differences between ranch and town life and, as Mark Busby remarks, gave the future novelist material for one of his leading themes (Busby 1995, 6). There were also predilections of character that contribute to an account of how Larry McMurtry became a writer. By his own testimony, he was a bookish boy who discovered the joys of literature at age twelve upon reading *Don Quixote*, a story of the disappearance of an earlier heroic life in Europe that must have resonated with McMurtry's observations of the passing of the Old West.

Larry McMurtry graduated with honors from Archer City High School in 1954, having been an editorial writer on the school newspaper, a member of the band for four years, a letterman in basketball and baseball, and an officer in the 4-H Club (Peavy 1977, 13). He enrolled for one semester at Rice University in Houston, but, failing mathematics, decided to transfer to North Texas State College in Denton where he became a formal student of literature (Busby 1995, 9–10). While at North Texas, he wrote from time to time for the student magazine *Avesta*. One of his contributions was a study of the Beat writers Jack Kerouac, Allen Ginsberg, and Kenneth Rexroth (Moritz, 276). He also published fiction, poetry, and essays in an alternative literary magazine called *Coexistence Review*, including a section of the novel he was writing that would be published in 1961 as *Horseman, Pass By* (Busby, 11). Two other stories McMurtry wrote while at North Texas also provided substance to the novel he continued to draft in the summer after graduation and finished the next fall when he went back to Rice University for graduate school (Busby, 14).

While studying for a Master of Arts degree in English at Rice, McMurtry began contributing book reviews to the *Houston Post*. He also married, on July 15, 1959, Jo Ballard Scott, a woman he had met in Denton where she attended Texas Woman's University. They had one child—James L. McMurtry—and divorced in 1966. James is now a prominent singer and composer, inevitably compared for his ballads to his father. After completing his degree at Rice in 1960, McMurtry won a fellowship that allowed him to enter Stanford University's creative writing program, then under the direction of the novelist Wallace Stegner. The quality of the Stanford program can be seen from the fact that some of McMurtry's classmates were Ernest Gaines, Tillie Olsen, Ken Kesey, and Robert Stone, each to become a noted and influential writer in later years (Busby, 16). While at Stanford, he also began to work as a book scout, an avocation that would lead him into a secondary career as bookseller and provide him background useful for the novel *Cadillac Jack*.

McMurtry took a teaching job at Texas Christian University in Fort Worth for the 1961–62 academic year; then in 1963–64 returned to Rice University for a faculty position that he retained through 1969, except for a year's leave in 1964 underwritten by a Guggenheim Fellowship. During these years, he completed a trilogy comprising the novel he began as an undergraduate student—*Horseman, Pass By*; an elegiac story of a love triangle, *Leaving Cheyenne*; and his satiric novel of small-town life, *The Last Picture Show*, which he ironically dedicated to his hometown of Archer City.

In 1969, Larry McMurtry moved into a new orbit. Settling into Waterford, Virginia, very near to Washington, D.C. and later into Washington itself, he taught at George Mason University in Fairfax and briefly at

American University in D.C., while he opened a bookstore called "Booked Up" with partners Marcia McGhee Carter and John Curtis. During this time, he also contributed book reviews to the Washington *Post*. But whatever other occupations he undertook, he continued to work on his writing with the proverbial assiduity of the McMurtry family. In 1971, the writing included work on the screenplay for *The Last Picture Show* with Peter Bogdanovich.

The notice he has received as a Western author, together with his evident ability to write quickly, has led McMurtry into a continuing affair with Hollywood. In the 1970s, he wrote a series of columns for *American Film* magazine, later collected in the volume *Film Flam* (1987). Stimulated by thoughts about the illusory qualities of movies to consider the matter of truth in fiction, he tells the readers of *Film Flam* that the day-to-day work of his life in writing fiction amounts to "a long and rather intricate cat-and-mouse game with Truth." Although it is sometimes hard to say if the author is the cat and truth the mouse, or the reverse, what he has learned is "that for a novelist to suppose that he is wedded to Truth is a flat absurdity. A novelist works with lies" (145). What does that suggest about the reputation of the writer of authentic tales? A tentative answer seems to occur a few pages later in *Film Flam*, where McMurtry is writing about fantasy. Fantasy is the very essence of films, he says. "One sees time and again [in the movie theater] how easily human beings can be made to accept with their emotions what they could never be made to believe with their brains. As long as there are human images to anchor to, emotionally, then the incredibility of the action not only doesn't detract from the film's appeal, but is crucial to it," because audiences "do not want to see movies in which people do what they might be expected to do . . . what they respond to most deeply is the heroic—the triumph over circumstance" (148).

Taking these comments with license to substitute literature for fiction in McMurtry's formulation, it seems that the affair with movies has given him the means to articulate a kind of "authentic" reality. His mode of writing is not what he terms "pedestrian realism," neither is it always marked by verisimilitude or the appearance of actuality—although McMurtry's descriptive powers convey palpable physical experience superbly well. Instead, he writes with an intention to relate some deeper felt reality, a reality conveyed largely through representation of the feel of experience, and feelings about it—feelings of the sort he expresses in "Take My Saddle from the Wall" and in his admission to a grandiose sense of loss of a god in the foreword to *In a Narrow Grave*.

Evidently, it has not always been easy for McMurtry to tap into that sort of Aristotelian truth—it was Aristotle who said that imaginative writing is more true than history. Critics view the books he published during the half-decade of 1978 to 1983 (*Somebody's Darling, Cadillac Jack, The Desert Rose*) as a low point in his career. Still, it was just a few years later that McMurtry's imaginative return to historical Texas won the Pulitzer Prize for *Lonesome Dove*.

Satisfying as the Pulitzer had to be for McMurtry, the period of time when he passed from an apparent critical decline to renewal of his reputation as a major author was an exceptionally difficult time personally. In 1991, Larry McMurtry was diagnosed with heart disease. He had just completed a term as president of the American Center of PEN, an organization dedicated to artistic freedom, during which he had worked especially strenuously in defense of Salman Rushdie, the Anglo-Indian author condemned to death by the Ayatollah Khomeni for the alleged blasphemy in his novel *Satanic Verses*. Despite the diagnosis made in June, McMurtry continued to work on his current novel-in-progress, *The Evening Star*, and delayed treatment for his condition until December, when he had a quadruple heart-bypass operation (Busby 1995, 26–27). The surgical procedure was a success, but the consequences to his state of mind were severely threatening. According to David Streitfeld, writing in the Washington *Post*, after his operation, McMurtry lost his appetite for reading, found it impossible to write, and had no interest any longer in traveling. He had nighttime terrors, insomnia that kept him from sleeping through till dawn, and a general feeling of disorientation. All he could do, Streifeld relates, was sit on his friend Diana Ossana's couch in Tucson staring into space and feeling, as McMurtry wrote in a later unpublished essay, "largely posthumous . . . my old psyche, or old self, was shattered—now it whirls around me in fragments" (Streitfeld, C1). One needs to look no further for explanation of the felt significance for the author of *Duane's Depressed*, the novel in which McMurtry shows Duane Moore, once a young man like McMurtry himself in Archer City, looking in middle age for therapy to repair his fragmented ego.

McMurtry's real-life therapy included collaboration with Diana Ossana on two novels and other projects, as well as reentry into the career of a bookman. When he was at Stanford, McMurtry had begun to work as a book scout, that is, a person who searches out editions and matches them with dealers or buyers. While living around Washington, he developed his avocation into a business. More recently, though, he has become something of an impresario of books. Home again in Archer

City, he is constructing a book city, buildings jam packed with books of all kinds—a destination, he expects, for buyers from all over the country, and one cannot help but believe, a project of reparation. In his novels, McMurtry turned Archer City into the fictional Thalia; now he is making the town also physically the locale of literature, by the ton.

McMurtry thinks he is now more than 75 percent recovered from his experience with death-in-life (Streitfeld). Indeed, since his heart attack he has published the novels completing the series begun with *Lonesome Dove*. These sequels and prequels show that his grasp on his Western project is as strong as ever. Together with the popular television miniseries taking the narratives to ever larger audiences, the recent publications of Larry McMurtry are sufficient to confirm the impression held by so many of his readers: He is authentic. By undertaking a rewriting of Western history, he has reengaged the sources of the Western myth, not only in the *Lonesome Dove* series, but also in additional projects. Novels about Calamity Jane, Buffalo Bill, and Billy the Kid recreate the foundations of the commercialized myths of the West. Meanwhile, McMurtry's habit of revisiting his characters' lives has resulted in a continuation of the story begun in *The Desert Rose* entitled *The Late Child*, and a return to the site of *The Last Picture Show* in *Texasville*. And, as if that were not enough to occupy a compulsive McMurtry, there are the collaborations with Diana Ossana, opening with a retelling of a latter-day outlaw's story, *Pretty Boy Floyd*.

Rightly enough, it has been said that a writer's biography has no exceptional importance in itself. We want to know about an author's life only because he or she writes books that are important to us. After details of education, prizes, marriage and divorce, illness, jobs, and residences are noted, we reach the conclusion that the writer's life is writing. To the writing of Larry McMurtry, then, we must now turn our attention.

2

Larry McMurtry and the Genres of the Popular Western and the Historical Novel

More than other popular literary genres, the Western shows its roots in a historic time and place. Although it can be argued that detective fiction arose in distinctly modern conditions or urban society, tales about sleuths cracking cases have been set in countryside and city, contemporary and past times, and many of the inhabited spots on the globe. The popular romance had its sources in the sentimental fiction written to address the interests of middle-class audiences of the eighteenth and nineteenth centuries, but heart-tugging accounts of the obstacles overcome before the eventual union of lovers have found locale and milieu in all sorts of societies. Only the most ingenious readers and critics, though, would account a story legitimately Western if it did not make use of the American landscape west of the Mississippi River and east of California. This is the land of the "Great Plains" and "The Big Sky," where the business of raising cattle fostered the special craft of the cowboy. Cattle have been basic to the economy of many other people, such as the Fulani of West Africa, other nations such as Argentina, and other American locales, such as Florida and Hawaii, but the literature of cowboys and cattle was created in celebration of a brief chapter in the history of the arrival of European-American settlement on the American plains after the Civil War.

That chapter opened after the consolidation of the national economy through the victory of the Union and after the routes of trade and population movement shifted from a north-south axis dependent upon river and coastal shipping to an east-west axis. Easterners spilled into new territories to take advantage of land secured from the Native Americans to increase agricultural production required by the industrializing cities that would soon experience a seemingly endless period of technological development and the growing pressures of populations relocating from the Old South and arriving from Europe. Richly detailed as it was, the chapter nevertheless spanned a brief period of time, from the arrival of the newcomers who displaced Indians (and in the Southwest, the Mexicans, whose territory was captured in the U.S.-Mexican War), and the closure of open land instigated by the spreading use of barbed wire, which by the 1880s was being manufactured at the rate of 10,000 pounds a year (Allmendinger, 43). During that window of time, the great trail drives of cattle from the lower states to middle western rail heads created the occupation of the cowboy herder. As railroads spanned the continent, the U.S. Army drove Native Americans onto reservations, and towns grew in the West, the window of cowboy glory times closed, changing the free riders of the plains into ranch workers.

That brief chapter of Western history resonates with meaning far exceeding its duration in time, for it seemed to epitomize the significance of the American frontier. In fact, one of the most famous essays in American historical writing bears a title pointing that up. In 1893, Frederick Jackson Turner, a historian at the University of Wisconsin, issued "The Significance of the Frontier in American History," arguing that the experience of the frontier had a determining and lasting influence in creating American institutions and character. The influence of Turner's thesis on American historical scholarship, and popular thought, can hardly be overestimated. The thesis became an article of fundamental belief in the American academy influencing the practice and study of history for generations, especially as it argued that the United States represented social developments and "offered a laboratory to study the evolution of society" in general (Foner and Garraty, 1090).

Turner's thesis most likely would not have had the effect it did, though, without considerable preparation of the popular consciousness of Americans. The first commercially successful novelist in American literature—James Fenimore Cooper—seized worldwide attention with his series of leatherstocking tales, the second of which in the order of composition was *The Prairie* (1827), a novel that recounted the passage of the frontier scout Natty Bumppo from eastern woodlands to open West. The formula developed by Cooper of an independent man at home in the wilderness but serving at the same time as the advance guard of settlement soon was applied by the writers of midcentury dime novels.

Yet another stream feeding the growth of popular frontier writing flowed from the stories of Indian captivities and wars. Older than the nation, these writings began as early as the seventeenth century when New Englanders such as the redoubtable Mary Rowlandson wrote of her capture in 1676 by Narragansett Indians in one of the campaigns that came to be known as King Philip's War. Published in 1682 under the title *A Narrative of the Captivity and Restauration of Mrs. Mary Rowlandson*, the work set forth in compellingly active prose an account of physical suffering and psychological terror that helped to foster the Manichean (i.e., a doctrine of eternal conflict between good and evil) conception of embattled settlers versus Indians that was common currency in frontier writing. Captivity stories on Rowlandson's model followed through the next two centuries as regularly as the waves of settlement moving West.

As so often happens in literature, change is not merely incremental. One day there are stories of frontier scouts, then suddenly a new genre seems to emerge; that was the case with the Western. Captivity and Indian war stories circulated. Derivations from Cooper's leatherstocking fiction appeared about other sections of the country. Then, in 1902, came the work that scholars and critics generally consider to be the first full-fledged Western: *The Virginian*, by Owen Wister (1860–1938), a Philadelphian of prominent family. At Harvard University, Wister became friends with Theodore Roosevelt, another easterner in whose career the West would figure. In 1885, Wister took a journey to the West for his health and became fascinated with the life of the section. According to Richard Slotkin, writing in *Gunfighter Nation*, Wister was a man perceiving a threat to the Eastern elite from the waves of foreign immigration into the United States. In the Cheyenne Club, a group of powerful Wyoming ranchers, he found a model for natural aristocrats operating outside the law by, for instance, lynching illegal cattle traders (170–71). Wister made annual trips to the West, even after he became a practicing attorney. Those visits provided him material for short stories about the disappearance of the Old West filled with the observations of local color that he collected in his journals. The transformation from Old West to a newer, settled West he embodied in the story of *The Virginian*, a man from the East as his title indicates, who scales the occupational ladder from cowboy to ranch owner. As an idealized hero, the Virginian is of "natural" nobility, his career signifying something on the order of the evolution which Frederick Jackson Turner suggested could be traced in the laboratory of the frontier West. The Virginian is a knight of the plains. His eventual bride is Molly Wood, a teacher come from the East (Vermont) to "civilize" the West. Of course, the tale also includes cattle rustlers and a villain, named Trampas, who serves as nemesis to the heroic Virginian.

The book was a great commercial success. Julian Mason, in *The Dictionary of Literary Biography*, reports that it was reprinted fifteen times within eight months. By 1911, it had been reprinted thirty-eight times, and by 1938, it was estimated that 1.5 million copies had been sold. Interestingly, the period of colossal sales of *The Virginian* was preceded by similarly impressive distribution of Western stories in pulp versions. In 1884, Beadle's Pocket Library introduced the series of tales about Deadwood Dick. Street and Smith entered the market in 1901 with their Buffalo Bill series that ran to 591 issues between 1901 and 1912. It was then followed by the *New Buffalo Bill Weekly* that ran until 1917. In 1902, the same year as *The Virginian* appeared, the mass market saw the appearance of the initial publications about "Young Wild West," a hero with a sense of right and wrong as solid as the Virginian's (Dinan, 11–12). The author of the Buffalo Bill stories was Ned Buntline (who appears as a character in Larry McMurtry's fiction), a well-known writer of latter-day frontier stories who functioned as a link between the earlier tales of Cooper and the captivity writers and Western pulp stories. Conclusive evidence of the enormous popularity of the formulas developed by the creators of the Western may be seen in the fact that the German author Karl May, who took over the formulas lock, stock, and barrel, sold more than 26 million copies of his German language stories of the West by the 1960s (Atherarn, 186).

Some insight into the composition of the Western stories that succeeded upon the appearance of *The Virginian* and the pulp stories is to be found in the testimony of editors and authors. Frank Blackwell, editor of Street and Smith's *Western Story Magazine*, reportedly tried to simplify the plots for his magazine to contain three components: pursuit, capture, and delayed revelation. Max Brand, one of the most famous and accomplished Western story authors, claimed that his rule of composition was to present a good man turned bad, and a bad man turned good. Frank Gruber, a master of pulp stories, classified the basic plots as follows: the Union Pacific Railroad story, the ranch story, the empire story, the revenge story, Custer's last stand, the outlaw story, and the marshall story (Dinan, 51 ff.). Of course, the insight yielded by such simplification is that the production of Westerns took on the character of factory work, with the stories composed of prefabricated, interchangeable parts.

Not all historians of the Western are satisfied by that characterization, however. John R. Milton, in *The Novel of the American West*, maintains that there is "a serious Western novel (as distinguished from popular Western)." The origins of serious authenticity Milton locates in derivation of an interest in the West that "is descended from the Western travel narratives and journals of exploration, from the nonformulaic side of Cooper and from the mixture of determinism and mysticism as found in the naturalism of Frank Norris" (106). The travel and exploration narratives supply to fiction the attention to physical detail and its impressive scale. The naturalism of Norris, as it appears, for example, in *The Octopus* (1901), dramatizes mankind subject to natural forces.

In contrast to Milton, some critics see no need to establish two tiers of Western writing in order to detect its power. John G. Cawelti in *Six-Gun Mystique* maintains that the Western crystallizes the frontier encounter of social order and lawlessness. Townspeople are the representatives of civilization who encounter outlaws or savages. In the middle are the heroes, the cowboy knights who are capable of violence but act in service of order (75–76). Indeed, Cawelti sees the dynamic position of the middle figures, the heroes, as a literary means of working out the philosophical justification for violent aggression (42).

The contrast between the approaches to Western story represented by Milton and Cawelti can be summarized in this way: Milton's apparent interest lies in the localized qualities of texts, that is, the techniques evident in singular texts allowing us to give them individualized interpretations. This approach becomes a path productive of the sort of quality judgments leading critics to select a canon or list of the "best" works. It is the approach that has created the idea that William Faulkner and Toni Morrison are outstanding American novelists, because their narrative prose displays unique accomplishments of structure, characterization, and theme. The approach to Western story employed by Cawelti for his study of the *Six-Gun Mystique* directs our attention instead toward summing up the habitual practices of Western writers so that the critic can establish a type distinctive from any other.

Each approach has its instrumental merits. Later in this book, the special construction Larry McMurtry places upon the Western will be the focus of discussion. The efficacy of that sort of discussion, however, will require the use of a background against which to display McMurtry's artistry. The regularized patterns or conventions of the Western story type establishes that background.

A survey of popular treatments of the West allows the stipulation of the following conventions: The leading figure(s) is/are resourceful individualists. Occupationally, the protagonist may be an official agent of the law or simply a man devoted to orderly ways of living. While he must possess the acquired skills of horsemanship marking him as a masterful cowpoke, he must also have learned methods of applying violence to outlaws, particularly the use of firearms. These skills are characteristically accompanied by great physical stamina. The cowboy might or might not be physically prepossessing because of his muscularity, size, and appearance, but, as C. L. Sonnichsen insists in his book, *From Hopalong to Hud: Thoughts on Western Fiction*, the chief trait of the cowboy shall always be guts (104).

Other conventions of the Western story place emphasis on the topography of the West. The treatment of setting can vary, in terms set by Max Westbrook, from description no more valid than a facsimile to an evident "denotative authenticity" that can summon a sense of actual place in the minds of readers ("The Authentic Western"), but reference to vast space and disinterested nature always signals the audience that they are witnessing a Western (Bucco).

The comments mentioned earlier by Frank Blackwell, Max Brand, and Frank Gruber about the construction of Westerns indicate that there are also clear conventions of plot. The chief of those is simplicity of conflict. As everyone familiar with popular culture has learned, there are good guys and bad guys who, by the necessity of narrative, must struggle for dominance. Very often, that struggle is attenuated in a lengthy pursuit across miles of landscape, or it can recur in a central spot, such as a frontier town. Conflict may not be limited to human struggle either, for the climactic conditions of the West so often turn inhospitable that struggle may also entail a battle by men trying simply to survive. An obvious result of the sorts of struggles spotlighted in the Western is that the plots invariably include extended physical action. The minds of cowboys receive reference, but the convention of Westerns is to sublimate psychology within outward behavior. Finally, the plots of Westerns are typically linear: events follow upon each other in the framework of sequential time. In other words, traditional Newtonian physics of time and space govern the universe of the Western.

Moving beyond the elemental conventions of the Western into matters related to theme, it can be seen that violence and aggression are always also distinguishing features of the Western genre. The violence may be enacted by outlaws or lawmen. Aggression is necessary in either case. Due to the violence, the Western story shows a preoccupation with death and the fragility of life. Sometimes a Western story will romanticize a protagonist—awarding him the manners of a courteous knight, for example—but the Western rarely takes a romantic view of life or human nature. The villains of a Western are not misunderstood victims of society; instead, they are studies in pathology, lacking any reasonable motive for their evil, unrestrained by ethics or superego in the commission of their assaults. The terrain is spotted with figures of evil, added to whom is the harshness of nature that typifies the geography of open land where beating sun, blasting chill, torrential storms, and wild animals threaten life regularly.

In such an environment where the fabric of society is rendered invisible, character is determined by individual traits rather than social influence. Heroes and villains alike are individualists. Values and motivation must be self-created, for there is no schooling from culture or society available to the lone self. The Western hero is, thus, very much like the existential hero of modern literature and philosophy, which accounts in part for the near-universal appeal of the Western story. At the heart of the genre's history, then, lies this paradox. The conventions of the Western genre yield clear traces of its origin in the specific time and conditions of the American West; yet, through the practiced manipulation of historically rooted conventions, the Western conveys a complex of themes with broader application.

By the reference to Frederick Jackson Turner, this discussion has suggested that the Western can be read as an exploration of the civic beliefs of American democracy. In this light, the cowboy. assumes the role of a hero of American expansion, carrying the special principles of American political values to wilderness lands. The cowboy president Theodore Roosevelt, who looked back upon his time in the Dakota Territory as a formative experience, embodied this outlook when he took Western inspiration for everything from his Rough Rider garb to his campaign as a trust buster. On this level, the Western operates as an allegory of American civilization, with the cowboy, who claims the land and rids it of outlaws and savages, serving as the agent of the progress presumed to inhere in the American way of life.

Still, it would be a mistake to take the Western's power to transcend its historical time and place as indication of its universality. One of the clearest signs that it is less than universal in its thematic concerns can be seen from the fact that the genre's major characters are uniformly male. Women can have a place in the Western, but always subordinate to men. Richard Slotkin reminds us in *Gunfighter Nation* that Zane Grey, the most popular Western writer of all time, frequently put the endemic violence of the genre to use in order to have the hero redeem the "white" woman from peril (214–16). Being victimized, the female character sets plot in motion, but her role is always as object, never as subject of the story. Lee Clark Mitchell develops the dominance of men in the Western into a thesis, claiming that the genre seems devoted to fretting over the "construction of masculinity." Noting the prevalence of scenes of injury and recovery in Western stories, Mitchell concludes that the physicality of the male body preoccupies writers and readers who intuit that the cowboy presents a figure on whom to play images of masculinity (27).

The fullest elaboration on themes of masculinity to date has been developed by Jane P. Tompkins in *West of Everything*. The evidence Tompkins summons in her study includes: the notable absence of references to church or deity in Westerns, even though the prevalence of death makes all other considerations trivial; the depiction of characters who show by their deadpan noncommunicative manner that they distrust language and sentiment; and the barren terrain where the cowboy rides without recourse to home or hearth. From the assembly of her evidence, she infers that the Western constitutes a rebuttal of the domestic female fiction of the nineteenth century. Although it may seem that Tompkins takes a negative view of the Western, she announces at the opening of her study that she is devoted to the genre. Her skill as a professional historical critic, however, has led her to produce one of the more illuminating investigations of the origins of the Western and the continuing subliminal appeal of its forthright masculine bias.

Larry McMurtry is a student as well as an author of works in the Western genre. Without doubt, he has made himself widely read in the literature of the West and on occasion has written about it in the manner of a critic. More important to his place in American letters than his extensive reading about the West and Westerns though, has been the thought he has given to all the genre relates about historical and contemporary America. He began his career and gained his initial fame with a series of novels that subject the mythic memory of the Wild West to an examination that is sometimes ironic, other times satiric. From his own commentary on *Horseman, Pass By*, *Leaving Cheyenne*, and *The Last Picture Show*, it appears that his purpose in those novels was to illustrate how the conventions of the Western, and the values they represent, have become anachronistic. The three novels that comprise the Houston trilogy—*Moving On, All My Friends Are Going to Be Strangers*, and *Terms of Endearment*—altered the setting of narrative from rural to urban Texas with an aim of examining the possibility for men and women to find in the contemporary American West new codes for life as viable as those that fading memory tells us arose from the legendary West. After a period when he seemed to have left thoughts of Western tradition behind, McMurtry began an extensive project in which he has set out to review and rewrite the history of the Old West. All of these works resonate against the patterns of the popular Western. In more recent books like *Lonesome Dove* and its sequels—*Streets of Laredo, Dead Men Walking*, and *Comanche Moon*—he reaches back in search of a West that has not been filtered through the selective practices of Western dime and pulp novels, the popular paperbacks, and the line of writers represented by Zane Grey and Max Brand.

By reconstructing the popular Western genre, McMurtry aims to reveal its concealed underside. Where the popular Western achieves a triumphal effect by leaving unstated whatever might diminish the scale of heroic adventure (hardships are tests of manly mettle and never tediously discomforting; combat is never ambiguous, but always a contest between the righteous and the profane), McMurtry's Westerns are notable for supplying their readers a ground-level perspective that supplants glorious allegory with a narrative of plausible experiences happening to probable people. To introduce this sort of realism, McMurtry draws upon yet another literary genre—the historical novel.

Narrative with historical furnishings and themes has long been evident in literature. The medieval romances, once their subjects were no longer contemporary, became "historical." The novel commonly cited as the first of the Gothic fictions, Horace Walpole's *The Castle of Otranto* (1764), employed costuming and incidents contrived to manufacture an odd antique milieu. What was lacking from narrative fiction set in the past until the nineteenth century was "precisely the specifically historical, that is, derivation of the individuality of characters from the historical peculiarity of their age" (Lukacs, 19). With Sir Walter Scott's novels of the Scottish adventure, the lack was remedied, for Scott made the events of the emerging nation fundamental to the plots of his fiction. In other words, the characters of *Waverly* (1814) and *Ivanhoe* (1819) and the rest of the popular series enact a story of historical process. The characters are both products of a historical time and projections of the historical forces Walter Scott discerns in the past. With the example of Scott before them, Charles Dickens wrote a novel of the French Revolution (*A Tale of Two Cities*, 1859); Leo Tolstoy wrote of the Napoleonic invasion of Russia (*War and Peace*, 1869); Alessandro Manzoni embraced the cause of Italian unity (*The Betrothed*, 1827); and in the United States, James Fenimore Cooper began a career as a historical author with *The Spy* (1821). By the third quarter of the century, writers encouraged by the wave of nationalism spreading across Europe and America made the historical novel, which proved so useful in affirming the origin of nation states, an established genre available to the applications of many popular authors. Within a short time, however, the genre's popularity went into decline as the realistic novel became increasingly an instrument for the examination of the massive changes occurring in contemporary society. While realism appropriated the formula of the historical novel to treat contemporary character as the product and projection of industrializing society, fiction about the episodes of past history became a rarity to be revived in such *tours de force* as Margaret Mitchell's glorification of the Confederacy in *Gone with the Wind* (1936), Robert Graves's resuscitation of ancient Rome in *I, Claudius* (1934), and William Faulkner's profound investigation of the South figured in his mythic Yoknapatowpha County, Mississippi. Otherwise, fictionalized history reverted to patterns of popular romance, casting a soft glow of erotic scandal over tales of past times that never were.

In his series about Texas Rangers, Larry McMurtry seeks to revisit the nineteenth-century genre of historical fiction. In the process, his work revives significant critical questions about the relationship between fact and fiction. Which is more profound, asked the ancients, history or poetry? Plato exiled the poets from his ideal republic, because their skillful ways of imaginative invention tempt listeners to disregard truth. Aristotle declared poetry to be more truthful than history, because, in its freedom from the rigor of particular factual reporting, it deals with universal truth. With the advent of the age of prose and the formation of the novel during the seventeenth and eighteenth centuries, the issue became rephrased as a contest between the empirical and the fictional. In the early novel, the "facts" might be thought to appear in the third-person descriptive sections of a narrative, while the fictional would be revealed in the authorial commentary that often accompanied the narrative. Thus, in the American best-seller of the eighteenth-century *Charlotte Temple: A Tale of Truth* (1794), the description of Charlotte's seduction by an army officer constitutes the "facts," and the author Susanna Rowson's direct assertion that she got her story from a reliable source and the words of caution she addresses to readers about Charlotte's behavior are to be taken as the invented portion of the book.

Of course, direct authorial address became in time inappropriate in novels, because the intention advanced by realism was to simulate reality on the page, that is, to create a veritable reality, the spell of which could not be broken by the admission of passages that would expose the creator behind the scenes. Rather than resolving an incompatability between the empirical or factual and the invented, the newer style of the novel compounded the problem of determining historical truth. One way to evade the problem was to introduce into the narrative references to events and personages that can be verified by other documents. By laying credible and certifiable details into the narrative, the whole becomes believable. This is the manner of writing known as narrative history, in which there is room for speculation—perhaps some invented but possible dialogue and some plausible exploration of motives—but the dependable details offer assurance that historical truth is the subject. Evocation of certifiably valid factual references comprises a basic technique of McMurtry's novels about Woodrow Call and Augustus McRae (the protagonists of *Lonesome Dove*), but it is a technique insufficient to relate the whole story.

Even as readers feel convinced of the accuracy of fiction in its outlines, they remain open to the persuasion of an interpretation of the dependable facts. Facts, it turns out, do not speak for themselves. They provide materials for reflection, or for a crafty writer to arrange in an effectively impressive way, but if the facts are only raw material, then the truth is arbitrary. How do we know the actuality we call history? We read about it somewhere. Searching texts, we form an idea of the past. The search is not altogether uncritical. We square what we read now with what we have read elsewhere before and make judgments about plausibility. Still, someone filtered the information we read through the structures of his or her mind. Subjectivity is unavoidable, and it is the seedbed of invention. The more we reflect upon the distinction between fact and fiction, the more it seems that, because truth eludes our grasp, there are only available to readers versions of fiction. And for authors, writing takes on the requirements of argument in favor of their own version.

Larry McMurtry's repeated challenges to the myths of the Old West appear in this light to be criticisms of historical arguments he judges to be false, because they have dressed the past improbably. Rather than presenting the actors of the Western story in the midst of routines that reason tells us must have been harsh and boring, at least at times, the mythmakers have omitted from their accounts the gaps between adventures. Then, exaggerating the valor of adventure itself, they plot their stories as either a string of triumphs or a glorious defeat. Like the paintings of Custer's last stand that once hung in barrooms across the country, the glorified stories of the Old West perform a feat of synecdoche (figurative language in which a part is used to signify a whole, e.g., "crown represents the institution of monarchy"). Were he to adopt the terms of the critical debate about the empirical and fictional, fact and invention, McMurtry might say that the legends and myths about the West have clouded our minds so that we cannot distinguish baseless invention from likely reality. By filling in the omissions from the myths, expanding upon the detail of ordinary experience, and by portraying his characters as products of the forces he sees as having made the West, rather than as borrowings from an all-purpose manual of heroic stock, McMurtry intends to advance an argument for a new history of the Old West.

In the body of his work, the new history emerges as a hybridization of the familiar genres of the Western and the historical novel. Devoted as he is to richly detailed and suspenseful storytelling, and as skillful as he is in creating a fully animate voice for storytelling, Larry McMurtry can compete successfully with any of the Western yarn spinners. And the bonus he offers the readers who will follow his sagas is the immensely satisfying experiment he conducts in reformulating a literature of the American West.

3

The Hometown Project—
Portrayal and Analysis
Horseman, Pass By (1961)
Leaving Cheyenne (1962)
The Last Picture Show (1966)
Texasville (1987)
Duane's Depressed (1999)

During the decade while he was a university student and a beginning teacher, Larry McMurtry wrote and published the three novels that first earned him a reputation as a voice of contemporary Texas. Some critics considered these works offensive. Tom Pilkington relates the story of one such critic, a professor at Texas Christian University (TCU), who checked out the library's copy of *Horseman, Pass By* on extended loan so that students would not be exposed to its coarseness (Reynolds 1989, 117). At the time, McMurtry happened to be an instructor at TCU. One wonders what strategy his unappreciative critic might have used to protect students from the author in his own classroom. Other friendlier critics of these early works saw an elegiac tone in them, a rueful view of life in a time when the ennobling romance of the Old West is only memory. Still other readers took these first works, particularly *Horseman, Pass By*, as dismissive of rather than nostalgic for a past way of life. This last position is notably represented in an essay entitled "Damn the Saddle on the Wall: Anti-Myth in Larry McMurtry's *Horseman, Pass By*," written by Mark Busby (in Reynolds 1989, 181–86).

Busby found support for an anti-mythic interpretation in McMurtry's own collection of essays, *In a Narrow Grave* (1968). Commenting in that collection upon the seeming inconsistency readers might see in his expressed attitudes about Texas, McMurtry writes, "I am critical of the past, yet apparently attracted to it; and though I am even more critical of the present I am also quite clearly attracted to *it*" (141). McMurtry labels his inconsistency "a contradiction of attractions," a phrase indicative of an unresolved set of feelings toward Texas, past and present. In another essay in the collection, entitled "Southwestern Literature" (31–54), McMurtry bemoans the absence of realism in Western writing; yet, when he wrote with the voices of his protagonists in *Horseman, Pass By* and *Leaving Cheyenne*, McMurtry could himself express regret, if not nostalgia, about past times.

The "contradiction of attractions" playing out in McMurtry's early writing may be taken as typical of the young writer's pursuit of the familiar admonition to "write what you know." Often what one knows cannot in honesty be reduced to a single, simple position. One may have disliked much about the experience and place of growing up, but then it was exactly those experiences and places that made the present self and provided it with a capacity to judge life. Certitude might be possible about experiences and places known at second hand, or even maybe about experiences later in life, but it seems downright impossible when the subject is the site of our own nativity. The personal past remains indeterminate, always waiting for a reworking, a re-creation that might make it finally certain; thus, Thalia, the fictional town named for the muse of comedy and the general setting for Larry McMurtry's hometown writing project, serves as locale for his repeated investigations of the modern Texan. How does the past figure in forming the present-day self? What can the future hold when repetition of past ways has become implausible and undesirable? Such are the questions addressed but left unresolved by the first hometown novels. When McMurtry returns to the project again in *Texasville* and *Duane's Depressed*, it is past time for resolution to those questions. The new query has become, what is salvageable for the self to cling to?

The presence of the first series of questions in the weave of the narration accounts in large part for the attraction of the initial hometown trilogy. They show each of the novels to be, in one fashion or another, a partial instance of what literary critics and historians term a *Bildungsroman*, that is, a novel of development or coming of age. This familiar genre has special importance to cultures that emphasize the singularity of individuals. When each person is adjudged unique, equality signifies equal value, not uniformity. All persons are expected to have distinctive qualities in a mix we receive as the personality. Personality in turn is declared by the culture to be a creation or product of nature and, very importantly, nurture. There is no exaggeration in saying this simple formulation represents a belief deeply structured into the cultural learning of modern societies. When literature accommodates that deep structure in its plots and characterizations, it delivers news about our own life's plot.

The questions at the heart of the later hometown novels—Why did life turn out to be so unsatisfying? And, what can I do about it?—are equally compelling, for as Dr. Honor Carmichael, the psychiatrist in *Duane's Depressed*, explains, "People who realize they had the capacity to do more than they've done usually feel cheated. . . . Even if they mainly have only themselves to blame, they still feel cheated when they come around a curve in the road and start thinking about the end of their life" (422–23). The same modern cultures that valorize the *Bildungsroman*, because that literary genre illustrates the belief in unlimited human potential, inevitably also foster disappointment with the common experience of potential unrealized. This accounts for the coexistence of the novel of psychic crisis in counterpoint with the *Bildungsroman*. As the latter genre speaks to our youth, the novel of crisis relates news of our middle age and later years. The rare accomplishment of Larry McMurtry's reworking of hometown material is the demonstration of how intimately connected the two genres are in portrayal of contemporary life.

The popularity of McMurtry's hometown novels has been further advanced by their adaptation to film. The story of *Horseman, Pass By* was rewritten for the screen by Harriet and Irving Ravetch and released under the direction of Martin Ritt in 1963 as *Hud*, starring Paul Newman, Brandon de Wilde, Melvin Douglas, and Patricia Neal. *The Last Picture Show*, directed by Peter Bogdanovich with a screenplay by McMurtry and Bogdanovich, was released in 1971, with Cybil Shepherd, Jeff Bridges, Timothy Bottoms, Randy Quaid, Ellen Burstyn, and Ben Johnson playing lead roles. *Leaving Cheyenne* in 1974 became *Lovin' Molly*, directed by Sidney Lumet, with parts played by Tony Perkins, Beau Bridges, Blythe Danner, and Edward Binnes. Finally, in 1990, Peter Bogdanovich issued *Texasville*, a sequel to *The Last Picture Show*, with the original cast reprising their earlier roles. Even though *Lovin' Molly* and *Texasville* were not well received by critics, the *fact* of the transfer of his books to the screen has had effect in confirming Larry McMurtry as an important writer of American hometown stories.

PLOT STRUCTURE AND NARRATIVE POINT OF VIEW

According to Lera Patrick Tyler Lich, McMurtry first put the material that would become *Horseman, Pass By* into fiction while he was an undergraduate student at North Texas State College (now University). Originally intending it to stand as related short stories, he wrote one story as an account of diseased cattle, another about the death of an old cattleman. In 1958, the year of his graduation from North Texas, he expanded and combined the two stories into the form of a novel. An examination by Charles D. Peavy of McMurtry's papers and correspondence housed at the University of Houston discovered that after taking shape as a novel, the manuscript was rewritten five more times with many changes adopted at the suggestion of an editor at Harper's, its eventual publisher (1977, 134). Many of the alterations in manuscript gave the plot of the narration a structure centered on contrasts. The occurrence of fatal disease in Homer Bannon's herd of longhorn cattle sets up a series of oppositions, between modern science and sentiment for the "heritage" type of animal that signifies the Old West, and between the integrity of Homer and the cynicism of Hud expressed in their varying opinions of how to handle the disaster. The basic opposition between integrity and self-serving opportunism, which it is suggested represents contemporary amoral society, gains reinforcement in the plot from Hud's abuse of Halmea and reaches its climatic expression in the ambiguity surrounding Homer's death. Did Hud kill him or not? As the plot oppositions develop, Lonnie Bannon is a feeling participant because of his emotional connection to his grandfather, Halmea, Hud, and the ranch hands, but his youth also sets him apart as an observer of the adults. The plot structure thus places him in a critical position. He can be the reader's representative in the sense that he is not fully responsible for decisions governing the ranch, but unlike the reader he is also expected to become in time one of the decisive adults. The experiences he undergoes are, therefore, versions of initiation.

Having reduced his narrative to a lean representation of opposition pointing up the issues facing Lonnie as an observer of the changing West, it must have seemed inevitable to McMurtry that his novel should become a coming-of-age story, which explains the next significant revision of the manuscript—conversion of the narrative point of view from general third person to the engaged outlook of teenaged Lonnie Bannon, who thereby was transformed from a bystander to the protagonist of *Horseman, Pass By.*

This alteration amounted to a reconception. "Who will tell my story?" is not only the first practical question a writer of fiction faces, it is also a question addressing the values that will be conveyed in the narrative, the intimacy that will become available to a reader, how the plot may take shape, and the genre to which the story will prove akin. With a first-person narrator, the reader has no other direct source of information. Everything, for better or worse, is filtered through the vision of the speaking narrator who is understood to select the details he or she feels are worth reporting. Receiving those details, and the coloration they are given in narration, the audience becomes acquainted with the person simulated as presenter of the story. Whatever else the story may concern, when it appears in the first person it is inevitably very much about the storyteller. Lonnie Bannon, thus, by McMurtry's revision of the narrative point of view, was no longer the object of scrutiny, becoming instead the speaking subject of *Horseman, Pass By.* As such, Lonnie responds to the world created for him by McMurtry, a world populated by family and acquaintances exemplary of outlooks Lonnie might choose to adopt for his own; people whose attitudes he can attempt to judge, but because they affect him personally, he cannot ignore. Grinding ranch labor occupies him physically, while a body of choices to be made about how life can (not necessarily should) be lived preoccupies the consciousness revealed in Lonnie's elaboration of the accounts of diseased cattle and the death of a rancher that were once short stories but have now evolved, through the application of McMurtry's craft, into a tight novel about coming of age in mid–twentieth-century Texas.

As though produced in accordance with the prescriptions for unity written by Aristotle and endorsed by generations of classicists, *Horseman, Pass By* employs a unity of place (Homer Bannon's ranch along Idiot Ridge), time (a matter of days, from discovery of the cattle disease until the world turns upside down following Homer's death and Hud's ascendancy), character (Lonnie presides in focal position), and action (the fate of the cattle pits Hud against Homer, while Hud's rape of Halmea constitutes further evidence of disintegration in the old ways). Together with the first-person narration, these unities give the novel emphasis that marks out the structure that our familiarity with literature reminds us is characteristic of the *Bildungsroman*: the young protagonist faces a crisis involving issues of maturity such as sex, death, and morality; passes through the trials presented by the appearance of those issues in his or her life; and emerges from the challenges as though reborn a different person.

Yet, *Horseman, Pass By* nags at us with a sense of its incompleteness as a *Bildungsroman*. Lonnie confronts the crises associated with the ranch community and his life, because he has no choice but to do so. He passes through them, because they are temporal crises to begin with. The cattle are gone at the end of the novel. Halmea is gone. Homer is gone. Lonnie has no control over those passages, nor, come to speak of it, does he have control over the historical changes of Texas represented by the oblique references to the newer oil industry, the power of government agents to direct range life, and, symbolically most striking, Hud's riding in a souped-up automobile to the blatant assignations that constitute the latter-day adventures of the appealingly masculine figure in cowboy clothes. These are aspects of modernity, and not only has Lonnie no power to alter them, if he even wanted to, he has no clear grasp either of how they will play out in significance to his life. In his epilogue, Lonnie tells of leaving Thalia with memories, but he is inarticulate, refusing, he says, "to get in a long conversation about it" with the trucker Bobby Don. The development or coming-of-age novel is sometimes described as an account of initiation, the events endured by the protagonist serving as rites of passage marking entry into autonomous adulthood. If the description is sound, then what Larry McMurtry has done in *Horseman, Pass By* is to write a novel of incomplete, perhaps forever-unfinished, passage showing us that in 1961, at the age of twenty-five, he saw the odds weighing heavily against a young man's going beyond adolescence in north Texas.

First-person narration also serves McMurtry effectively in his second novel, *Leaving Cheyenne*, except that in a *tour de force* of narration he awards the presiding role of narrator to three different characters: Gideon Fry, Molly Taylor, and Johnny McCloud. Different as they are, the three are closely related through a triangular love affair that endures for decades. With the intimacy of their affair at the center of each character's narration, the shift from one speaker to another makes clear the obvious point that individuals feel a mutual experience differently. For example, Gid wrestles with the demands of propriety making him feel at times tawdry in a physical relationship unsanctioned by marriage, while Johnny expresses no interest whatsoever in matrimony. Although Molly actually does marry a third man, the goal of her sexual and emotional desires is a self-validating love. As she explains to Gid, she means "just you loving me . . . and nothing else. Just pure me and pure you. But you're always thinking about Johnny or Eddie or your ranch or your dad or what people will think, or what's right and what's wrong . . . Or else you're thinking about yourself, and how much you like me . . . Or else you just like to think about having me for a girl. That ain't loving nobody much. I can tell that" (137).

If registering varying attitudes was the sole reason for McMurtry employing a split narration, it might be received simply as a trick of technique meant to confirm an elementary psychological observation. In the economy of the novel, though, the narrative movement among the points of view of three participants adds complexity and value. First, each narrator is allotted a different time period in the love affair. Gid, who speaks first and for the longest duration, tells of the early years of the relationship and, in the course of his story, establishes the traits of all three characters. Molly, coming second, presents them all in later years when their irregular relationship is tested by the loss of Molly's sons—Joe, whose father is Johnny, and Jimmy, whose father is Gid—and by the roles forced upon them by Gid's achieved prosperity and respectability. Molly's narration thus covers life *after* initiation into adulthood, testing the efficacy of the youthful rites of passage related in Gid's narration. Finally, Johnny's account covers the aging of the three lovers until their companionship is broken with Gid's death. The temporal spread of the three interrelated narrations achieves the dimensions we often see in a "family" saga. Acknowledging the parallel, we recognize that McMurtry has stripped the "family story" down to its essential core, namely, the interplay of emotional affinities that, apart from legal sanction, bind people together.

The second level of value added to the economy of *Leaving Cheyenne* by McMurtry's tripartite narrative structure concerns historical reference to the settling of the western lands. The earliest European arrivals on the Great Plains were adventurers seeking whatever treasure the land might hold but showing no interest in permanent residence. Their resources were bodily endurance, physical skills, and swift horses. Encountering the native inhabitants and appropriating their territories, the doughty newcomers, whether conscious of the matter or not, were preparing the way for a later wave of Europeans, and Euro-Americans, who saw the new lands as their opportunity to plant and reap. The second wave meant to become permanent builders on the land and held hopes of founding families and communities, finding fortune by working the land, and forming a society that would satisfy a yearning for ownership.

The success of the second wave did not eliminate traces of the individualistic adventurers, because the adventurers' skills were readily adaptable to the new uses to which the land was put. The emergent class of builders became ranchers and farmers, the residual class of physically hardened individuals became cowboys and ranch hands. These historical lines of descent resonate in McMurtry's portrayal of Gideon Fry and Johnny McCloud. As Molly tells Gid, he is always thinking of the ranch or of the respectability expected in a man of business. He marries unhappily because he must be married, and he moves to a brick house in town because it is suitable to his station and to his wife's ambitions. Except for moments of release with Molly, he has taken to heart his father's philosophy that life is not to be enjoyed, or even endured, but fought (25). Johnny, on the other hand, has no desire to appropriate or possess either land or Molly. Fatherhood does not alter his ways. He comes and goes by apparent whim, living much of the time on wages earned as an employee on Gid's ranch. In his essay "Take My Saddle from the Wall: A Valediction," McMurtry describes the relationship between cowboy and farmer as inimical (*Narrow Grave*, 141–73). In *Leaving Cheyenne*, Gid and Johnny are not personally inimical, but their ways of life are irreconcilable in the values they express. Together, though, they achieve a synergy in the economy of the ranch, just as McMurtry has them do in the economy of his novel.

A further allusive quality the novel derives from its tripartite narration may be found in a symbolic formulation of the relationships of Molly, Gid, and Johnny. Observing that "Gid's powerful concerns for being responsible correspond to his equally strong conscience and the guilt he feels about his desire for Molly," Mark Busby finds the novel limning Sigmund Freud's "tripartite division of human psychology, with Gid representing the superego; the wild and free cowboy Johnny corresponding to the id; and the ever present Molly as the Ego being forced to mediate between the two" (*McMurtry and the West*, 89–90). In Freud's system, the three divisions exist within a single individual, with the superego being that portion of mind conditioned to social definitions of right and wrong, the id representing the basic drives normally repressed so that they emerge only in mediated form, and ego being the manifestation of conscious awareness and control. Busby makes no claim that the Freudian system dominates the novel. Rather, his observation explains a further source of structural unity in *Leaving Cheyenne*. On one level, the main characters narrating the story are bound together emotionally as a "family." On another level, they are linked in a relationship descending from historical settlement of the land. Then, too, just as their distinct narratives assemble into the novel's wholeness, character behavior intertwines in a representation of basic human psychology.

For the third installment of the saga about his fictionalized hometown, Larry McMurtry adopted the omniscient third-person point of view for the narrative. For writers, the attraction of this narrative point of view lies in its possibilities for privileged entry into the experiences of a cast of characters who can be revealed as less aware of significances than is the presiding, impersonal voice. Such a narrative must not be mistaken for a transcription of the author's feelings or beliefs, let alone the personal experiences of the author, but it can take a bird's eye view of events employing tone and selective reporting to issue judgments quite distinct from those of the characters. The consequence of such total access is the introduction of distance between narrator and the objects in narrative vision. A third-person narrative does not encourage audience identification with characters in the way that a first-person narration does, because it does not encourage the belief that the storyteller stands in for the reader. The distance can be useful, however, when an author wants to present a broad picture, perhaps a group portrait. Although Sonny Crawford, Duane Moore, and Jacy Farrow are major actors in *The Last Picture Show*, it seems evident that McMurtry wishes to subordinate their particular destinies to portrayal of the ways of life available in common to them and their contemporaries in the teenaged cohort of Thalia.

The group portrayal works to displace the sense that we are reading another *Bildungsroman*, although each main character's career in the novel can be read as an initiation and an education. The element obsessing each of their careers—namely, sex—instead encourages us to take the novel as a broadened study of manners and follies. A description of the structure issuing from McMurtry's selection of the third-person omniscient narrative viewpoint is found in an essay by Donald E. Fritz, entitled "Anatomy and *The Last Picture Show*: A Matter of Definition." McMurtry writes often about sexual behavior, indicating that it provides an avenue for depiction of character and society. In Fritz's argument, however, *The Last Picture Show* is less a presentation of characters acting within a society—an all-purpose definition of the ordinary novel—than it is "a novel strongly pulled in the direction of an anatomy, that is, toward an encyclopedic investigation of one specific human concern, specifically, the sexual attitudes and activities of Texas in the 1950s" (in Reynolds 1989, 187). The structure of the novel, then, becomes a tapestry of case studies of characters absorbed by sex.

Writing about the novel nine years before Fritz, whose essay first appeared in 1978, Thomas Landess drew attention to the similarities between *The Last Picture Show* and the writings of Sinclair Lewis, America's first Nobel Prize laureate for literature. The tally of congruence includes the hypocrisy about respectability in both Thalia and Lewis's Gopher Prairie, a rigid social hierarchy in both fictional towns, and a set of values "retarding the intellect and blighting the joy of living" (23). The importance of the parallels for an understanding of the novel's structure rests in the evidence offered for taking McMurtry's purpose in the novel as satiric. To be sure, the construction of the book as a series of vignettes— quick revealing scenes—and the tendency to caricature in the presentation of Coach Popper, Lois Farrow, and Abilene are expected elements in prose satire.

The commentaries of Fritz and Landess have come to represent the majority critical opinion of the novel's structure, as may be seen in the statement by Lera Patrick Tyler Lich, written in 1987, that the novel is a debunking of small-town life (20–21). In this light, the novel's inscription—"lovingly dedicated to my home town"—adds irony to a treatment of life leaving small room for nostalgia.

A satirically comic tone remains prominent in *Texasville*, the treatment of the same central characters twenty-seven years after events of *The Last Picture Show*. Because the novel takes up the story of people who have taken different routes in maturity, the wide-angle lens provided by a third-person narration has the utility of permitting a gradual reengagement of their lives without sacrifice of information about what they have been doing for a quarter-century. The narration has space for an update, telling readers that Duane Moore is now a forty-eight-year-old oil man with a $12 million debt due to a slump in demand resulting from OPEC's influence on the market; Sonny Crawford is the owner of a convenience store; and Jacy Farrow is a small-time movie actress who has recently returned to Thalia to live in an imposing mansion. The breadth and inherent detachment of the third-person narration also serves to allow McMurtry to develop newer relationships among characters. After his return from the Korean War, Duane married and had four children with Karla, who had recently moved to Thalia. One of their children, thrice-married Nellie, has returned home with her two children. Another child is Dickie, a hapless, dope-dealing young man with no discernible ambition except to score sexually, which he does with two married women. The final two children are constantly scuffling twins, born late to Karla and Duane. The Moore household is completed by Minerva, a housekeeper over eighty years of age, who had once been rich herself until her father lost his money in a previous oil bust. The household does not exhaust the variables for relationships, though. There are lovers for both Karla and Duane, as well as employees. This large cast cannot be managed with any other point of view than the wide, third-person narration.

While *Horseman, Pass By* develops its structure around the destiny of the ranch in a changing economy, *Leaving Cheyenne* centers attention on the unconventional "family," and *The Last Picture Show* employs the institution of Thalia High School as an organizing principle—all relationships radiating out from the characters who are associated as classmates—*Texasville* reflects a more tentative social organization in its structure. The occurrence event of a centennial celebration works as the enabling event that joins the characters in momentary common cause, which, in turn, plays the tales of random amours, purposeless time wasting, and spiteful conflicts on the broader canvas of social satire. Aptly, the centennial celebration ends in an orgy of egg-throwing vandalism; the townspeople, adults and children, reduced to players in a slapstick comedy, while they pelt each other with five thousand dozen eggs— sixty thousand eggs (546). The effect is to indicate that the characters have aged in years since their appearance in *The Last Picture Show*, but are no closer to becoming productive and satisfied adults than they were twenty-seven years before.

Frequent reference to dissatisfaction among the characters marks *Texasville* as a novel of psychic crisis. Duane, who appears in the opening of the novel aimlessly shooting a gun at a doghouse while he sits in a hot tub, drives pointlessly around the countryside, and engages in sex that costs him more in anxiety and self-loathing than it returns him in pleasure. Ruth Popper describes Sonny as "resigned" (29), and he is given to periods of mental absence, appearing in one sad scene seated in the balcony of the ruined movie theater while he runs an old film in his memory (189 ff.). Karla patterns her life on shopping expeditions and the selection of tee shirts with taunting slogans on them. Jacy suffers from the loss of a child. Even the frequent comic scenes contribute to a sense of underlying disturbance, as when Duane, who admits to feeling depressed, and Karla, who is disturbed about her marriage, visit a psychiatrist who turns their therapy session into a manic attack on Karla.

The Last Picture Show and *Texasville* finally serve as prelude to their sequel, *Duane's Depressed*. Here again, McMurtry employs a third-person point of view, but this time he lessens the distance between narrative voice and character, so that the novel posits a sympathy for Duane resulting in a break from the satiric outlook of the previous two novels. Structurally, *Duane's Depressed* represents a diagnostic investigation of Duane, starting with an account of his uncommon desire to walk everywhere rather than to ride around in a pickup truck or car as everyone else in town does. Such behavior is as inexplicable to Duane as to Karla and other people in town, but it leads Duane into episodes constituting a serial presentation of symptoms of mental distress. First of all, he finds that on foot he can see a contrast between nature and what humans have made of it. He is struck by litter everywhere, but also by beauty. Evidently, Duane has been suffering the endemic alienation of a society that has cut itself off from its origins in the Western landscape. Soon, he comes to realize that his physical tramping enacts an inner journey. He admits that his knowledge has been limited (77), and that he wants to simplify his life, so that he can grasp it better (81–82). A further symptom the narrative relates occurs when Duane becomes fixed on securing order: in his family life, to be achieved by leaving the family; and in his daily routine, to be achieved by preparing lists of things to do.

Evidence that McMurtry means to infuse this narrative with a tone more deeply caring than the ridicule and irritation he exhibits in earlier hometown stories emerges when he sets Duane on a path of therapy with a visit to the psychiatrist, Dr. Honor Carmichael. The first visit saps his strength, and he begins to feel he is having a "nervous breakdown" (222). The tabulation of symptoms accelerates: he takes long baths (240), has morbid thoughts about his death (279), feels himself on the edge of life (279), repeatedly dreams of frustration (246, 280), and erupts in fits of anger (257). McMurtry presents none of these episodes under the aspect of satire, nor does he hesitate to inscribe the seriousness of Duane's condition by making him face Karla's death in an auto accident (284). In fact, McMurtry intensifies the circumstances for Duane's despair by showing that despite his and Sonny's long association, they have so little real friendship that they have nothing to say to each other, and, then, by ending Sonny's life as absurdly as he had Karla's. She dies as a result of a string of chance happenings (296), he keels over in his store when nobody is around (375).

Critical and despairing as the circumstances of Duane's life in this novel are constructed to appear, McMurtry has analysis rather than lament in mind. The analysis, which is to say the therapy that must grow out of analysis, results from Duane's interaction with Dr. Carmichael. In an episode that professional therapists describe as "transference," Duane becomes fixated on Honor Carmichael and feels he is in love with her, even though he is aware that she is a lesbian in a lifelong companionship with a woman described by Honor's father as her husband (348). When Honor deflects his romantic overture, and gives it a clinical explanation, he breaks into uncontrollable tears, but he also drops his romantic feelings. He has reached the point where Dr. Carmichael can say, "if you really want to be my *patient* [rather than lover], I'm ready to begin" (421).

The structure of psychiatric diagnosis that McMurtry gives to *Duane's Depressed* requires close attention, because it is nothing less than presentation of the results of the hometown novel project. The earlier novels may be thought of as formulating the characterological problems McMurtry believes that life on the cusp of change from Old West to New West creates. *Horseman, Pass By* sets up Lonnie as the feeling representative of young persons facing the uncharted future without the aid of instruments to suggest a way to follow or a goal to attain. *Leaving Cheyenne* introduces a fantasy resolution of the problems in the form of the attempt to find fulfillment in a quest for an enclave for erotic satisfaction apart from the conventional world. *The Last Picture Show* is another take on the vexing question of determining a worthwhile life. Together with its sequel, *Texasville*, the story of Duane, Sonny, Jacy, and the other Thalia citizens succeeds in *reinscribing* the condition of aimlessness, but there was no further to go with the satiric treatment of hometown ways and not much satisfaction in presenting, one more time, how life in a technologically advanced and prosperous society can be reduced to misguided pursuit of ephemeral physical gratification and comic turns. Dr. Honor Carmichael might be thought to state the author's new view on hometown life when she insists that while Duane must consider that he did not get to choose his life, and cannot change what he *has lived*, still there are decades *to live*. It's time to figure out how to do it (422–24). So, the construction of *Duane's Depressed* ought to be understood against a background of the books about Thalia preceding it as a sign of resolve to examine, at last, how to make do with the circumstances so effectively described by the earlier novels.

CHARACTER DEVELOPMENT

The literature of the West inscribes a largely male world. The mythic characters of cowboy and rancher are men. Plots relate adventures about riding horses wildly, driving cattle, or gunplay that are almost exclusively enacted by men. When not absent entirely, women are work-worn wives, widows, harlots, objects of men's lust, or, in the case of somebody like Annie Oakley, a woman miscast in what is understood to be a male role. McMurtry creates many interesting women in his hometown project: Halmea, Molly, Jacy and Lois Farrow, Karla, and others, but appearing as they do in fiction still rooted in Western literary tradition, they usually appear as characters instrumental to men's lives. McMurtry acknowledged something of this when he wrote in an article on the film *Lovin' Molly* that the triangle with Molly was a male fantasy ("Approaching Cheyenne . . . Leaving Lumet: Oh Pshaw!" in *Film Flam*).

Fantasy or not, McMurtry introduces women characters in ways that modify the masculinist slant of Western literature. Halmea in *Horseman, Pass By* is a true companion to Lonnie, although he cannot live up to the implications of that kind of relationship with a woman, because her physical attributes have greater attraction than her being. Molly in *Leaving Cheyenne* becomes the sole spokesperson for unqualified intimacy. In that regard, she may be taken as a normative character offering readers a standard by which to measure the behavior of others. Still, the plot of the novel consigns her to the position of mothering five men unable to value her. Her father beats and terrorizes her. One son rejects her before his death; another passes out of her life even before his death. Her husband, for all his electric attraction, treats her as property he can abandon at will, but expect to remain receptive when he returns. Her lover, Gid, is ashamed of his relationship with her, and her other lifelong lover, Johnny, has no ability to form a couple and, thus, no capacity to assist Molly in realizing love.

The women of *The Last Picture Show* may seem to be caricatures. Charlene Duggs, of the large insensate breasts, is merely one-dimensional. Other female characters, though, are conditioned by social constructions that make men, whatever their weaknesses, gendered to rule. It takes some probing and speculation to see through those constructions, which is, of course, McMurtry's point about what cliches of gender do to women. Jacy, who seems to lack any ambition but to gain greater luster for her personality, and Lois, who uses sex as relief from boredom, are developed with a complexity that exceeds typecasting. Although the narration does not allow readers to enter the subjective feelings of either daughter or mother, it is not difficult to see that their behavior is conditioned by the society that presents sexual submission to men as the route to attaining identity and ego satisfaction. Lois, like any other person, wishes to have control of her life. If that can be attained only within a circumscribed circle where attachment to one man grants her status, and a sexual affair with another reassures her that she has the option of choice, well, so be it. Like her male counterparts, Jacy is at the age when she must begin to define a path to autonomy. Theoretically, anything may be possible to her—rocket science, the law, writing fiction—but practically, the circumstances of her existence as a beautiful female in a testosterone-charged environment will determine what she becomes. Intuitively, then, she directs her intelligence and her nascent skill in interpersonal relationships to secure a position as Miss Desirable. It may seem a lowly ambition, but fulfilling it takes wit and nerve. Ruth is another character with concealed complexity. An unhappy wife in a foolish affair, she is nevertheless a person with the courage to test herself in rebellion against convention. Unwilling to remain stifled emotionally and unable to express her need for intimacy otherwise, she has an affair with a boy who, because of his youth and inexperience, is likely to be responsive. There is a paradox to be glimpsed in these female characterizations. Playing their roles in the sexual follies of Thalia, they follow conventional scripts, but the amassing of singular details in their portraits gives the characters an unexpected individuality. There is a suggestion of McMurtry's sympathy in their portrayal, sympathy which encourages readers to discover that the motivation of their scripts actually is an urge to struggle against the conventions of constructed views of women as men's appendages.

Nevertheless, the traditions of Western literature thrust male characters into the spotlight of these novels; consequently, it becomes important to note the formulas McMurtry is disposed to use in their portrayal. For instance, Lonnie Bannon is an orphan, and Duane Moore and Sonny Crawford might as well be. Johnny McCloud has no evident connection to a parent. Among prominent male characters, only Gideon Fry lives with a biological father. This is not to say that the others lack elder mentors. Sam the Lion cares for Duane and Sonny like a parent, even leaving his pool room to them in his will. Homer Bannon, Lonnie's grandfather, serves as a nominally supervisory male. It is guiding fathers the younger males lack. This goes as well for Gideon Fry, whose father is present in the early section of the novel, but whose mentoring consists of cynical remarks about women's love (123), comments on the limits of cowboys like Johnny (23), and the example of his suicide. By severing the connections ordinarily expected between the generations of fathers and sons, McMurtry may be suggesting the absence of an immediately felt legacy of cultural norms for behavior. More surely, he is placing his characters in a condition of negative freedom. There is nothing inevitable

about selections they make of worthy models. They must search their
cultures for suitable examples, and, if they are to follow examples, they
must freely commit themselves to those models.

That is the problem, of course—making commitment. A second part
of McMurtry's formulation of male characterization consists in description of peer bonding: Sonny and Duane in *The Last Picture Show* are
companions, but their closeness cannot withstand sexual jealousy over
Jacy; Gid and Johnny in *Leaving Cheyenne* work out a way to share the
object of their love, but their careers as rancher and cowboy set them
increasingly apart; Lonnie Bannon in *Horseman, Pass By* has momentary
affinities with the ranch workers Jessie and Lonzo and a guilty admiration of Hud, but bonding with any of them is impossible either because,
in the case of the ranch hands, of an impassable gap between backgrounds and experience, or, in Hud's case, because the model he offers
is both too aloof and too brutal. None of this suits the romance of male
bonding. On the contrary, McMurtry's presentation of failed bonding
reinforces the characters' emotional and moral isolation in a culture that,
despite celebration of male pairs, retards the development of the self-
security and sexual affection necessary for bonding in intimacy.

Thinking of numerous instances of archetypal male pairing in American literature—Huckleberry Finn and the slave Jim, Ishmael and Queequeg in Herman Melville's *Moby Dick*, Chingachgook and Deerslayer in
the leatherstocking series of James Fenimore Cooper, Jack Kerouac and
Neal Cassady in Kerouac's *On the Road*, the Lone Ranger and Tonto, and
on and on—one cannot doubt that Larry McMurtry consciously took
them as the field upon which to paint his stories of a contemporary
breakdown in the possibility of free, unqualified association such as is
idealized in American masculinist myth.

This is to argue that male characters in the Thalia novels are to be
taken as representative types to be measured against a mythy origin.
Certainly that is true of Hud and Abilene, examples of cowboys without
any of the values of their predecessors, or of Johnny McCloud, a cowboy
lacking an open range to ride freely as earlier cow punchers did, or so
the stories we all know tell us. Similarly, there is typification to be seen
in the young male protagonists Lonnie, Sonny, and Duane. Each is a
searching adolescent (does that sound like *Catcher in the Rye* or *The Adventures of Huckleberry Finn* or *Two Years Before the Mast* or radio dramas
of the 1940s about Jack Armstrong, All American Boy?) open to suggestion, wondering what to be when he grows up. Finally, typification extends to elder characters also. Sam the Lion in *The Last Picture Show* is a

man devoted to older ways of behavior he has little hope of finding renewed. Homer Bannon of *Horseman, Pass By* is, of course, the cattleman from a time that has passed.

There is a tendency to read type characters as cliches, worn-out flat figures. That is fair treatment when the writing is poor, but when the writing is careful, as it is in McMurtry's Thalia novels, the presence of type characters represents a conversation the author has with many other texts about subjects similar to his or hers. Readers come to fiction already prepared by their absorption of dozens of previous readings to hear echoes. This preparation gives us the substance of the literacy that has educated us about genres—so that we know at once the difference between, say, a detective story and a story about coming of age—and gives us possession of a store of models thrown up by our culture—the romantic lead character, different kinds of heroes, and, of course, the cowboy and the rancher. Naturally, writers come to their texts just as well prepared and knowing that what they write is never entirely new. The latest story may modify its models, as McMurtry does when he truncates the *Bildungsroman*, but the original remains vital as a reference point for both writer and reader. Larry McMurtry opened his career writing what he knew, and that includes the literature and cultural conversation about the West.

Had the hometown project concluded with *The Last Picture Show*, it would have been necessary to observe that the idea of character development, in the usual understanding of the term, is misplaced in regard to characters in these novels, because the point about these leading players seems to be that they do not develop. That is why the coming-of-age stories seem truncated. There is no outcome, no product from the experiences the characters suffer. The hometown project did not end with *The Last Picture Show*, however, and because it did not, McMurtry had opportunity to communicate how he imagines development to occur. First of all, as he sees it, character development takes considerable time. Nobody experiences epiphanies of understanding causing immediate rebirth in a McMurtry novel. Nor do characters become worse or better, morally considered. The changes they do undergo come from a model of pathology. As time passes, and they age, characters' traits exaggerate. If they were impetuous about sex as youths, they are fools about it as middle-aged adults.

What does happen to indicate development in the characters is an increasing sense of futility that breaks through the protective tactics that numb them to their reality. In *Texasville*, the lead characters seem worn down, sometimes frantic, near to breaking. In *Duane's Depressed*, of course, the one that survives does break down, and therefore moves into position to alter his life. Possibly, McMurtry is suggesting that for some people the breakdown of old ways may occur when they are younger than Duane, providing that they experience disruptive shock. At least that is one reading to make of the report in *Duane's Depressed* that Duane and Karla's children begin to shape up when Duane withdraws the support that has made them dependent (324–25). In any case, the promise of character development, and promise is all that McMurtry allows, occurs in these novels through psychic trauma.

In a profound sense, this treatment of character signals the realism of McMurtry's writing. The genre of *Bildungsroman* has in it more theory than reportage. As a literary form, it embodies our culture's values concerning individual malleability, which reinforce our civic faith, but in no way can the genre be thought to have statistical application to a large population. It serves as a metaphor more than it does an account of actuality. Underlying the genre of the conventional coming-of-age story is a notion that transformation may be dramatic and sudden, but there is little evidence outside of studies of brain injuries to substantiate a belief that alteration occurs in a flash. Even if a retrospective view of our own experience makes change look to have been quick, when we check recollection against observation of change in other people, we cannot sustain the notion that we are that exceptional. When McMurtry cuts his coming-of-age stories short, he comes down on the side of actuality rather than the metaphor.

Although novels of crisis typically are less given to rapid change—characters do not usually find themselves just suddenly in the doldrums, nor are they often cured overnight—McMurtry's use of the form has its own special quality, namely, the implication that the way to despair is long and the way out incremental. The final hometown novel announces Duane's depression in its title, but in *Texasville*, about a time approximately thirteen years earlier, he is already exhibiting some of the symptoms he shows in the later novel. Research about mental depression indicates these important facts about the ailment: its ultimate cause is obscure, but it results from chemical conditions in the brain, and while administration of chemical or other therapy may control depression, it usually is a lifelong condition. These research findings bear directly upon McMurtry's novels in this way. The circumstances of life in Thalia do lack the ballast of values, but the novels trace no direct causal line between those circumstances and the moods of the characters. Moreover, the dissatisfaction the characters exhibit is endless, as though they have a chronic condition. The realism in Larry McMurtry's portrayal of character would suggest that is exactly right.

THEMATIC ISSUES

The ideas of the West hovering insistently in the atmosphere of the Thalia novels are, like the precedent novels and films and other cultural representations to which they allude, constructions. As C. L. Sonnichsen instructs us, the historical period immortalized in the popular literature we call the "Western" presents "the West that wasn't" (*From Hopalong to Hud*, 1978). It is a creation of publishers, dime novel writers, journalists, showmen, entertainers, and moviemakers who recast gritty reality in the pattern of celebratory epic. The creation has durable appeal, because it ennobles the cowboy as archetypal individualist and protagonist of a struggle to subdue the chaos of nature manifest in Indians, outlaws, and the land itself. It endorses American expansion by the fictional demonstration of the heroic roots of national destiny. And because the vacancy of the land permits elemental plotting, the images of the Western reduce social and historical complexity to a contest of stark opposites, good and bad.

In his Thalia novels, McMurtry collapses the Western construction, showing it to be no longer sustainable as the reality that provided raw material to the glorious image recedes into the past. In his study of McMurtry's novels, Raymond L. Neinstein describes the theme of the earliest works as displacement (*Ghost Country*). Neinstein's thesis is that the first three Thalia novels illustrate a move from a regional literature where the land, as an actual entity, is the locus of values to a literature he terms "neo-regionalism" that is about a fictive place. His analysis of such characters as Lonnie Bannon, who "has no decent model of manhood at a time when he crucially needs one," supports the idea of displacement, while some of the strongest evidence for reading the novels in terms of lost values can be found in the elegiac use of titles. *Horseman, Pass By* takes its title from the line that concludes William Butler Yeats's suggested epitaph at the conclusion of his "Under Ben Bulben," which, as Mark Busby points out, "suggests the comparison between Yeats's mythic horseman and the death of the cowboy god that Homer Bannon represents" (*McMurtry and The West*, 71). The title *Leaving Cheyenne*, McMurtry explains at the opening of the book, represents the earliest and best part of a cowboy's day circle and is taken from the song "Goodbye Old Paint." Each section of that novel bears an allusive title. For example, Lonnie's narration employs the phrase "blood's country" from Judith Wright's *South of My Days*. The section Molly tells is headed by the quotation "Ruin hath taught me" from Shakespeare's sonnet 64. Johnny's narration uses the title "Go Turn My Horses Free" from a song by Teddy Blue, to which McMurtry adds impact by adding a passage from Geoffrey Chaucer's Wife of Bath lamenting the passage of youth. The third novel of Thalia varies the practice of allusion by referring to the departure from town of the movies that literally projected for its residents images of the adventurous West. Of course, then, *Texasville* evokes the image of the pageant celebrating in a debased fashion the lost history of seizure and settlement of the land, and *Duane's Depressed* announces the reason for the therapeutic treatment meant to allow Duane to see his past for what it really was.

The term "displacement" and McMurtry's use of elegiac references point to a further thematic concern, the sense of personal disconnection or isolation. Male characters lacking fathers, female characters with scant opportunity for autonomous realization, and passages to maturity that are never completed underscore the fact that the protagonists are emotionally homeless. They have a native place, but, metaphorically speaking, it gives birth only to their physical being. Critics, among them Christopher Baker ("Death of the Frontier") and Tom Pilkington (in Reynolds 1989, 118–19) have found it convenient to explain the loneliness that pervades the lives of the youth in Thalia by employing the concept of "the marginal man" developed by the sociologist Robert E. Park. The figure is marginal because, according to Park, he lives between tradition and a newly emerging culture. In the years about which McMurtry writes in the Thalia books, the traditional society is represented by the mythic West, the intrusive new culture by such signs as the oil industry giving employment to Molly's husband, Eddie, and to Sonny Crawford, the attractions of urban excitement in Fort Worth, and increasing friction between those who live on accrued wealth and the wage earners who serve them. The binary options of a life between a used-up past—symbolized in the deaths of Homer Bannon and his cattle, or the dissolution of the cowboy figure in the portrayals of Hud and Abilene—and a yet-uncharted future leaves Lonnie feeling "like he was the only human creature in the town" (*Horseman, Pass By*, 5), Sonny relapsing to a child in the embrace of Ruth Popper, Molly and Johnny preferring memory of the past to present life.

The critics cited in this discussion made their interpretations of the

Thalia novels when only three of them had been published. If we extend the insights of their analysis to include the last two entries of the home- town project, the thematic issues will be seen to devolve from the broad issues associated with the Western past to the narrowed perspective of the life of characters who are less definable by their roots in Texas than they are by residence in a modern society that might as well be found in Iowa or Connecticut as in the Southwest. Despite the topical references in these final novels to the particular history commemorated by the Tex- asville pageant or the booms and busts of the oil economy, the conditions of life are described in terms applicable to anywhere that accelerated social mobility and a consumer culture may be said to exist. The home- town project therefore becomes in its last installments a thematic explo- ration of the anxieties and discontents of individuals definable simply as contemporary American.

With the hometown project completed by *Duane's Depressed*, we see confirmation that from the start, McMurtry disallows the judgment that his characters are hapless victims, because they are born too late to par- ticipate in a meaningful Western past. His use of a first-person narration in two of the Thalia novels, a narrative perspective closely identified with Sonny and Duane in *The Last Picture Show*, and the even tighter focus on Duane in *Texasville* and *Duane's Depressed* does not portray the protag- onists as passively whimpering. The premise of the narrative viewpoint in every case is that the speakers are agents for their stories, selecting the incidents and memories they relate, admitting to confusions as though they know the ambivalence they are feeling holds the possibility of eventual resolution. They simply cannot yet see resolution. Lonnie's response to Halmea's rape offers a hard but instructive example from the first hometown novel. The physical description, which is given by Lonnie, shows Hud's violent assault on Halmea's spirit, dignity, and body all at once. Moreover, the speech of Halmea about nobody ever stopping Hud, which is quoted by Lonnie, directly states that because of her gender and race, Halmea is viewed by the Bannon household as "other," that is, excluded from the decent treatment reserved for whites and men. But what bothers Lonnie, he says, is not just the horrifying deed, but the recognition that "he had wanted to do pretty much the same thing to Halmea" (*Horseman, Pass By*, 117). Shock builds upon shock in the episode. So, too, does insight. McMurtry has given Lonnie power to select the facts that document racist sexual abuse. This the reader grasps, or so we hope, but Lonnie does not think the matter all the way through. He tries to take action by leveling his gun at Hud, but loses aim as he shoots. "I guess I thought any shot would end it," he says (113). The thematic drama of the episode is that of uncompleted choice. Moral issues are plainly present in the events, but the will to declare for the right is lacking in Lonnie. So it is not that he has no choice, but rather that he does not make a choice.

The incident of the rape in *Horseman, Pass By* can be taken as representative of further incidents in that and the other novels. Gideon Fry's agony about his relationship with Molly places him almost endlessly at the moment of choice. When finally he decides to cut off the physical affair, he appears to be making a choice for rectitude. Upon a reader's reflection, though, it turns out to be more like a refusal to choose the path his heart would follow. In that regard, his action can be interpreted as a shunting of the responsibility to choose. The mess Sonny makes of his relationships with Ruth Popper and Jacy Farrow also lend themselves to analysis in terms of faulty choice making. He becomes involved with Ruth originally because, as she understands very well, he is ruled by sexual hunger. When the affair goes beyond physical sensation into serious emotion, Sonny turns his gaze toward Jacy as an object of desire. Hormones impel him, but he is making a choice, just as he does when, frustrated by Jacy's shenanigans, he submits to her mother's advances and eventually returns to get comfort from Ruth. All of it is despicable behavior, but it is also an enactment of choice, however faulty. Similarly, the sexual diversions of Duane and Karla and Dickie and his married paramours in *Texasville* must not be received as the actions of characters whose environment provides them no other choices. They may be bored, decentered characters with apparently limited understanding of their own motivations, but still they elect the way they live and, for that reason, must be held accountable. The eruption of sympathy toward the lead character in *Duane's Depressed* and the structure of his story as an analysis of mental symptoms offers understanding, not exculpation.

Finally, one is led to the conclusion that in his five Thalia novels Larry McMurtry has undertaken the ethical project of investigating right conduct. More often than not, his characters muddle the ethical issues, and their marginality makes them see the issues opaquely instead of crystal clear, as ethical matters were once presented in the older, mythic West. Still, the world they live in—the fictional world of Thalia—holds right conduct possible. Why else would the characters peopling the world of Thalia express the ambivalence they do?

A PSYCHOSEXUAL READING OF THE THALIA NOVELS

Critics or other readers who charge McMurtry with coarseness point to the frequency of sexual episodes, suggesting that they are gratuitous insertions in his texts or, worse yet, evidence of a nasty view of humanity. In censorship cases brought to a court of law, the standard commonly applied to portrayals of sexuality demands "redeeming social value." Sex for its own sake evidently cannot pass muster in a court of law, or at least that used to be so. McMurtry's case has not been brought to a court of law, but in the court of literary opinion, the standard of social value can have relevance, because what McMurtry depicts by his references to sex is our socially interactive nature.

We need not scour the pages of McMurtry's novels looking for encoded references to Freud to believe that he thinks sexual practice is an index of personality and that sex is primal to human relationships. The discussion of character in *Leaving Cheyenne* indicated the possibility of reading the love triangle as a rendition of the Freudian depiction of Mind. Neat as that formulation appears, there seems to be a broader and less precise conception of sex at work in the Thalia novels. The lovemaking between Sonny Crawford and Ruth Popper in *The Last Picture Show* will serve to illustrate.

As they come together naked for the first time, Ruth waits "trustfully for a beautiful thing to happen to her." Her husband, Herman, either knows nothing of the beautiful thing or won't give it to her, but she is sure Sonny will. While the two proceed to attempt a coupling, the third-person narrative underlines their inexperience with comedy. "Sonny was not absolutely sure of the target." They cannot tell who is feeling what, pain or pleasure. Then the bed squeaks, louder and louder, making Ruth think that the whole town can hear it (*The Last Picture Show*, 118–19). By the time of their third tryst, Ruth is more comfortable, and she has an old blue quilt for them to lie on. Now they are more at ease with nakedness, and when Sonny naps after ejaculation, Ruth finds it lovely. "It was almost as if he were a child inside her" (124).

Because the narration is third person and presumably controlled by the author, we can hazard the thought that it comes near to representing the way McMurtry, rather than the characters, envisions the scene. His comic tone, starting while Ruth is waiting for "the beautiful thing" and continuing through the imagined scene of the whole town pausing to listen while bed springs squeak, replaces any salacious possibility the sex

act might hold, with a distancing look at the couple's mechanical inep-
titude and nervousness. In effect, it is more innocent and beguiling than
anything else. Having already established their inexperience, the couple's
third tryst might be thought to be "natural" and without artfulness. So
when the narration introduces maternal imagery, it can reasonably be
expected to describe an intuitive feeling. The same is equally true of a
later scene of Ruth and Sonny in sex when "he was removed from her
legs, and afterward lay at her breast." And yet again, when on the next
day Ruth experiences an orgasm described as a "delivery" (*The Last Picture Show*, 129).

Is this mother-child description a severely satiric treatment of copu-
lation between an older woman and an adolescent boy? Perhaps, but the
unease we might feel at that possibility is easily matched by the startling
effect of McMurtry's conjuncture of orgasms and their issue in childbirth.
What could be the intention of the effect? Surely it is a declaration of the
significance to identity of the primal act. Just as Sigmund Freud posited
a narration of a child's desire for its mother or father and rivalry with
the opposite parent in order to root character in earliest experiences,
McMurtry might be said to have deployed his narration of Ruth and
Sonny making love to indicate that sex is, so to speak, a terrain where
we seek a self. At the start of their affair, neither Ruth nor Sonny has
more than secondhand cliches they expect to be reflected in the mirror
of their sexual intercourse. In time, Ruth's femaleness offers her a truer
option—she might be a mother. That's always associated with sex. More
than that, she might learn in the school of sex a way to intimacy that is
modeled in the mother-child relationship but which could be found in
other relationships as well. Compared to Ruth, Sonny is a slow learner.

The burden of the analysis, though, rests on the repeated use of sex
as a way to occupy oneself in Thalia. Without question, sex is a creative
act. That it feels good is an inducement to seek sex and, in terms of a
psychosexual view of humankind, it can be seen as a means of self-
enactment. We define ourselves in marriage, courtship, or in the absence
of those arrangements sexually. We are wives and husbands, parents,
lovers, bachelors, gay, "old maids," once-married-now-divorced—all of
these terms denominate a sexual status. Of course, sexuality is not all
there is to a person, but only severe conditions deprive a person entirely
of sexual feelings, while practically all other attributes are malleable.

Ordinarily, we expect sexuality to exist as an undercurrent in life as
we live it. Creativity has other outlets also. In literature, too, we expect

to use a text like Sigmund Freud's *Interpretation of Dreams* in a search for symbols, and knowledge we may have of clinical findings, to unpack the subordinated sexual meaning in events. The striking thing about life in fictional Thalia is that no search is necessary. While it sounds extreme to apply the term primitive to the characters, in a sense that is exactly what they are, and McMurtry knows that is the impression he creates.

Not that it is an expression of distaste on his part, although there is bite to his satire in *The Last Picture Show* and *Texasville*. It is instead a function of the theme of an absence of cultural or familial moorings for him to present the characters stripped of any other terrain for defining the self and reduced to strutting themselves largely in the roles of sexual players alone. In confirmation, think of the details of the lives of Duane and Karla's children as they are presented in *Texasville* and *Duane's Depressed*. Their oldest daughter's marriages last no longer than the period of initial sexual arousal. Their oldest son has honed all of his talents as aids to seduction. And the parents themselves persist in analyzing their own relationship as the setting for sexual satisfaction, or the lack of it.

The significance of *Duane's Depressed* to the Thalia project lies in its revelation that sexual behavior has a symbolic content masking unconscious motives or needs. His psychiatrist explains Duane's dissolving into tears, an occurrence described as a "flash flood of tears that had swept his personality away" (418), as the crumbling of his defensive strategies. She goes on to say that, because Duane lost his father when he was five years old, his mother was very poor, and he had to work from the time he was thirteen, he feels subconsciously the loss of opportunity to choose his own life (422). From that analysis, it is only a short step to recognition that in sexuality, precisely because it is so primal, so consuming, Duane has been seizing the freedom to choose, which he has felt otherwise denied. In sexual affairs, he achieved brief command of his destiny; he would be doing what he, and nobody else, chose to do. As the affairs were also violations of commitment to his wife and family, they represented rebellion against the life "unfairly" forced upon him. What is true for Duane can readily be applied to other characters in McMurtry's Thalia. Accompanied as they are by elaborate description of their sexual behavior, their portrayals equally indicate that we are to take the physical actions of sex to be enactment of personal psychological drama. In fact, patterns similar to the defiant pseudochoice revealed by psychiatric analysis of Duane can be discovered in outline among such other residents of Thalia as Hud in *Horseman, Pass By*; Gideon Fry in

Leaving Cheyenne; Jacy Farrow in *The Last Picture Show*; and Suzie Nolan, Jenny Lester, Janine, and Karla in *Texasville*. The personalities of all these characters show similarities for which the portrayal of sexual behavior is the index.

4

City Saga
Moving On (1970)
All My Friends Are Going to Be Strangers (1972)
Terms of Endearment (1975)

In an interview conducted by Patrick Bennett and published in *Talking with Texas Writers* (1980), Larry McMurtry expressed the sense that his first six novels bear a thematic relationship. In the first three books—*Horseman, Pass By*; *Leaving Cheyenne*, and *The Last Picture Show*—he explains that he was writing from a small-town perspective about "the move off the land toward the cities and the gradual disintegration of the rural way of life . . . and the small-town way of life too." Next, he adopted "the perspective of people who have left the country and found themselves in the city, a sort of transitional generation," and it is this outlook that informs *Moving On, All My Friends Are Going to Be Strangers*, and *Terms of Endearment*, uniting them as a group into what he, and the critics following his lead, have taken to calling the Houston trilogy.

Lera Patrick Tyler Lich maintains that McMurtry began *Moving On* as early as 1964 and developed the book through several title changes (28). According to Charles Peavy, McMurtry knew from the beginning that his study of the transitional generation would require three novels, with *Moving On* intended as the conclusion, *All My Friends* the first of the series, and *Terms of Endearment* the middle volume (1977, 37). Chronologically, *All My Friends* relates events occurring eight years before those in *Moving On*, while *Terms of Endearment* concludes with the death of Emma Horton in 1976 (the year after publication of the book!), but also covers events during the same years as the previous volumes.

At times, the intended order of the stories becomes confusing, which is a natural result when a writer undertakes composition of such broad scope. The order of publication for James Fenimore Cooper's leatherstocking tales is contrary to the order of the adventures they relate, and William Faulkner's imagined history of the fictional county of Yoknapatawpha, Mississippi was written backwards, forwards, and sideways, all three. Still, when we finish reading about Cooper's or Faulkner's frontier, the complications in chronology are of little consequence. What counts instead are the evident interconnections among characters and careers, providing the books a thickly textured quality resembling the weave of lives and events in the world that is not literature but "real life." Reading *Moving On*, one comes across mention of Danny Deck in a conversation between Patsy Carpenter and her lover, Hank Malory. He's a writer, it is said, who was a friend of Emma and Flap Horton until he disappeared. Patsy didn't like his book (276). The fragment of reference is all . . . in that book. But when one turns to *All My Friends Are Going to Be Strangers*, there is Danny as the book's protagonist telling his story, including the incident of his betrayal of the Hortons. And taking up the story of Emma's mother, Aurora Greenway, in *Terms of Endearment* the reader finds Danny surfacing again, first as a man Emma seduced when they were undergraduates at Rice University and then as a subject for Emma's intermittent brooding for the rest of her life (71–72) until, at the point of death, she realizes that Danny and her son, Teddy, were the only two people who "had liked her entirely" (408). The example of appearances and disappearances by Danny Deck can be matched by examples of such other characters in the trilogy as Aurora Greenway, who is briefly mentioned in *Moving On* and becomes the dominant character in *Terms of Endearment*, or Patsy Carpenter, who holds the center of the narrative in *Moving On* and receives bare mention in the final work of the Houston trilogy.

It is important to observe that the interconnections McMurtry develops in the Houston novels are neither the first nor the last example of the practice. The Thalia novels also cover ground more than once as they register the waning of rural Texas life. One of Danny Deck's companions, Jill Peel of *All My Friends*, is presented as a star of a later novel, *Somebody's Darling* (1978), along with Joe Percy, who debuts in *Moving On*. The Las Vegas showgirl named Harmony, whom readers meet in *The Desert Rose* (1983) when her life seems to be at its lowest ebb, returns in *The Late Child* (1995) to show us that things can never get so bad that they can't get worse. The characters featured in McMurtry's Pulitzer

Prize novel *Lonesome Dove* reappear again and again, in sequels and pre-quels. And so it goes, until it must be concluded that McMurtry's is an art of multiplicity.

His first works were carefully edited by the publisher, but once his reputation was secure, McMurtry could resist the intrusion of other hands. McMurtry was free to be McMurtry when he issued the Houston trilogy, presenting his work just as he conceived it. Unaltered by editors, these books teem with characters, each embodying a story that might be told once as a minor, even grotesque, episode serving as an aside or as just a part of the main interest, but at another time, when the vision is narrowed, the character becomes the subject of primary attention. This is not an art of well-proportioned narrative design. The works sprawl, flooding their pages with detail uncontrollable by the classical conventions of symmetry or economy, wending their ways in plots that show no regard for neat balance among the beginning, middle, and end, and driving home their themes through a rotating selection of literary modes—sometimes the narratives are comic, other times tender, mostly realistic, yet also in the same volume displaying the capacity for vituperative satire that usually comes from disappointed idealism. Because his is not a carefully crafted way of writing, its characteristic spontaneity reveals McMurtry's writerly self. What we get in the Houston trilogy is something along the lines of a record of the storyteller's process of sorting through all that he knows, searching for ways to give his audience the experience of life as he feels it.

SETTING AND MILIEU

An often-repeated story has Larry McMurtry sporting a sweatshirt bearing the caption "Minor Regional Novelist." Whether or not the story is true, the display of such a label indicates a sardonic attitude McMurtry might well have adopted toward his being pigeonholed by book reviewers in the minor category of regional novelist. For some critics, the strong flavor of Texas in McMurtry's first three books meant that he was not simply an American novelist, but an author of fiction, serving to report the peculiar manners of an out-of-the-way place for readers in the center of things. There is, however, a positive content to the practice of writing about a region. Dozens of skillful prose writers have taken the states of the old Confederacy as the site for fiction, and demonstrated that in terms of the myth of race and the history it spawned, the South is the most American of regions. The West, as a locale of fiction, transcends provincialism in its special way as the locale of the durable myths of the cowboy riding the wild land and lawmen taming anarchy, myths that represent core values of the way that America portrays itself to the world. McMurtry's first novels resonate with allusions to the mythic images of the West, for it is the transition from the days of ranching to a contemporary economy that gives substance to the Thalia trilogy.

Raymond L. Neinstein's *Ghost Country: A Study of the Novels of Larry McMurtry* captures the significance of McMurtry's regionalism by formulating a theme of displacement for the first five novels. In Neinstein's formula, the protagonists of *Horseman, Pass By* and *Leaving Cheyenne* are searching for a way of living that will suffice when the land is no longer the locus of values, and *The Last Picture Show* renders the emptiness of a culture in which sexual adventure is the insufficient replacement for the waning myth of the Old West. For such regional fiction, setting or place assumes fundamental importance, because geography—the land and the life it can support—determines the culture. As John Graves puts it in *The American Southwest: Cradle of Literary Art*, the sense of place that is found in regional writing "is bound up with the way people are in that place and with the history of the people, and it's bound up even more with physical and natural detail, with trees and grass and soil, creatures, weather, water, sky, wild sounds, the way some weed smells when you walk on it" (11).

That sense of place pervades *Horseman, Pass By*, as when Lonnie recalls in the prologue to the novel, "how green the early oat fields were that year, and how the plains looked in April, after the mesquite leafed out" (3). It characterizes the rural setting of *Leaving Cheyenne* also, but a tangible sense of place has receded in *The Last Picture Show* until the land is simply the piece of ground where Thalia is located. Setting, which is defined in handbooks of literary terms as "the where and when of a story or play" (see Cuddon), in some cases can be so physically tangible that protagonists, and readers of their stories, always aware of its presence in the narrative, find setting to be as functional as a major character. To a critic like Neinstein, this development of setting distinguishes regional literature from other types. It is what gives this passage from Danny Deck's story the feel of regional writing: "It was the sky that was Texas, the sky that welcomed me back. . . . It had such depth and such spaciousness and such incredible compass, it took so much in and circled one with such a tremendous generous space that it was impossible not to feel more intensely with it above you" (*All My Friends Are Going to Be*

Strangers, 170). Danny's response to the sky of Texas is so striking, because it is so rare in his narrative and in the other works of the Houston trilogy.

Instead of the tangibility of physical setting that is so important in the Thalia novels, place in the Houston novels is more like "the where and when of the story," simply an inescapable necessity for the narrative. Of course the setting is Houston, not Denver or Dallas, but urban settings are more abstract than rural ones. They can include specific landmarks and street names, but urban settings of fiction are typified by their social conditions and cultural behaviors—a nonphysical environment or medium. For this reason, it is more appropriate to use the term milieu to describe the location of events in a body of work like the Houston trilogy. Milieu suggests atmosphere, conventions of behavior, learned responses, attitudes the qualities of occupational and social groupings that have little or no connection to geography or topography.

In a preface he wrote in 1986 for a new issue of *Moving On*, McMurtry affects puzzlement at the number of rodeo scenes in the book. "Few novels," he writes, "have attempted to merge the radically incongruent worlds of graduate school and rodeo. I am now completely at a loss to explain why I wished to attempt this" (x). He is certainly right about the unusual pairing of worlds. It is hard to think of another example besides *Moving On*, but their incongruity is only apparent. Each is a realm of stylized artifice. Both are objects of McMurtry's scorn. Apart from the treatment in *Moving On*, the best indicator of McMurtry's views on rodeo can be found in the notes he wrote for the book of photographs and text published by Louise L. Serpa as *Rodeo* (1994). Serpa loves rodeo, McMurtry does not, partly because he considers it show biz with little relation to actual ranch work. In fact, he explains, "real" ranch hands deride rodeo hands: "No one on a working ranch would ever have any reason (or desire) to ride a bull, Brahma or otherwise," nor would a real ranch hand ever "race a horse around three triangularly placed barrels, an activity that quickly ruins the horse for more productive activity. Bull riding and barrel racing are rodeo *kabuki*—their relation to anything that might happen on a ranch is confined to costume." Besides the lack of authenticity to rodeo, the general anachronism of contemporary cowboy play irritates McMurtry: "Cowboys, sensing—like gorillas—that their time has passed, cling ever more desperately to anachronistic styles, not willing to admit that the myth has degenerated, the traditions eroded to a point where attempting to sustain them falls somewhere between silliness and the outright ridiculous" (82). Sending the idle, rich Jim Carpenter off to play as a rodeo photographer in *Moving On* is, then, McMurtry's way of indicating that Jim is engaged with a sad parody of working life. Jim sees the rodeo cowboys much as McMurtry says Louise Serpa does, as noblemen. McMurtry testifies that "I see them as physically competent but emotionally limited men who are in most cases sexist, chauvinist, xenophobic, quasi-fascistic, and not infrequently dull" (Serpa, 83). If the rodeo milieu in *Moving On* presents us the world of practitioners of skills so irrelevant to contemporary life that their deeds have become ridiculous stylizations of the cowboy myth, its connection with the academic milieu lies in their common deracination. The Rice University English Department created by McMurtry has no serious scholarly or critical business on its agenda. Using Patsy Carpenter as a foil to the graduate students, the novel shows their shoptalk to be ill-informed and insipid. Setting forth the licentious, self-promoting Bill Duffin as the students' role model of a major professor, the narrative makes the advanced study of literature seem as artificial, insignificant, and parasitic of the genuine craftsmanship employed by professional novelists as any rodeo could be. Together, rodeo and graduate school are McMurtry's indices of lost value in the urban life of the new West.

Much the same can be said about the literary world Danny Deck encounters when he becomes a published author in *All My Friends Are Going to Be Strangers*. That world is awash in written and spoken histrionics. Besides Danny's published novel, *The Restless Grass*, there is the second novel he hijacks from Jill Peel, the screenplay he is invited to write, and talk, talk, talk by Godwin and Sally and others in the book. By plotting the novel as Danny's encounter with the show biz of literature and movies, McMurtry gains thorough opportunity to reveal and mock the milieu as yet another example of life abstracted from a sense of place.

Although the milieu in *Terms of Endearment* seems to bear no direct relationship to the worlds devised for the first two novels of the trilogy, the representation of Aurora Greenway's environment makes a subtle connection. Aurora, the New Englander attempting to transfer her sense of propriety to widowhood in Houston, struggles with her suitors and daughter to naturalize and thus control a haphazard, traditionless existence. Using her escapades to isolate a sample of life among the rootless, McMurtry succeeds, as Ernestine P. Sewell expresses it, in making Aurora seem "the embodiment of Houston, a city vested with the trappings of wealth, whatever is shiny and new and extravagant" (in Reynolds 1989, 202). Setting, as a sense of place, has disappeared in this novel as much as in the others of the trilogy, and milieu—the "where" of the story—has been absorbed into the narrowing frame of character. Lacking sufficient reference for value beyond itself, bizarre personality has become both site and subject of the fiction.

PLOT DEVELOPMENT AND GENRE MODELS

Moving On seems such an apt title that it comes as a surprise to find that McMurtry deferred to his publisher in its selection. According to Mark Busby's research, McMurtry wished to name the book after its leading female character, Patsy Carpenter (1995, 120). The publisher's intuition was sound, though, because *Moving On* suggests the restlessness seen in the episodic plot. When the book begins, Patsy and her husband, Jim, are rodeo groupies. Jim is trifling with a career as a photographer of the stylized reenactments of cow punching and bronco busting, while Patsy passes her time as a disengaged observer of the scene. Her gender-determined role as second fiddle in their marriage act continues when Jim shifts his aspirations to graduate studies in English at Rice University. From there he turns to filmmaking, which leads him to California and an eventual job with IBM. For the Carpenters, the journey they follow has no predetermined purpose or appropriate end. They are always just moving on, because no locale can satisfy the needs they are unable to articulate, and no occupation can engage characters who possess neither motive nor moral purpose.

The journey motif, however, does provide the plot with contrasts between the rough environment of the rodeo world, the dreary life of university graduate students, and the vacuous realm of Hollywood. The contrasts, however, produce a curious sense of repetition, rather than progress, because at each stopping place the characters continue to meet experience at secondhand. The rodeo is vestigial, an imitation of skills and a way of life that has become anachronistic in modern Texas. Graduate study of literature appears to be parasitic nattering about someone else's creativity, and movieland depends on illusion.

The plot of *All My Friends Are Going to Be Strangers* also follows a pattern of restless physical movement, signaling, no doubt, McMurtry's conviction at the point in his career when he was writing the Houston trilogy that the authentic journeys of life are internal. Making Danny Deck (the lead character of the novel) a writer underlines the plot's meaning, for no matter where he travels or with whom he takes up—

whether Sally inveigled from the control of Godwin Lloyd-Jons early in the book, or Jill Peel with whom he lives later in the novel in California—Danny has the same malaise as Jim Carpenter, a feeling of inauthenticity manifest in feelings of separation from the natural world and society. Appearing in a narration about an author at work on a novel, the sense of estrangement introduces a plot pattern that one critic has defined as the same as that of a mythical hero (Busby 1995, 131–38). The stages of this particular movement, as outlined by critics Northrop Frye, Joseph Campbell, and others, include separation, return, and final departure. In Busby's reading, the escape occurs at the end of chapter 6, when Danny leaves Houston with Sally and Godwin. In chapter 12, he returns to Texas. Then, in the final chapter, he departs again, this time into an indefinite state much like a borderland.

Terms of Endearment confirms the notion that journeys for McMurtry signify the attempted passage of a character from confusion to knowledge. This time, though, the plot eschews representation of physical movement in favor of the fixed setting of Aurora Greenway's Houston, the vantage point from which she addresses a surrounding chaos. Her daughter, Emma, seems reckless, her suitors unpromising, her future uncertain. She feels detached from her body, out of touch. Life is a mess, and the plot of Aurora's story concerns her attempts to give it coherence and symmetry, attributes of a product of human control. The plot, thus, presents Aurora in episodes where contingencies are beyond her control, each making her more and more determined to bring them into her grasp.

The physical motion of the journeys in space seen in the two previous Houston novels allowed McMurtry to introduce contrasts by the simple expedient of moving his characters into a new environment. In the comparatively fixed location of *Terms of Endearment*, however, the contrasts appear more artificial. The farce in scenes with Rosie and Royce jar with their sharp change from the comic tone of the Aurora scenes. The final section of the novel presenting Emma's death disturbs unity to the extent that, in the words of Robert Towers, it "dangles from the rest of the novel like a broken tail" (*New York Times Book Review*, 19 October 1975).

For a fuller sense of the development of plots in the Houston trilogy, it is useful to consider them in relation to genre, even though they are difficult to classify. Apart from the resemblance of *All My Friends Are Going to Be Strangers* to the *Bildungsroman* that serves as template also for *Horseman, Pass By* and *The Last Picture Show*, the Houston works generally are amalgams of literary types. This is particularly true of *Moving*

On. Ernestine P. Sewell indicates the mix of types present in that novel when she explains that it is many other things besides a sprawling fiction: "a novel of manners with random satire, a sociological study of urban life and marriage, and an existential tome, complete with absurdities . . ." (in Reynolds 1989, 196). Sewell also describes *Moving On* as a chronicle, explaining that "one can say 'chronicle' for McMurtry seems to have taken a sociological rather than a narrational stance toward his characters" (195). Elroy Bode judges the sprawl of *Moving On* a sign of its basic failure. Claiming that "the reader becomes desensitized to events from the barrage of minutiae," Bode remarks that the manner of the novel appears "as though Hemingway had decided to write a Sears Roebuck catalogue and thereby obligated his readers to follow page after page of carefully chosen words about linoleum and sundresses and wicker baskets" (in Reynolds 1989, 228).

The remarkable length of *Moving On* (847 pages in the Pocket Books edition of 1988) accounts in large measure for the critical judgments it has received. A novel of that length seems impossible to structure in any other way than linearly: it simply must ramble on and on. Still, a work of its sort has precedence. Miguel de Cervantes rambles too through the adventures of *Don Quixote* (1605, 1615)—in a book McMurtry says he first encountered as a boy of twelve (*Narrow Grave*, 139)—as does Daniel Defoe in *Moll Flanders* (1722). These works have come to be known as picaresques, after the Spanish word *picaro*, designating a rogue, and are typically both accounts of adventure and satires of their contemporary societies. The main characters of *Moving On* are not uniformly rogues, but they are all at least marginal to the society through which they move and, in that respect, of a status that makes them unconventional in comparison to the majority of citizens in Houston or wherever they journey. Furthermore, the linear structure of *Moving On* presents its characters always journeying either physically or emotionally, just as do the protagonists of the early picaresque stories. From the vantage point of the history of novels, we see, then, that McMurtry's saga of twentieth-century Texans is unusual only by comparison with an entirely different kind of writing, perhaps the tightly constructed fiction of John Updike. When viewed against a background that includes the earliest examples of long prose fiction, however, *Moving On* looks like McMurtry's recovery of the original loose form of the novel.

There is yet further indication of novelistic tradition to be seen in the realism of *Moving On* and the other novels in the Houston trilogy. In the United States, William Dean Howells, author of *The Rise of Silas Lapham* among other influential works, was accorded the position of a leader in the literary war of realists against the sentimentality they felt had infected fiction. Howells acknowledged that realism was not an entirely new way of writing, but he did insist that it was the only authentic way to treat life in fiction. In developing the example of realism he hoped would reign in American letters, Howells stressed that fiction should be concerned not with ideal portraiture, but with the way people in the majority live here and now. He meant to make literature attend to everyday events and to adopt as its subject the doings of a largely middle-class public. In his own fiction, marriage and divorce figure prominently, along with the experiences of business, householding, and public affairs. In order to enforce the program of realism, Howells, and his colleagues in the movement, took frequent opportunity to include in their texts contrasts between the ways that life has been imagined (often they called this way "romantic") and the way people actually experience their lives. Love affairs are not often blessed. Business may fail. Children can disappoint their elders. Happiness can be minor. Life is rarely truly tragic.

Allowing for the seeming exaggeration resulting from his depiction of unusual characters such as Aurora Greenway and some of her suitors, one can see realism is the prevalent mode of the Houston trilogy. A less precise term than genre, mode denotes manner and style; thus, the mode, or manner and style, of realism can occur in a wide range of types of fiction. There is realism in *The Last Picture Show*, that is, rendition of everyday experience and an anti-romantic viewpoint, but the novel is also satiric. The same can be said about the Houston novels. The scene of the jealous Royce Dunlup driving his truck wildly through the J-Bar Korral in *Terms of Endearment* reads comically, but the relationship of Rosie and Royce that produces the scene is founded in a realism of ordinary characters, who are in their foolishness and limitations recognizably human types. The tale of Danny Deck is replete with comic scenes—Sammy Solomea dousing his wife Jenny and Danny with soapy water as they are coupling, the dinner of Viking food Leon O'Reilly hosts for Danny at Thor's ice-bound restaurant, and all of the scenes with Godwin in them—but the novel remains rooted in the manner of realism portraying Danny's increasing disappointment and despair with his writerly life.

CHARACTER DEVELOPMENT

Ernestine Sewell's observation that *Moving On* is a collection of partial literary genres can be applied, in fact, to the entire trilogy. Each of the novels has a strong story line about a lead figure. It is Patsy Carpenter in *Moving On*, Danny Deck in *All My Friends Are Going to Be Strangers*, and Aurora Greenway in *Terms of Endearment*. The story line is supported with a cast of secondary characters such as Emma Horton, Rosie Dunlup, Jill Peel, Hank Malory, and many others. These events serve as the ground against which McMurtry plays his variations. With the free form of a jam session, he swings from one narrative tone to another and back again, embellishing the story line with the artist's varying perspectives on the human condition and its follies.

While the novels play their variations through character appearances, they also form a composed singularity through the interconnection of characters in the three novels. Danny Deck has a reference in *Moving On* and then takes the lead in *All My Friends Are Going to Be Strangers*, which is placed in time before *Moving On*. Aurora Greenway appears in *Moving On* before becoming the dominant figure of *Terms of Endearment*, in the last part of which Emma's husband, Flap, originally presented in *Moving On* along with Emma, reappears, as does a memory for Danny. The effect is to create an "extended family" of fictional characters whose inter-weaving destinies in the Houston trilogy, and in novels McMurtry would write later, produce the same impression as the collected Thalia novels—that of a saga-in-progress, like life itself, never to be finished entirely.

As the previous examination of milieu and genre models indicates, the appearance of some characters of the Houston trilogy seems intended to serve a typifying function. Sonny Shanks, the rodeo champion in *Moving On*, is not dull, but otherwise he illustrates McMurtry's description of rodeo cowboys as emotionally limited, sexist, and quasi-fascistic. His outsize personality fills the prescription for a rank authoritarian whose sadistic treatment of Patsy Carpenter and careless handling of Eleanor Guthrie are as much a part of his self-centered style as the trademark automobile he uses for seductions. Similarly, Ed Boggs, who urinates on Patsy's car at the opening of the novel, surely is a sexist boor, and other minor rodeo characters in the narrative have little to recommend them for the ranks of noblemen. Just as McMurtry says about the competitors on the circuit in his notes to *Rodeo*, these subjects of Jim Carpenter's admiration are exemplars of degeneration.

Novels like McMurtry's massive works about Houston devote so much space to reporting the events of major characters, and thereby making them come alive, that it becomes important to remember that these figures have as much thematic function as do the minor characters. Patsy Carpenter is a case in point. In a later part of *Moving On*, Patsy Carpenter, a voracious reader but, unlike her husband and his graduate school fellows, a self-taught student of literature, decides to read Tolstoy's *Anna Karenina*, a book she had started but failed to finish while in high school. She becomes completely absorbed in Anna's story, skipping the parts of the book about other characters, and taking in the narrative "as if it were a medicine." But when she returns in mind to her own present circumstances, she feels a discrepancy between them and Anna's fictional experience: "Her own sins had been so small-time; her marriage and her affair as well, so weak and short-term. . . . She was not even meat for a good case history, much less a novel. It had all been trivial, and probably in the end amounted to nothing more than that she had run into someone she liked sex with better than she liked it with her husband. Society didn't care what she did—not really" (735–36). Plainly, the significance of Patsy's perception lies in the noted distinction between the intensity of the Russian fiction and the ordinariness of Patsy's "real" life. A similar contrast between real and artificial occurs in *All My Friends Are Going to Be Strangers*, when Danny Deck says he only went to third-rate movies, explaining that "I didn't want to see films that reminded me about life—I wanted to see films that bore little relation to it . . . anything unreal" (85). This sort of self-conscious reference of literature to art was in the nineteenth century a familiar technique of the realists whose program was to record life as they believed it actually was. In the twentieth-century novels of Larry McMurtry, such references serve to highlight the motivation of the major characters whose feelings of emptiness spur them to ceaseless journeys in search of a reality more meaningful than can be found in the lives they seem fated to inhabit.

Of course, no character is more dissatisfied than Danny Deck, who gives the manuscript of his new novel to the drift of the Rio Grande in *All My Friends Are Going to Be Strangers*. Only about a third as long as *Moving On*, this book is just as much a composition of episodes within a journey. Because the story tempts us to take it as a quasi-autobiographical work, several critics have made extended interpretations of the character of Danny Deck as a portrait of the artist.

Barbara Granzow has read the novel as a reflection of Wallace Stegner's definition of the Western writer. Stegner wrote "Born a Square: The

Westerner's Dilemma" in 1964, and according to Granzow, McMurtry brought the generalizations to life in 1972 with *All My Friends*. The dilemma Stegner proposes lies in the Western writer's "naivete when confronted with worldliness, his meliorism when surrounded with apparent nihilism, and his struggle for a new personal identity when faced with literary success" (in Reynolds 1989, 242). The dilemma proceeds through stages of alienation from the homeland, beginning with the sale of a novel and proceeding through the writer's attempt to assimilate the values of the "Eastern publishing and critical establishment." The positive resolution of the dilemma would be, according to Stegner and others, the writer's acceptance of his own native values and a return to a new beginning in the West. Granzow makes it easy to witness Danny's move through the stages of separation from the ways of his homeland, his exile, and his confrontation of such alien ways as those exemplified in Los Angeles by the movie producer Leon O'Reilly. In the process of demonstration, she characterizes Danny's work on the novel *The Man Who Never Learned*, which he cribs from Jill Peel, as an attempt to assimilate Eastern values. By this formulation, with reinforcement from places in the novel's text where Danny says he is not mad at life and does not feel sorry for himself, Danny appears to Granzow to be orphaned in a borderland between West and East, rejecting the latter and unable to return to the innocence of the former.

Aurora Greenway, the dominant and major character in *Terms of Endearment*, sparks responses in readers and critics, ranging from delight to impatience. Michael Meshaw, reviewing *Terms of Endearment* in *Texas Monthly*, comments on Aurora's "hugeness of spirit" harboring "an infinity of contradictions." The unconventional arrangements she constructs—for example, indulging suitors who individually cannot satisfy her, but who collectively add up to "the perfect mate"—come to appear sane and reasonable when compared to the catastrophes that her daughter, Emma Horton, and her maid, Rosie Dunlup, produce (in Reynolds 1989, 237–39). Robert Towers, treating the book in the *New York Times Book Review*, finds Aurora, "who is supposed to be so charming . . . little more than a termagent" (Reynolds 1989, 240–42). Clay Reynolds in *The Southwest Review* (1976) considers Aurora a stereotype, and Roberta Sorenson in *Western American Literature* (1977) thinks Aurora saves a novel that otherwise lacks insight. The diversity of opinion about Aurora seems irresolvable until one realizes that McMurtry develops his characterizations guided by two purposes. The most obvious purpose, of course, is portraiture that captures the peculiarities of character. The author also has in mind to convey the thematic resonance of the character, which is less apparent in a work as sizeable as *Terms of Endearment*, simply because there is so much detail.

A key to discerning the presence of the two purposes in the characterization of such a figure as Aurora Greenway lies in giving some thought to what it means to say a character is eccentric. Geometers use the term eccentric to refer, for example, to circles that are not concentric, because their centers are differently placed. Certainly, Aurora suits the meaning of the term; she seems to be erratic or decentered, because in her desire to control the lives of those around her she deviates from expected behavior. She is extreme in her infuriated response to Emma's marriage and pregnancy, as well as in her frustration with the inadequate suitors who present themselves to her. Her reactions are stronger than we believe from our observations of real-life people to be normal. She behaves eccentrically. She does not center her responses the way others do. As we read episode after episode dominated in one fashion or another by Aurora (and in the Touchstone edition of *Terms of Endearment*, they fill 360 of the 410 pages), we begin to respond like the book reviewers did, as if Aurora Greenway were an actual person, which is to say that we have so much experience with her presence that we come to know her in a consistent way. She irritates or enchants us, much like real people will sometimes attract and sometimes bother us. But this is literature, and Aurora is a deliberate creation of fiction, not an acquaintance from life. Now it dawns on us. The art of McMurtry has rendered Aurora Greenway in so many dramatic episodes that readers feel they have lived with her. At the same time, though, the episodes have repeatedly made the same point of her vanity and controlling personality, so that character and theme are now inseparable.

THEMES AND STRUCTURE

The Houston trilogy revisits the theme of the lost past McMurtry had developed through his three Thalia novels. Two years after completing that initial trilogy in 1966, McMurtry published his collection of personal essays, entitled *In a Narrow Grave*. In one of those essays, he makes a telling contrast between the lives of an earlier generation of Texans and himself. His grandfather, he reports, was sent to town at the age of twelve with a herd of steers and an assignment to sell them, buy new animals, bring them home, and show a profit. When Larry McMurtry was twelve, "he would have been hard put to drive a very docile herd of steers forty yards." Actually, the death of the Old West was even more recent than his grandfather's generation, for when his uncles were young, they could see a cattle drive from their barn roof, while the scene he watched from the same barn showed pickup trucks going by. Still, that older way of life, McMurtry says, "has not quite died in me—not quite. I missed it only by the width of a generation and, as I was growing up, heard the whistle of its departure" (139–40).

The whistle sounds for the characters of the Houston trilogy also. They know the older West mostly by the bastardized pretense of rodeo competition, but their stories also contain a more direct treatment of the age of ranching by the notable introduction of Roger Wagoner in *Moving On* and Danny Deck's Uncle Laredo and the Hacienda of the Bitter Waters in *All My Friends Are Going to Be Strangers*. As a West Texas rancher, Roger Wagoner has retained his connection to the land as a setting of tangible influence on his life and a source of traditional values. When he appears in the novel, strong feeling accompanies him, and the feeling carries over to the ranch. Visiting it, Patsy senses it to be a vital place. Spending time with Roger at the ranch, she takes his set ways as indicators of his integrity. In a generous gesture of continuity, Roger wills his ranch to Patsy and Jim, but neither is capable of resuming the rancher's way of life. Their alienation from the old ways is too complete, their condition too lonely to endure the isolation.

By contrast to Roger, Uncle Laredo appears in his novel like a gross mockery. His ranch house is a Victorian mansion, his livestock are a medley of camels, goats, buffalo, and antelope. One of his ranch hands has sex with any vacancy he can find, including post holes in the ground. The cook, Lorenzo, joins Laredo every night in a vigil awaiting the return of Emiliano Zapata. If Roger Wagoner gives *Moving On* a feeling of nostalgia for lost ways, Uncle Laredo makes it apparent in *All My Friends Are Going to Be Strangers* that, as McMurtry wrote in *Rodeo*, attempting to sustain tradition past its time "falls somewhere between silliness and the outright ridiculous" (82).

The theme receives extended treatment in the Houston trilogy. From the perspective of theme's influence on narrative structure, the episodic construction of *Moving On* and an ending in which the story trails off seem completely apt, because a strongly plotted and patterned narration would suggest the opposite of what the experience of Patsy and the others indicates, namely, that their living has no discernible points of accomplishment or inherent purpose. The universe inhabited by the characters of the novel suggests an existential philosopher's conception of a universe without meaning. What purpose or significance is to be found in life must be the consequence of purposeful decisions. The will of the younger Houstonians in *Moving On*, though, seems to have been sapped. They are adrift.

In addition to giving Danny Deck a career similar to his own, Mc-Murtry has also encouraged critics to interpret *All My Friends Are Going to Be Strangers* as the artist's portrait by remarks about his own feeling of ambivalence about writing. In an interview with Si Dunn conducted for the *Texas Observer* in 1976, he said that reflecting on your writing creates ambivalence: "You get to wondering what it is doing to you, sitting in a corner with a machine, projecting your emotions [through characters on paper]" (quoted in Busby 1995, 129). The year before the Dunn interview, McMurtry wrote in an article for *Atlantic* that novelists "exploit a given region, suck what thematic riches they can from it, and then, if they are able, move on to whatever regions promise yet more riches. I was halfway through my sixth Texas novel [*Terms of Endearment*] when I suddenly began to notice that where place was concerned, I was sucking air" (quoted in Busby 1995, 129).

This statement by McMurtry suggests yet a further theme of importance, namely, the authenticity of writing. Its pertinence derives not only from the fact that McMurtry has developed a reputation as a writer of the "authentic" West, but also from a sort of natural order in the career of the novelist. Our culture gives writing a luminous effect. To be a writer is tantamount to being a genius and, thereby, different from everyone else. To rise from the desk where one is fixed upon technical problems of narration and to see the physical book on sale, getting reviews, being purchased and read is a heady experience entirely unlike any other. Then, the marketing of books takes the writer into another alien experience. No wonder writers feel a sense of separation. No wonder also that they have a feeling of ambivalence about it. If popular success comes fast and early, as it did for Larry McMurtry, it seems entirely natural to develop self-doubt and then anxiety about what to do next. Surely, the evidence of this pattern in *All My Friends Are Going to Be Strangers* gives the book much of its appeal. Despite the episodic quality it shares with *Moving On*, the novel gains from the identifiable account of a writer's struggle a meaningful structure that relieves the existential angst of its predecessor.

As *All My Friends Are Going to Be Strangers* lends itself to being read as a partially autobiographical narrative of Larry McMurtry's becoming a professional writer, *Terms of Endearment* may be seen as the writer's tentative resolution of the problem of an adequate subject. When the Old West has become material for myth or parody, and the writer feels estranged from the tastes of the East, he must make the best of that limbo as his literary material. Two passages from *In a Narrow Grave* help to illuminate McMurtry's position as he began work on the Houston trilogy. The first speaks to his disposition as a writer and confirms the subject readers find him exploring in the books about Houston. "Not long after I entered the pastures of the empty page," he writes, "I realized that the place where all my stories start is the heart faced suddenly with the loss of its country, its customary and legendary range" (140). The second passage occurs at the conclusion of the critical essay entitled "Southwestern Literature?" in which McMurtry appraises figures responsible for creating the prevailing (largely false) images of Texas. A fear of being thought provincial, he says, has made too many Texas writers fearful of rendering the particularity of their own place: "If this is truly the era of the Absurd, then all the better for the Texas writer, for where else except California can one find a richer mixture of absurdities?" He then goes on to say that while the physical life of Texas, historical and contemporary, has been presented reasonably well in literature, "our emotional experience remains largely unexplored, and therein lie the dramas, poems, and novels" (54).

The heart facing loss . . . absurdity . . . emotional experience—these are the themes found in *Terms of Endearment*. Surprisingly, in light of his comments on Texas particularity, McMurtry's preface to the 1989 Touchstone edition of the novel says he thinks of it as his most European novel. Part of the reason is that the book was written in Europe, but more important is the fact that he wrote *Terms of Endearment* after rereading such nineteenth-century novelists as Balzac, Tolstoy, and George Eliot, each of whom took "a very searching look at the fibers and textures of life" (5). There lies the explanation of accidental European kinship. Those masters of the novel, who happen to have been Europeans, took social networks as their material. So, too, does Aurora Greenway, who imperiously seeks to direct the lives of family, suitors, employees, and anyone else who comes into her orbit. It is in social networks that she confronts loss and absurdity; thus, while reviewers are naturally drawn to comment on the individual whose figure is so prominent in *Terms of Endearment*, the structuring of the novel shows us its theme to be the way an individual defines herself in relation to the social web. One may feel alone—as Aurora, Danny, and other characters do—and one may be eccentrically singular as is Aurora, but the true self, the self that one hopes to make authentic, is the product of interrelationships with other people.

A major theme of McMurtry's Houston novels reveals that there is no innate essence to character, for character results from interaction. The negative remarks about Aurora Greenway in reviews, therefore, are really statements of failure to discern the connection between theme and the episodic structure the novel shares with the other works of the Houston trilogy. Perhaps by giving over a final brief section to the story of Emma's hapless life and unfortunate early death, McMurtry meant to give the narrative a tear-jerking ending, but it is more likely that he introduces the affecting scenes of Emma's dying to enforce the theme of absurdism, for the fictional world of *Terms of Endearment* lacks evident purpose or design. In such a place, what is there to prevent a daughter dying before her mother? What happens, happens, and the point of life is to cope as gracefully as possible with the circumstances life presents. Emma's pregnancy threatens Aurora's chances for remarriage, she thinks, and it infuriates her. Emma's marriage to the unsuitable Flap is a disappointment to a mother's hopes, and it constantly irritates Aurora. Her suitors are inadequate, and it frustrates Aurora. What is a body to do in the face of such chancey happenings beyond one's control but try to find a graceful means of coping. For Aurora, those graceful means are the rules of conduct she tries to impose on those around her with the force of her personality.

One critic considering how puzzling the book is when a reader tries to discern the logic of its organization is Kerry Ahearn, who recommends thinking of "marriage as the major theme and widow Aurora Greenway the aging prophetess. Like *Leaving Cheyenne*, this novel presents not a vision of life as it is lived but a fantasy antidote: men's savage and possessive love is somehow lulled by a strong woman who charms them so completely that she occupies the center, loved by all but controlled by none" (287–88). So far as there being a theme of marriage in the novel, Ahearn's interpretation is all well and good, but the judgment of the action in the novel as fantasy is unfair. It may be implausible that a woman would be able to keep so many men on the string, but it is not unlikely that she would attempt to do so in order to counter personal loneliness and existential absurdity. Much of the puzzlement felt by readers and critics of McMurtry's writing arises from an unwillingness to follow the logic of literature that says behind any structure, or lack of it, and behind every style lies the author's conception of reality. That conception can be that there is scant ground for believing life has evident purpose. *Terms of Endearment* defies attempts to discover an inherent design to the narrative, because the underlying proposition in McMurtry's trilogy is that after the land has been fenced and gated and drilled with oil rigs, there is no longer a compelling design to be found, or at least not yet to be found. It is possible to doubt the proposition, but the novels cannot be judged as something they are not.

A MULTICULTURAL READING OF THE HOUSTON TRILOGY

Literary criticism cannot be confined to study of all that is present in a text. Sometimes what is not present is also worthy of study. Feminist critics have made this point as they have examined such popular genres of writing as the hard-boiled detective story that features a strong masculine presence in the person of the sleuth but, until recently, has excluded females from any but supporting, and often demeaning, roles in fighting crime. When the women are only victims of crime or *femmes fatales* luring men to destruction—see, for example, the stories of Philip Marlowe by Raymond Chandler—then the critics rightly judge the genre as preoccupied with fostering social stereotypes of both men and women.

A similar investigation of obvious absences is possible for Larry McMurtry's Houston trilogy. For all of their concern with a lost history of the West and their fixation on the contemporary scene of urban life, it is striking how closed the societies of these open-ended novels are. Without exception, all of the major characters and all of the minor characters of consequence are White people. There is a mix of social and economic class in the rodeo scenes and in Aurora Greenway's immediate household, but the few Mexicans play ludicrous roles in association with Uncle Laredo. And there are no African Americans; their presence in the world noted only when a character makes an occasional racial slur.

Of course, neither Hispanics nor African Americans are absent from the real world that these novels purport to represent. Approximately 10 percent of the population of Texas in 1970 was African American; the Hispanic population was many times that. Moreover, both Hispanics and African Americans have had notable parts in the history of the Southwest. Texas was once part of Mexico. It also became a producer of cotton, a crop dependent on Black labor, and part of the Confederate States of America formed to preserve Negro slavery. All-Black cavalry units, the famed Buffalo soldiers, fought in the Indian wars. Black and Mexican cowboys rode the plains. But the place of these ethnic groups is unmentioned in the novels as part of the history of Texas in its mythic days, nor are present-day Hispanics and African Americans in the Houston of the McMurtry novels. Why is this so, when verisimilitude (the appearance of reality), so crucial to the mode of realism, would demand that Hispanics and African Americans appear?

The effect is easier to describe than the cause, for the consequence of the exclusion of non-White characters and culture is to repeat the decades of misrepresentation when non-Whites were written *out* of the national history, leaving the impression that America was exclusively a European enterprise and European Americans the inheritors of the land. In this version of history, people of color became the "other" people, aliens in the midst of the real Americans.

It is beyond McMurtry's control that the absence of people of color from his novels concurs with racially determined ways of writing about America as a White country, unless it could be shown that he has deliberately tried to falsify his representations of reality. Since there is absolutely no evidence of that, the explanation of the absence must be found by determining what his deliberate literary purposes were, if not to practice racial exclusion.

Once a multicultural consideration of the Houston trilogy is undertaken, it becomes clear that there is a paradox in the reputation the novels have for breadth and inclusiveness. These large, episodic novels freighted with so much detail are nonetheless works of preoccupation. They are centered only on a body of people McMurtry knows well, because he has been one of them—graduate student, apprentice writer, urbanite bereft of his past. They are not, in fact, fully novels of Texas; instead, they are novels of Anglo Texas alone. While the themes and philosophical conception of reality have been applied by other writers in fiction about other groups, for McMurtry they can only be lodged in the niche of Anglo experience.

Multicultural criticism is an analytic and descriptive mode of analysis. It does not prescribe subjects for McMurtry or any other author. It is, however, a sobering kind of criticism. Used for perspective on the Houston trilogy, it leaves one aware that there is an even bigger story of Texas yet untold.

5

Interlude
Somebody's Darling (1978)
Cadillac Jack (1982)
The Desert Rose (1987)

Larry McMurtry's disposition to repeat the appearance of characters from novel to novel makes it convenient for critics to cluster his works, as they do with the Thalia novels and the Houston trilogy. The habit is hard to break, even when the novels in question do not display the same kinds of extended interrelationships among the narratives as the first two groupings do. The three books McMurtry published during the nine years from 1978 to 1987 offer a case in point. If you look hard enough, you find evidence that McMurtry conceives his stories on a scale larger than a single novel.

Somebody's Darling links most clearly to *All My Friends Are Going to Be Strangers* from the Houston trilogy because, while it employs Joe Percy, who appears in *Moving On* as one of the first-person storytellers, it elevates the character of Jill Peel, who is one of Danny Deck's lovers in *All My Friends*, to a central narrative position. In his preface to a paperback edition of *Cadillac Jack*, McMurtry once more evokes Danny by declaring that the character Jack McGriff most reminds him of is the "young writer who raced across the lawn of imagination some twelve years ago, in a book called *All My Friends Are Going to Be Strangers*" (ix). *The Desert Rose* does not reincarnate characters, but it has a loose connection to earlier McMurtry novels through the fact that its lead figure represents what he terms a dying craft: "I have always been attracted to dying crafts—cowboying is one such. It became clear [while writing *The Desert Rose*] that the showgirls were the cowboys of Las Vegas" (x).

McMurtry's reintroduction of characters and events is not, however, what finally allows readers to connect *Somebody's Darling, Cadillac Jack,* and *The Desert Rose*. Instead the link appears through the novelist's examination in each novel of a milieu of popular culture. Jill Peel is a screenwriter and director. All of her associates are movie people, engaged in one way or another in the business of creating those artifacts of illusion marketed as Hollywood's product and America's dreams. Cadillac Jack works in the vast economy of antiques, the cast-off goods that acquire value to the degree that they become physical objects of desire for collectors. And Harmony, performing in feathers before Las Vegas audiences, participates in a business that in its maintenance of an idealization of female sexual availability illusory as the Hollywood movies and as fraught with the desire for possession as the antique economy.

Where the Thalia novels set their action in the gap left as Texans lost their heart's land, and the Houston trilogy shows its characters without mooring in urban emptiness, this next group of novels ventures into the new world of significations (which, in the previous trilogies, is delineated as the myth of the West) that human beings create to make sense of their existence. This relationship, however, is generally unremarked by reviewers; instead, they have grouped together in leveling criticism more abusive of these novels than of any of McMurtry's earlier writing. That treatment, in combination with the glitzy environments the novels describe, has led to their reputation as the "trash trilogy" (see, for example, the heading for treatment of these works in Reynolds 1989, 151). Despite the critical opinion, though, an examination of these three novels in the context of McMurtry's development shows them to have considerable importance for the evidence they contain of the novelist's intuitive discovery of a new landscape.

NARRATIVE STYLE

In his preface to *Somebody's Darling*, McMurtry comments that he had wanted to write the story in the third person, although he began the novel in the first person. Once before, in *The Last Picture Show*, he had rewritten a first-person draft as third person. This time, for reasons including his lack of confidence about the details of Hollywood necessary

for a third-person rendering, and the relative ease of catching the into-
nation of Joe Percy's voice, he left the narrative unaltered (ix–x). Had
McMurtry, in fact, made the translation from first person to third person
that he claims he contemplated, obviously it would have been a significantly different book. A third-person narration can tell readers much
about characters, but it is always from a distance and always mediated
by a narrative voice demanding attention to the nature of the persona
behind it, as well as challenging readers to decipher the reported character's way of viewing experience. What is the age or gender or background of the third-person narrator? What assumptions about human
nature are guiding that speaker's portrayals? These are questions inevitable to a third-person narration that may be deflected by a first-person
presentation. When a character speaks for herself or himself in narration,
a level of mediation is removed, with the effect that the speech of the
character becomes an element of characterization.

This is so in *Somebody's Darling* where even while Joe Percy is presenting biographical facts about Jill Peel in the first section of the novel
that are intended to introduce her to readers, the voice of his exposition
also works to establish Joe's preoccupation with a self-pity he expresses
in voluble mockery. An interesting complexity results from the use of
the first-person voice in the section of the same novel said to be narrated
by Owen Oarson. Dedicated to self-justification and the settling of scores
with those who have offended him, the cynicism and vindictiveness of
Owen's account unintentionally transform it into self-condemnation. Finally, McMurtry demonstrates with Jill's narration of the novel's third
section how a character who has been elaborately discussed by others
nevertheless will reveal depths of insecurity and feeling unimagined by
her acquaintances.

McMurtry employs first-person narration to good effect once again in
Cadillac Jack. Clay Reynolds, noting that his speech is sprinkled with
unlikely words for a cowboy such as "bethought," "beringed," and "lu-
bricity," thinks Jack is a caricature of the westerner gone eastern (1989,
284). Word choice is not the whole of language, however, nor is fidelity
to actuality always the wisest possibility in narration. A work of docu-
mentary realism would not contain a character who is a thirty-three-year-
old, six-foot-five-inch, twice-married former rodeo bulldogger who deals
knowledgeably in Sung vases, ancient truncheons, all manner of chests,
as well as cowboy boots. But a work of fiction concerned to posit a
relationship between the artifice of latter-day rodeo and the conventions
or decorum of antique artifacts can make a character like Jack McGriff

seem entirely appropriate to the story. It can do so especially when the
character's creator gives him immediate presence in the text through the
sublimation of all the pertinent information about his nature in the character's own voice. Were he presented in a third-person narration, perhaps he would seem as implausible as Reynolds believes him to be, but
in speaking for himself, Jack's unusual voice acts to certify the narration.
A man doing the kind of things Jack does, the reader feels, probably
would talk in language as heterogeneous as his fields of knowledge.

Curiously, McMurtry prefaces *The Desert Rose* with a discussion of the
book as through it were written in the first-person point of view. Explaining how the character of Harmony seized his interest, he writes that
"Harmony's voice won me at once; I felt I had rarely, if ever, made a
happier choice of point of view." A few lines later, he adds that the
energy he gained when he took a break from the composition of *Lonesome
Dove*, which he left unfinished until well after this novel, enabled him to
complete Harmony's novel in three weeks. In explanation, he says that
he believes he was energized by switching his attention from the third-
person novel about men to Harmony's story (x–xi).

This preface cannot help but confuse a reader, since the novel starts
right out in what looks to be third person: "Harmony is driving home,
eastward out of Las Vegas, her spirits high, her head a clutter of memories. Harmony loves to remember bits of her life, it makes her feel well,
anyway, it's all been interesting" (3). The second sentence of this passage
adds complication. Having started out in a reporting voice typical of an
omniscient third-person narrator, the run-on sentence then makes a shift
near its ending to language that could be a simulation of Harmony's
voice, if she were narrating. The sliding standpoint of narration continues throughout the novel. To take a random example, here is an account
of Harmony after a show. "From behind the bar Giorgio was smiling at
her with his big white teeth again." That's more or less reportorial, but
it is followed immediately by this passage: "He was quite a nice-looking
guy really, very Italian. Now that he was out of baccarat he always wore
bright shirts, they looked like silk, with the sleeves rolled up to show
his muscle, he was always sort of smiling and showing off his muscle,
it was kind of charming really, you could just see him thinking how
could any woman resist me" (47). The voice of this passage possesses
information about Giorgio's circumstance—that he no longer works the
baccarat table—prior to the reported event of his smiling. That seems to
characterize a third-person narration. The shirts looking like silk, though,
presents an immediate perception by someone looking at Giorgio smil-

ing. The inference about his showing off muscle and thinking he is irresistible, then, carries the perception forward to offer a comment tantamount to gossip, as Harmony might say it under her breath to a table companion. But she is not saying it, at least not directly.

What McMurtry has devised for *The Desert Rose* is a type of narrative technically known as indirect discourse. The perceptions and peculiarities of language usage may belong to a character in such narration, but rather than have the character speak in quotation marks, the author reports what the character says in a style that retains the cadence and word choice of the speaker, while setting the gist of the speech free from the conventions of written dialogue, such as the tag lines "she said" and then "he said." Indirect discourse introduces a level of subjectivity into narrative, while the omniscient voice, which determines when to allow subjective expression, retains command of all the information. The subjective passages are illustrative, but character remains distanced. In *The Desert Rose*, the technique communicates the fact that development occurs in terms of Harmony's situation rather than in her character.

CHARACTER DEVELOPMENT

In the opening section of *Somebody's Darling*, as Joe Percy gives the details of Jill Peel's life necessary to create the impression that the novel concerns real people who naturally have biographies, Joe's voice also tells readers that he is a contract writer for movies and author of a by-now-forgotten novel. More importantly, the voice shows him to be at once a man of learning and a man with an injured ego. Telling the episode of a reception he attended, he characterizes himself as like Dr. Brydon, the lone survivor of a retreat in the British Afghan campaign. The last of 15,000 British lost in a foray, Brydon straggled back to his garrison to report the loss of 14,999 of his colleagues. Looking at the new faces surrounding him at The Lincoln Center reception, Joe figures he is the only remaining member of the band of old-time movie people, fallen (in a manner of speaking) in the canyons of southern California (97). The fanciful self-description extending in simile for a full page manages to be a typical Joe Percy display—gabby, self-pitying, and self-denigrating all at once. On another occasion, following intercourse with the much younger woman who is his current sex-mate, he waxes like John Keats: "Page at twenty-five was more perfect than anything that would ever happen to her, and she should never have to change, grow up, grow old, grow pale, or tired, or bitter. It was the thought that those states would come to her too that made me sad" (54).

Despite the disclaimer—Joe maintaining that he is sad for Page, not for himself—at age sixty-three and writing now for an unpromising television series, Joe is surely lamenting his own transitory life. Perhaps if he had satisfying work, he could be content, or if he had an intimately complete relationship with another person, the work could be less disappointing. But he has lost his wife, Claudia, and not gotten over her death, and the work he does now is pretty much as he describes it, hack work. Jill Peel, who provides balm for Joe's condition of emptiness, can be his best friend but not his life's mate. Sex that once enriched his life with Claudia is now, in the time of Joe's narration, so necessary to him as distraction from anxiety and sadness that he seeks out women who will be no more than physical partners.

Still, despite Joe's evident spiritual malaise, McMurtry inscribes his character with such sympathy that his fate in the novel engages readers as much as Jill's. The case is entirely the contrary with Owen Oarson whose first-person voice presents the second section of the novel. Hud in *Horseman, Pass By* set the pattern for Oarson's type of skeptical character. Centered on his own pleasures and status, cynical about the values of others, resentful and vindictive, the foul-mouthed Oarson's part of *Somebody's Darling* lacks any evidence of authorial sympathy. He functions in the overall narrative to illustrate the rapacious figures attracted by the glamour and wealth proffered by the film industry, and in the developing portrait of Jill Peel, he serves to introduce an inexplicable element. How, we ask, could she be attracted to him? Perhaps in preverbal, physical ways he communicates a virility she wants, or an escape she needs.

Surely, as her character develops through the first two sections of the novel and into the final part she narrates herself, Jill appears to be a needy person. Described as Hollywood's first woman director, thirty-seven-year-old Jill Peel, due to the success of her film, *Womanly Ways*, is what agents call a hot property. Success in the film industry must always be reinforced, though; and since the bottom line for a production turns so quickly from black to red, an artist such as Jill intends to be lives a life of constant stress. Like other characters in McMurtry novels, Jill seems driven to complicate her life with hopeless sexual alliances that forestall the possibility of developing a complete personal life. Jill has had more lovers than she can recall. She has a child she does not see. But she does have her friend, Joe Percy, and it seems to be the aim of

McMurtry to make the sexless relationship with Joe the site for revelation of Jill's vulnerability, and her association with the novel's secondary characters Tub McDowell, Elmo Buckle, Winfield Gohagen, and Mr. Mond occasions to round out her personality. Tub is the bookseller who brings her to tears and rueful memory with talk about river books of the sort Danny Deck loved and the presentation to her of Danny Deck's novel, *The Restless Grass*. Buckle and Gohagen are the wildly successful script writers who join her in the abortive theft of her film, *One Tree*. Mr. Mond is the film magnate who acts as Jill's sponsor in the business. These minor characters are well and fully detailed enough to earn them intrinsic interest in the Hollywood gallery of types. In relation to Jill, however, they work to evoke her capacity for affection, her possession of nerve, and her sometimes madcap manner. Collectively, the major and minor characters of *Somebody's Darling* demonstrate the richness of McMurtry's storytelling. His ear for the cadences of speech that distinguish one person from another grasps his readers' attention, while his eye for the bizarre yet plausible detail always gives the speech a subject worth noticing.

Jack McGriff is a vagabond of the interstate highway system. As Jane Nelson puts it in *A Literary History of the American West*, the Western land holds no emotional importance in *Cadillac Jack*: "Now the Western past is represented by a cattle rancher who is a drug addict; the modern West is run by a network of female real estate agents who are directed by a powerful and dynamic woman living in the East" (618). His automobile's trunk packed with a hodgepodge of swaps and purchases from auctions and yard sales, Jack carries with him on his tour of the milieu of antiques the fulfillment of customers' wishes—pieces to fill in collections of this or that, objects to affirm someone's standing as a collector, or to furnish the phenomena which provide a sense of commanding a material reality. Through his relationships with his former wife, Coffee, Cindy Sanders, and Jean Arber (neé Tooley), it develops that Jack's physical journeying back and forth across America replicates an interior quest. Impressively exotic as he appears to be, the women are not bowled over by him; instead, they use him alternately for adventure and social management. Coffee demands that Jack telephone her regularly to hear of her troubles with boyfriends. The incorrigible social climber, Cindy, requires his service as an escort to all the events where she simply must be seen. Jean, a genuinely decent and affectionate woman with Jack, nonetheless judges him as the wrong man for her and her daughters.

Jack's experiences in love increasingly seem to be symptomatic of a deep spiritual fatigue. He has a wonderfully clear eye for the beauty of objects and can even see the beauty of composed landscapes (*Cadillac Jack*, 153), but after completing the telling of slightly more than half of his narrative, he relates that he has suddenly grown tired of objects. He is in Bryan Ponder's garage inspecting his enormous collection of birds' nests when he feels the loss of his "appetite for the bizarre. . . . I had just O.D.ed on objects" (215). The emptiness he feels extends to the world around him. He wants somehow to center himself in life, but the people he sees in federal offices and the Washington suburbs who might be thought typical and centered in life seem to him, in their drab synthetic clothes and desperate manners, way off in some zone where he does not wish to drift (223). Following the example of James Joyce, who describes certain evanescent moments in *A Portrait of the Artist as a Young Man* as epiphanies, literary critics have taken up the term epiphany to denote scenes with a sudden revelation of a spiritual state. Of course, the term originates in the festival of the Three Kings that celebrates on January 6 the appearance of God in the world. Putting the term to use for these experiences of Cadillac Jack McGriff, we have the suggestion that McMurtry is marking the development of Jack's character by a series of negative epiphanies, during which Jack feels significance draining from his world.

   Cadillac Jack is, again, a McMurtry novel filled with a cast of odd and interesting secondary characters, among them Boog Miller, owner of Winkler County, Texas, and collectors like Benny the Ghost of Baltimore. These figures populating the milieu McMurtry is exploring function, like the subjects of an anthropologist's study, to create a texture of characterization to embody the acquired cultural habits and practices of their culture. In a significant variation on the cast, though, McMurtry also introduces the charming Belinda and Beverly, Jean's small children, who are meant to be taken as normative figures, the best of ordinary folk before their innate goodness has been fully conditioned to conformity with the guarded and selfish ways of adults. Because the normative figures are children in this novel, it has a romanticism indicative of McMurtry's regard for his hapless protagonist.

   As analysis of the technique of narration in *The Desert Rose* has shown, development occurs more through situation than character. The story relating the end of Harmony's career as a showgirl, and the start of her daughter Pepper's, shows the changes to occur through choices made by the manager-producer of the Las Vegas casino show rather than through any actions taken by the women. From first to last, Harmony possesses the unchanging traits of a survivor: she is surprisingly optimistic and more or less resourceful. Pepper's character—ever impatient, self-centered, and limited—also shows constancy. The result is a novel of circumstantial reportage, where the characters do not undergo internal change, nor, for that matter, do their characters resonate with significance beyond themselves. It is hard to imagine that McMurtry intended them to represent any particular female accomplishment or type, and they are not given a capacity for reflection that would make it possible to see them as commentators on the culture they inhabit. In fact, they seem to be entirely the products of show-biz culture that establishes women as commodities for the entertainment trade. They are rarities in McMurtry's fiction, because their makeup lacks any reference to a past before Las Vegas became a capital of glitz. Living always in a tawdry present, they are redeemed as creatures of interest for readers by the same quality that enabled their author to complete their narrative in a record time of three weeks—plausibly human voice.

PLOT DEVELOPMENT AND DESIGN

The emphasis in this discussion upon plot *and* design is intended to direct attention to complexity that can be overlooked in a strictly categorical analysis of texts. Separate consideration of narrative style, character development, plot, and theme has utility, but, as has become apparent, these elements synergistically relate to form a finished narrative in which all the parts contribute to the enduring effect. It is especially true that the matter of plot needs regard for full understanding of other features of narration. Handbooks of literary terms correctly define plot as the sequence of occurrences in a narrative more or less linked in a causal chain. Pure summary of plot would state the order of fictional happenings. It would be the skeletal residue when all else is boiled away, just as bare and inanimate. Like a skeleton, a fiction's plot becomes evident in the play of the elements that clothe it. The whole may be thought of as a design, in the formation of which the writer has combined many inseparable features.

While the flow of voice in these three novels accounts for much of their appeal, they must not be taken as shapeless transcriptions of talk. The speaking voices constitute the immediate present of the novels relating the ways the narrators perceive their experiences while telling their stories. Beneath this surface, however, lies the larger design. The present moments of speech satisfy the author's obligation to give a semblance of actuality (verisimilitude) and to record character in action, but the novelist also creates destiny in the fictional world. As the maker of all within the book, the writer comes equipped with a vision of the whole. He or she knows, when characters do not, how they will come through the events of the story and what those events will be. Plot comprises a pattern serving as the armature for the general design.

The plot or sequence of events in *The Desert Rose* representing the termination of Harmony's career as a showgirl and her ironic replacement on stage by Pepper embodies the understanding that the rise and fall of a career in the flesh trade is beyond the control of will. Before the novel begins, Harmony has become a successful showgirl, not because of any innate or developed talent, but because her body conforms to sexually charged notions of physical beauty. When, due to age, she can no longer meet those standards, her career ends.

Other characters play supporting roles. In the second section of the book, though, one of the supporting cast—Harmony's daughter, Pepper—comes forward to take more attention than is usually accorded to a supporting player. Soon, she seems to be presenting a story equal in length to her mother's. What's happening? McMurtry has begun to turn his plot toward the purpose of revealing the fuller design. Pepper speaks more, and her life secures more coverage, because her story is counterpointing Harmony's. Eventually, the plot and design of the novel assume the form of a large X. At the top of one axis is Harmony, who begins a downward descent in her showgirl career. At the bottom of the other axis, Pepper is located at the start of her career. The axes cross when Jackie Bonventre fires Harmony, making his purpose of replacing her with Pepper clear when he crassly explains, "I don't want to put a mother and a daughter on the same stage, it could mean some tricky publicity." The spell of illusion in a show that strips women not only of their clothing but also of their awkward real-life circumstances, so that they are objectified as sexual goals, would be broken: "You could be a grandmother soon, you know. Topless grandmothers just aren't what the public wants to see" (182–83). With that speech, it becomes evident that in *The Desert Rose* Larry McMurtry has rewritten the film story *A Star Is Born*, which recounts how a young understudy replaces an older performer, as biting satire.

Patterns of rise and fall also provide plot and structure for *Somebody's Darling*, although without the stark clarity of design found in *The Desert Rose*. From the beginning of the novel, Joe Percy is in decline in his career and psyche. As he puts it late in the novel, he wished his life to be like a good script with the incidents adding up, characters complementing each other, the story line clear, but in his experience there was no important story line (399). Meanwhile, Jill Peel, despite personal dissatisfaction that leads her to promiscuity, appears to be rising to artistic prominence in the movie business. In his own tawdry way, Owen Oarson parallels Jill's rise by opportunistically attaching himself to women he can use for personal advancement in return for stud service. Again, the writer uses the pattern in a critical way, for advancement in McMurtry's Hollywood has much less to do with the integrity or quality of art than it does with commercial manipulation or ego gratification. And again, there is the understanding that talent and will seem to amount to less than chance, along with another dose of McMurtry's irony, deriving from the fact that the writers of satisfying plots cannot find a plot sufficient for their own lives.

To further complicate plot and design in *Somebody's Darling*, McMurtry accompanies the tale of falling and rising Hollywood reputations with a subtext of human companionship between Jill and Joe. While the movie careers of the characters hold the center of the frame, a story of the long-term effort to sustain friendship plays along the margins. Jill and Joe banter almost like a married couple, have times of emotional intimacy, break up, and reestablish companionship in awkward ways, each always valuing the other with an affection unlike any they feel for anyone else. As the novel arrives at its end, things in the center of the frame could hardly be worse. Joe does only hackwork, and his sexual escapism is stymied by impotence. Jill has lost control of her film. At that point, McMurtry subordinates the plot of film careers and replaces it at the center of the novel with the plot of Jill and Joe's relationship. They have never slept together, but now they lie abed and Jill gratuitously gives Joe an erection. It is an odd, but for McMurtry, not an out-of-place scene. From the start, he has defined his characters largely by their sexuality, making their sense of identity depend heavily upon carnal performance. In this scene, then, occurring shortly before Joe's death, Jill has momentarily restored what identity he has been able to retain during his career decline. It seems that these two characters have risen to a level of human caring quite apart from the decline they suffer in their film careers. To make too much of this thematically would be sentimentality, which may be why McMurtry gives the scene an awkward earthiness, not to mention a decidedly male image of gratification, but still it does work to bring the novel's underlying construction to its surface.

The design of construction in *Cadillac Jack* lies in the same plane as the surface narration. The causation for the sequence of events making up the narration arises in Jack McGriff's character itself. He roves the interstate highways because he is the rootless man he is. His trade as antique scout suits him exactly because it gives him an outlet for his gregariousness while requiring travel. And he becomes involved with Cindy Sanders and Jean Arber for the same reason that he hits on women all the time—he relishes sex, feels confirmed and vital when he has sex. The plotting of the novel so that Jack enters the lives of Cindy and Jean seems determined, therefore, by the construction of *Cadillac Jack* as a literal road novel.

MODES OF NARRATION

The movement requisite to a road novel in *Cadillac Jack* also proves functional to the mode in which it is conceived. Representative scenes of the Georgetown party near the opening of the novel with attendant dogs on the dinner table, the embassy reception described in terms of hungry hordes awaiting access to the food, Boog Miller's household and his flirtations with nubile masseuses—together with the range of characters, including the columnist, Ponsonby, and Cindy herself—mark it as written in the mode of a comedy of manners. This type of literature concerns the behavior of people presented in terms of codes peculiar to their class or group. Comedies of manners often treat the wealthy and privileged, because their codes of conduct are so elaborated and precise, and the comedy frequently derives from the clash of an interloping character with the established conventions of behavior or manners. For fiction having to do with cultural artifice—as do the Hollywood film world, Las Vegas show biz, and antique collecting—the comedy of manners proves an effective instrument for examining milieu.

The mode of manners comedy allows a writer to adopt any one of a variety of possible stances. In the hands of a conservative exponent of established society, the comedy can make an outsider the butt of criticism. This is the case when the social climber or the nouveau riche character acts, in comparison to his betters, like a crude buffoon. This is a source of humor in *The Gilded Age* (1873), the novel by Mark Twain and Charles Dudley Warner about post–Civil War American society. Manners comedy can equally well mock the overly conservative character or anyone else, such as characters in Molière's plays, who may be presented as overzealous or otherwise in violation of a balanced norm of behavior. If the sympathies of the writer are with the outsider, as is the case with William Dean Howells in telling the story of a businessman who meets aristocratic society in *The Rise of Silas Lapham* (1885), then comedy comes at the expense of the establishment. The latter position informs *Cadillac Jack*. To the people he meets in Washington, D.C. through his affair with Cindy, Jack is the odd duck, but McMurtry invests Jack with control of the narrative so that his outlook becomes normative, besides which, Jack shares with his creator an eye for the unusual. The result is ridicule of the society that Cindy aspires to enter.

On the other hand, while in *Somebody's Darling* and *The Desert Rose* McMurtry devotes much description to the behavior of secondary characters we understand to be meant as typical of their milieu, the censorious tone takes those works into the mode of satire. Satire is a kind of exposure and protest. It demonstrates duplicity, falseness, guile, or immorality in a manner meant to ridicule offenders of the author's code of conduct and standards of ethics. As examples of satire in *Somebody's Darling*, the scenes of the press conference for Jill's picture and the party at Elaine's illustrate, in the first instance, McMurtry's view of film critics intent on grinding their axes and taking satisfaction at others' expense, and, in the second instance, gives in Joe's voice an account of vapid conversation and maneuvering egos. Further satire appears throughout the novel in the form of such characters as Oarson, whose portrayal excoriates talentless hangers-on, and the circumstances of film production as in the accidental success of the misconceived *Doom of Rome*. Character also carries a burden of satire in *The Desert Rose* where Jackie, the producer, exemplifies cold calculation in the flesh business and Pepper's betrothed, Mel, illustrates in a milieu that so insistently objectifies women that it makes love possible only in the form of voyeurism and spectacle.

Invariably, satiric writing implies the existence of the opposite of the behavior satirized. If selfish characters are denounced, then there will be indication in the text or exposition of generous behavior. In *Somebody's Darling*, the satiric text of movieland ambition is contrasted with the quite different subtext that tells of the abiding affection of Joe and Jill. That affection, forming first a margin to the centrally framed story, finally takes on the function of a norm of human feeling against which the satirized behavior in the remainder of the novel is contrasted. In *The Desert Rose*, the presumed norm—the way people, in the writer's opinion, ought to be—must lie with the resilience of Harmony and the demonstrable affection of her friend, Gary. Harmony's decency seems unblemished despite the uses to which the show-biz milieu puts her. Limited as she is, and as unattractive her occupation, Harmony, in contrast to Pepper who fully embodies the exploitative values of Vegas, has been drawn by McMurtry with a sympathy to make readers feel the shame of the treatment she is given in a dehumanizing milieu.

THEMATIC DEVELOPMENT

The discussion of character presentation and style, construction and mode should by now make it clear that these novels are indivisible. Consideration of the techniques of McMurtry's presenting character in the permutations of a first-person narration leads to observation of the significance of wandering Jack, disappointed Jill, and betrayed Harmony, while exploration of the modes McMurtry manages for the construction of the novels opens the way to draw conclusions about his view of the milieu in each work. Narration and mode both make it clear that the characters of McMurtry's "trash trilogy" reside in a world without a viable past and, in some cases, without any knowledge or memory of a grander Western way, actual or mythic. Their environment is the abstract realm of a landless, presentist culture. They exist within a reality secondary to the natural world, amid styles generated by commerce rather than organic nature or the seasons. In a practical sense, they are as without place as they are without a history, for their trades have to do with the desires and movements of febrile dreams created for the consciousness of those seeking illusion by those whose business it is to pre-form reality into appealing packages. To state that this is the case with the environments and characters McMurtry draws in these novels is also to state his theme of dissatisfaction with what the milieus of characters and occupations signify in contemporary culture—its reductive inhumanity, its mediocrity and insipidity.

Leading to a more specific consideration of this general theme: What determines value in *Somebody's Darling*, *Cadillac Jack*, and *The Desert Rose*? Jill Peel's film, *Womanly Ways*, receives acclaim, but then as the narration provides entrée to Hollywood talk, it seems that the ruling standards are either commercial or derivative of personal bias. The film industry, as its members like to term their business, operates through exchange of unreal images. Since movies are a visual storytelling medium, it could seem natural that deals would be consummated on the basis of visuali-

zations—spectacular scenic effects, fundamentally appealing stereotypes—but McMurtry seems to mean more than that. The product of his
Hollywood has no fundamental use value. The movies do not provide
dependable reports of reality or truth, nor in their provision of the experience of diversionary escape do they offer moral commentary or instruction. The telling significance of McMurtry's view of movieland
culture arises from the fact that his novel deals almost entirely with off-
screen affairs and matters, precisely that sector of life where artistic motivation and goals would most likely be evident. Yet, instead of aesthetic
development, social purposes, or thematic content, the talk is all about
the process of assembling the capital and crew, the hot writers, and appealing stars. The folks might as well be in the business of dispensing
opiates, as indeed McMurtry implies that they are.

What is value in *Cadillac Jack*? It is measured by scarcity and oddity.
Jack has some appreciation for his wares, but the artifacts—all of them
uprooted from the provenance where they had a utility—have become
objects of acquisitiveness. Value in *The Desert Rose*? There, too, it is constructed out of illusion. The idealized sexual bodies of Harmony and
Pepper bear no relation to productive sex and intimacy. In an ironic twist
to the theme of value, their female bodies are served up to viewers of
their casino acts as objects to use in fantasies of exploitation.

Substitute for value the word truth. Where is truth in the environments
of *Somebody's Darling*, *Cadillac Jack*, and *The Desert Rose*? The movie mo-
guls have no interest in truth. They profit on falsity. Las Vegas? In
McMurtry's book, it is all about misrepresentation. Truth for many of
the people Cadillac Jack encounters is simply an irrelevant issue. Beneath
the comedy of manners, within the satire of these novels lies a quiet fury
and frustration, because McMurtry views the conditions he reports as
more than a problem for his select protagonists. They are endemic to the
American popular culture.

Placing the characters of each of the three novels in an enveloping
milieu, McMurtry makes the books into broad social criticism. There is
no alternative economy for Jill and Joe, Jack, and Harmony and Pepper
to work in, no other medium for the expression or development of creativity and integrity. They are captives of a consuming cultural system.

What gives poignance to the critical theme is the worthiness of the
central characters, conveyed through McMurtry's sympathetic rendering
of their voices and his sketching of them as redemptive figures—insistent
believers in norms, opposed to the debased kind of value that typifies
their milieus. Jill Peel, Cadillac Jack, Harmony, and some others are char-

acters capable of more than the world allows them to be. If they falter, as all of them must in a truthful story, the fault is not theirs alone.

If only McMurtry did not grant his sympathy to his characters. Then the works could be dismissed as the trash some critics have felt them to be. But in his discovery that popular culture can be another landscape for his exploration, McMurtry held onto the essential humanism of the realist. He cannot give up on his people, and neither can his readers.

A BIOGRAPHICAL READING OF THE TRASH NOVELS

Teachers of literature will always take the opportunity to discourage their students from reading works of fiction as though they were taken from the author's own life. Right they are to do so, too, because writing always has more to do with thoughts about facts than about the facts themselves. Even when we are writing firsthand accounts of the way events really were, we engage in a process of selection and emphasis that converts raw data into story. The freedom to do this becomes all the more pronounced in fiction, where the genre one chooses and the plot devised introduce their own demands that help to shape story. Still, writing cannot be completely detached from experience. There is some connection and, providing a critic is careful not to insist upon one-to-one correspondence between fictional events and a presumed biography of the author, there can be legitimate use made of biographical interpretation.

There is, however, an important distinction to be made between types of biographical criticism: One looks for analogues between the fictional experience presented in the literary work and the life experiences of the author, while a second type treats the works as signifiers of the author's mood or state of mind during the creation of the work.

An example of the first type of biographical criticism is to be found in Janis Stout's "Cadillac Larry Rides Again: McMurtry and the Song of the Open Road." In this article, Stout maintains that Jack McGriff "is very much a projection of McMurtry himself, who in his capacity as rare book dealer, is known to wander the width of America in his own Cadillac, departing on marathon drives at a moment's notice, carrying his treasures in his trunk. The hero's occupation, too, is an apt projection of McMurtry's bits-and-pieces kind of novelistic virtuosity" (244). Such a connection as Stout draws between Larry and Jack is easy enough to entertain, since it is never surprising when a writer uses familiar material, and what is more familiar than personal experience? The idea might even be hazarded that the sympathy with which Jack is drawn on his unending voyage derives from the pleasure McMurtry has felt book scouting.

A more hazardous, but then also a richer, excursion into this type of biographical criticism can be made by noting that each of the so-called trash novels concerns the matter of authentic artistic expression. His tenure in Hollywood, and the reports he gives of it in *Film Flam*, seem provocative evidence that truthful expression has remained one of McMurtry's challenges since he labored over the revisions of *Horseman, Pass By* and the screenplays for others of his works. Considering the collective pressures of the profit-driven enterprise of movies, how is it that one holds onto a vision? Jill Peel and Joe Percy facing this issue plausibly seem to be surrogates for McMurtry, whose popularity has made him subject to both the beguiling promises of success and the demands of those who claim to know how to guarantee it to the writer.

The second type of biographical criticism that takes the works to signify a writer's state of mind, even when the subject or design of the works seems to bear no direct relationship to the fictional texts, appears to be stimulated by some of McMurtry's statements of feelings about the "trash" books. In his interview with Patrick Bennett conducted in 1980, after he had published *Somebody's Darling* and two years before the appearance of *Cadillac Jack*, he said he did not feel engaged by the story, that it was forced, because although he had wanted to do a novel about Jill Peel since writing *All My Friends Are Going to Be Strangers*, when the time came to do it, he had lost his initial energy (29–30). The comment does not completely contradict the idea suggested by the example above of the first type of biographical criticism claiming a surrogate relationship between Jill and McMurtry, but it does indicate that the critic needs to be wary of the analogues he or she may see.

A further addition to the evidence of McMurtry's feelings about *Somebody's Darling* appears in the preface to the paperback edition of the novel issued in 1988. There, he reiterates that the book was not timely and adds that he feared repeating himself by using the three first-person structures he had previously introduced in *Leaving Cheyenne*. Concluding the preface, he says he usually is depressed when he finishes a book and becomes separated from his characters, "but I was happy to be done with *Somebody's Darling* . . . I left it with a weary sense that it was a book I had essentially finished several years before I got around to writing it down" (ix–x).

That remark about weariness throws another light on an effort at biographical criticism. Our analysis is revealing that there are two levels of biographical significance. One may be that the tale of Jill and Joe was once, before it was actually completed, an exploration of the struggle for artistic integrity conducted through surrogates' stories, while the second level is addressed by placing the novel into the chronology of McMurtry's career. The conclusion thus becomes that the book had relevance to the author's feelings about Hollywood writing, but he had grown tired of lamenting the matter.

For at least one critic, the dissatisfaction McMurtry states that he felt about the experience of writing *Somebody's Darling* turned into a writer's crisis when he wrote *Cadillac Jack*. That critic, Clay Reynolds, reports that since his earlier works, "a feeling has grown that insofar as he is a representative of the Southwest, McMurtry is dead." The cause of the feeling was "a certain flatness, a loss of the inspiration that gave his early books their freshness and appeal." But, again according to Clay Reynolds in the same piece from 1985, there may be hope, for "McMurtry may be signaling, perhaps unconsciously, his awareness of this authorial identity crisis, and the careful reader can perceive a recognition on McMurtry's part of the need to return to his roots and make peace with his homeland" (1989, 281). Clay Reynolds finds the allure of his interpretation not in any independent evidence, but in his own opinion that *Cadillac Jack* is a "disorganized and ungainly tale." This opinion leads Reynolds to dispute the idea advanced in the discussion above that Jack serves as the satiric norm by stating that Jack is "neither normal nor believable," and what's more "is not even original," being loosely drawn from the figure of Vernon Dalhart in *Terms of Endearment* (283).

What can the two types of biographical criticism and contesting opinions about the execution of narration in the "trash" novels allow one to conclude about the relationship between McMurtry's three novels and his life? Larry McMurtry unquestionably abandoned the familiar Texas settings in these three novels. Without doubt also, he states an unease about *Somebody's Darling*. Equally incontrovertible is that McMurtry sees *The Desert Rose* as a book that reawakened his writer's energy. As he puts it in the 1984 preface to the Pocket Books edition, ordinarily writing fiction seemed to him "a semiconscious activity. I concentrate so hard on visualizing my characters that my actual surroundings blur. My characters seem to be speeding through their lives—I have to type unflaggingly in order to keep them in sight." But in 1983, he was "laboring away on a long novel about the 19th century West called *Lonesome Dove*. Some twelve hundred pages were in hand at the time; the narrative was not exactly stalled, but it was slowing." Instead of speeding along, "my characters seemed to be moving at an ox-like pace up the great plains . . . and still had a thousand miles to go." Then came the opportunity to write about a Las Vegas showgirl. A producer wanted a script. He accepted the chance "and before I had written a paragraph I knew I was writing a novel" (viii–x). Here is powerful evidence for biographical criticism. McMurtry was fatigued with writing, feeling in a slump. Then Hollywood called, and he regained energy. This is the same author speaking who had ridiculed Hollywood in *Somebody's Darling*, and whose collection of pieces on the movie business would blast it again when *Film Flam* was released in the same year as *The Desert Rose* appeared. Obviously biographical criticism cannot yield an elementary direct relationship between life and story. The evidence shows McMurtry too ambivalent for that.

What it can do is offer opportunity for some limited speculation about McMurtry's state of mind during the period when the first Thalia novels were well behind him, the Houston trilogy complete, and *Lonesome Dove* still in process. His prefaces state dissatisfaction, perhaps frustration, and fatigue. Besides the causes he gives in the prefaces for those feelings, he may have been facing a challenge that comes to any serious writer when he or she reconceives his or her project. McMurtry had written extensively about people bereft of their past, and equally extensively about people feeling displaced in the city. He set out to process other subjects he knew: the movie world where he had spent time while his early novels were being filmed, the milieu of book scouting which shares the milieu of antique scouting. And he took up the subject of Las Vegas unequipped by personal experience but already skilled in storytelling and qualified to do any investigation that the stimulation of his subject might lead him to do. In short, McMurtry was altering his direction as a novelist when he wrote these three novels, at the same time that he was embarking on a major historical project with *Lonesome Dove*.

There is no evidence to dress up this period in McMurtry's career as some "dark night of the soul," but there is enough biographical information to allow a characterization of this interlude between the novels of contemporary Texas and the start of his historical project about the older Texas as a time of reconsideration and retooling. Uncertain as biographical criticism turns out to be, it has the not inconsiderable value of returning works that we have read as freestanding to the context of the writer's career where they take their place as part of an extended work-in-progress.

6

A New History of the Old West

Lonesome Dove (1985)
Streets of Laredo (1993)
Dead Man's Walk (1995)
Comanche Moon (1997)

By the time that *Lonesome Dove* was published, Larry McMurtry had spent nearly a quarter-century in a mental struggle with Western history. In *Horseman, Pass By*, the book he began writing while still a college undergraduate, he had inscribed the irreparable condition of a young man who cannot transfer the values of the Western past into the grim future. The novels of the City Saga that he wrote after completing *The Last Picture Show*, his fierce satire of the small-town sexual follies that substitute for the enterprise of land settlement of earlier days, represents Western life as a never-ending journey away from an illusory myth of a way of life that never was. The books he published following the Houston trilogy appear to have dismissed at last the Old West as material no longer suitable for much more than parody. Yet, even during the interlude when he rendered modern Las Vegas in *The Desert Rose* as a place where women's bodies have become the livestock for sale, savaged Hollywood's stumbling production of fakery in *Somebody's Darling*, and portrayed cowboys and ranchers as marginal eccentrics in *Cadillac Jack*, Larry McMurtry seems to have been at work re-viewing the Western past that had been receding into the distant background of the body of his published work.

Lera Patrick Tyler Lich, whose study, *Larry McMurtry's Texas: Evolution of a Myth*, pays special attention to the genesis of his publications, maintains that, in fact, *Lonesome Dove* was begun as early as 1972—the same year that he published the Houston novel *All My Friends Are Going to Be Strangers*. According to Lich's account, McMurtry started the novel while working for Warner Bros. on the screenplay *Streets of Laredo*. Also, McMurtry himself testifies in his introduction to *The Desert Rose* that his story about the woman Harmony was written while he took a break from the very long book about men on a cattle drive. So, it seems that despite what the published works may have suggested about a removal from the West, in all of his journeys, Larry McMurtry, much like his fictional protagonists, never lost the desire to create for himself a usable history of the West.

The effect of the publication of *Lonesome Dove* was to create a new reputation for Larry McMurtry. The novel became a *New York Times* best-seller within weeks of its appearance. Reviewers acclaimed its authenticity and objectivity, which was a way of stating that the book is anti-mythic but not belittling. The Pulitzer Prize Committee gave *Lonesome Dove* its award for fiction. The Western Writers of America bestowed on it the Spur Award, and the Texas Institute of Letters presented the novel its own prize for fiction. It became a television miniseries, and by 1998 had gone through twenty-seven Pocket Books paperback printings. As the write-up on McMurtry in *Contemporary Authors* puts it, he "no longer wears the sweatshirt with 'Minor Regional Novelist' emblazoned on its front."

No author with the readership and approval that McMurtry has achieved can be treated any longer, even in self-deprecation, as minor. He is now a major interpreter of the West. But what about "Regional"? Is the West not a region? America has had many interesting regional writers. Sarah Orne Jewett's stories of Maine, and Hamlin Garland's fiction about Middle Western homesteaders are regional works, as are Alice Dunbar-Nelson and Kate Chopin's tales of New Orleans, and Bret Harte's stories of Western mining camps. These works concentrate attention on provincial characters and circumstances, offering readers "local color." Some authors taking regional life as their subject, however, give it a treatment that exceeds the particulars of a locale. Mark Twain exceeded particularity in *The Adventures of Huckleberry Finn*, drawing from his Southern narrative of slavery issues of morality and humanity that speak for democracy in all American regions in any time. McMurtry exceeds the particularity of regional place and local color, not so much because the issues addressed in *Lonesome Dove* and its successive novels transcend the West, but because the historical West holds a unique place in popular consciousness where it is seen as the terrain for realization of American heroism. The stock figure of the cowboy serves the American imagination as the archetypal individualist, just as the marshall serves as archetypal lawman, and the Western villain as either likeable rogue or unqualified scoundrel. Furthermore, the confrontation of settlers and Indians in the West has come to model the frontier expansion that Frederick Jackson Turner, Theodore Roosevelt, the authors of hundreds of popular stories, and the makers of the cowboy films about Destry, Hopalong Cassidy, Shane, Roy Rogers, and Gene Autry have persuaded us is America's core narrative. Writing about the figures and geography which contribute that legend to the American popular consciousness, McMurtry is no longer the regional scribe. He has a national story to tell.

The story begun in *Lonesome Dove* eventually runs to nearly 3,000 pages in paperback editions of the four novels relating the adventures of Texas Rangers Woodrow Call and Augustus McCrae. The first work in order of composition, *Lonesome Dove* presents Call and Gus as retired rangers. The plot treats the central drama of the cowboy legend—the cattle drive from Texas to the northern territories of Montana. Its sequel, *Streets of Laredo*, continues the linear movement of the narrative to present Call in the period after his return to Texas and the death of Gus. Having carried the story to the end of the lives of its leading characters, McMurtry reversed in *Dead Man's Walk*, to take up Call and Gus as young rangers and, then, carried them through their middle years (predating *Lonesome Dove*) in *Comanche Moon*.

OLD MATERIALS FOR THE NEW HISTORY

The pattern of composition by sequel and "prequel" so characteristic of McMurtry conditions readers in this instance to realize that his revisionary history of the West begins as the story of ordinary individuals. As preparation for reading the texts of his lengthy volumes on the Old West, the idea is unremarkable; of course, the narrative from start to finish presents the representative experiences of a band of men, and a few women, undergoing an unrelieved test of their physical and mental endurance as the hostile Indians are pacified and the land changes from open range where the buffalo roam to the locale of the beef industry. Looked at another way, though, the relating of the history of the West through the adventures of individuals suggests the formula for a major literary development dating from the nineteenth century—the historical novel (discussed in chapter 2).

The new history inscribed in McMurtry's four novels surrounding the adventures of the Hat Creek outfit of Lonesome Dove depends to a significant extent upon materials that have long formed the substance of Texan narrative history. To begin with, in the background of the novels there are the broad patterns of occupation and settlement described by the esteemed historian of the Texas frontier, Walter Prescott Webb, who opens his record of the Texas Rangers (*The Texas Rangers: A Century of Frontier Defense*, 1935) with a chapter of exposition entitled "Texas: A Conflict of Civilizations" (3–15). Larry McMurtry is no fan of this book as an arbiter of truth. In his essay, "Southwestern Literature," included in the collection *In a Narrow Grave*, he accuses Webb of producing a "glaring whitewash." McMurtry's diagnosis of the book is that it is flawed in attitude. The facts he does not "presume to dispute" (40). The comment suggests that his readers, like McMurtry himself, may accept Webb's facts as stipulated, reserving differences for later interpretation.

The narrative historian thus offers a gloss for the writing of the novelist. For the Western historian, the land is primary, so Webb presents the incontrovertible information that the expanse known by the Caddo Indian word *texas, texias*, or *techas* (meaning "allies" or "friend") is crossed by the ninety-eighth meridian, which divides it into eastern woodland, with a climate much like Louisiana and other southern states and the Western Plains running to the Rocky Mountains. The indigenous people of east Texas were agricultural, while those of the plains, notably Comanches and Apaches, were hunters and warriors. Cherokees driven from further east arrived in Texas in 1824, but then were expelled in 1839. Yet other tribes, among them the Kickapoos who are represented in the McMurtry novels by a skilled tracker called Famous Shoes, also passed through Texas in flight from European settlement to the East.

In the seventeenth century, the Spanish empire extended north from Mexico to Santa Fe in the west and to mission settlements in the area adjacent to Louisiana in the east. In 1718, the Spaniards established San Antonio. The native peoples frustrated Spanish settlement so successfully with continual warfare and resistance to religious conversion that the Spanish government withdrew from the plains in the later eighteenth century, but not without leaving an evident cultural presence and a population of Spanish-speaking residents.

Steady Anglo-American movement into Texas began with the Austins

(Moses the father, Stephen the son), who established a colony between the Colorado and Trinity Rivers in 1820–21, the year that Mexico secured independence from Spain. After Mexico officially chose to encourage emigration in 1825, Anglo settlement increased so steadily that, according to Webb, the Anglos outnumbered Mexicans and Indians combined by 1830 (10).

The version of Texas history related by Webb, and other traditional historians, is an exclusively Anglo one, initiated in the rebellion of settlers in 1835 that led to declaration of the independent Republic of Texas in 1836, the proclamation of annexation by the United States in 1845, and the ensuing Mexican War of 1846–48. All that preceded the uprising of the doughty American revolutionaries was preparation for circumstances ratified by the Treaty of Guadalupe Hidalgo (1848), whereby American authority was extended to the Rio Grande.

This preparation included a resolution passed by the council of the government in rebellion in 1835 ordering establishment of a corps of rangers (Keating, 22). The original mission of the rangers, numbering 150 men at first, seems to have been to provide defense against Mexican forces, but soon their efforts were directed toward the Plains Indians, especially during the presidency of Mirabeau Buonaparte Lamar, who organized the army attacks that expelled the Cherokees from Texas in 1839. It was President Lamar of the Texas Republic who also dispatched an expedition to Santa Fe in 1841 with the aim of seizing the province of New Mexico (37–38, 50).

This futile expedition to Santa Fe serves McMurtry as the basis for the second book of *Dead Man's Walk*, the novel that in recounting the first experiences of the fictional rangers Woodrow Call and Augustus McCrae offers the novelist's view of the historic rangers. The project evidently licenses literary invention, for it seems that McMurtry has conflated the Santa Fe foray with an expedition sent by President Sam Houston, who succeeded Lamar and began his second term in 1841, to invade Mexico under the command of General Alexander Somerville. This latter campaign, also a failure, concluded with captive Texans being marched across northern Mexico (the Dead Man's Walk) to be rewarded with a ceremony in which the Mexican dictator, Santa Anna, ordered the survivors to draw from a pitcher of white and black beans, the black ones marking death, the white ones life (Keating, 50–55).

This use by McMurtry of recorded history in *Dead Man's Walk* provides excellent illustration of the technique of adapting the sources of old historical materials to the purposes of a novelist's new interpretation for history. For those who care to investigate, the outline of events can be independently verified, which is sufficient to establish that the novels are based on what may be taken as the actual past. More than that, the solidity of references to the historical record works to give readers the effect of history reanimated by more detail than nonfiction normally offers.

The extent to which McMurtry employs this practice of improvising on the historical record can be gauged by noting that in the novels devoted to the rangers there are more kernels of fact. Buffalo Hump, the Comanche nemesis of Gus and Call in the novels, was, in the historical record, a leader who, in 1840 led an army of warriors in a raid on Victoria and Linnville (near San Antonio) and engaged the Texas militia in a losing battle at Plum Creek on August 12. Buffalo Hump's army was "larger than any seen before on the western frontier," and the defeat at Plum Creek decisively concluded attempts to mount large attacks upon settled towns (Keating, 44–47; Webb, 62). It was the historic Buffalo Hump also who, on November 15, 1850, signed a general council treaty of peace with Texas government authorities, including Captain J. B. McGown of the Texas Mounted Volunteers (rangers), that was declared nonbinding a month later (Webb, 138–39). Among the characters from the novels with historical counterparts there are Big Foot Wallace, a legendary ranger; Governor Pease, the man to whom Call and Gus report in the pages of *Comanche Moon*; and John Wesley Hardin, a villain who enters scenes with Judge Roy Bean, another historic figure, in *Streets of Laredo*.

Holding a special place of attention is Charles Goodnight, who appears and reappears in the novels. McMurtry brought Old Man Goodnight to his readers' attention when writing about the movie *Hud*, and with the mention of him as a god who abandons Texas in the introduction to *In a Narrow Grave*. That book also directed readers to the biography *Charles Goodnight: Cowman and Plainsman* by J. Evetts Haley (175). This man, who drove cattle into the Palo Duro Canyon in 1876, built a great ranch, and blazed trails from Fort Belknap on the Brazos River to Dodge City, Kansas, into Colorado, and north to Cheyenne, Wyoming, plays numerous cameo parts for McMurtry. He is an evident representative of a cowboy ethic, and through his periodic emergence in the fictional narrations comes as close as McMurtry will allow himself to presentation of an inspiring spirit of the West. He was, though, an actual historic person, and, for that reason, has utility in the way that King Charlemagne has in old French epics. He presides from the margins of the story as a model of cultural values.

As historically informative as Goodnight for McMurtry and the readers of his new history is Teddy Blue, another cowboy whose life story McMurtry recommends. In this case, the historical source is *We Pointed Them North: Recollections of a Cowpuncher* by E. C. Abbott and Helena Huntington Smith (1955). Smith was the interviewer of E. C. Abbott, who came to be known as Teddy Blue. Abbott, born in England, came to this country to join his father who emigrated in 1871. The experiences related in his *Recollections* proceed from the time he was fourteen years of age and give an invaluable account of the origins of cowboying. As he explains it, cattle ran wild in Texas when many ranchers were away fighting in the Civil War. After the war, prices for beef fell, so there was no alternative but to drive the cattle north to seek markets, which were provided by the railroad running east to the cities. Herds of cattle crossed the Red River in 1866. The following year, the Kansas Pacific Railroad reached Abilene, and from then on cattle drives became an annual occurrence. By 1880, Texas cattle had reached Miles City, Montana, "and Texas cowboys with them" (Abbott and Smith, 5).

It is such a history of the cattle drives that McMurtry references in a scene of *Comanche Moon*, where Call and Gus complain about feeling reduced to mere police constables good for "hanging bandits and putting drunks in jail" but supplanted by the army in Indian fighting. They know that cattle ranching is the new thing and once witnessed a herd of four thousand cattle being driven by vaqueros. To Gus, the scene is less interesting than "watching weeds turn brown," a comment to which Captain King rejoins with a remark to Gus to use his mind's eye to think of the "teeming East." "Beef," he explains, "is what will bring Texas back from the war. Cotton won't do it. There's too damn much cotton in the world now. But beef? That's different" (*Comanche Moon*, 717–18). And, of course, it is the joining of economic and all the other changes wrought by the war that instigates the cavalcade of episodes on the cattle drive making up *Lonesome Dove*.

COMPOSITION OF THE NARRATIVES

In identifying the kernels of fact giving Larry McMurtry's fiction of the West its credible references to recorded history, a reader has to guard against a tendency to assume equivalence. If events or characters in the novels were in direct correspondence with the happenings and persons described in works we think of as "history," we might reasonably wonder why a writer would choose to repeat the established record. It would be another matter if a writer was a professional historian who has located previously unknown evidence, such as official papers, court reports, letters, memoirs or other documents termed primary materials. Then the writer would be able to expand the factual record. Clearly, though, McMurtry makes no claim to expand the record of primary materials; instead, the process he undertakes in these four novels about the Old West produces a *reconsideration* of the historical record. This involves interpretation, of course, but McMurtry's interpretation emerges from story. He embeds his meaning through constructions of written narrative, or, to put it another way, the devices for presenting an imagined reality are employed by McMurtry to communicate what he is convinced was the actual reality for representative people, mostly Anglo, in nineteenth-century Texas.

Taken as a body of connected fictions, McMurtry's four novels are reminiscent of the previously mentioned body of associated works known as the leatherstocking tales. Thematically, they bear a resemblance to McMurtry's series in their shared purpose of imagining the history of American settlement and change. In addition, there are similarities about the composition of the two series, for neither Cooper nor McMurtry seems to have begun his series with a plan for a chronological account. McMurtry's hopscotch through history begins in *Lonesome Dove*, which relates the trail drive from Texas to Montana, described by Teddy Blue as being completed by 1880. *Streets of Laredo* follows this chronologically when Gus is dead, the Montana enterprise has failed, and Woodrow Call is "edging seventy" (4). McMurtry then reverts in *Dead Man's Walk* to the period predating the Mexican War, when the Texas Rangers were founded. The final installment in McMurtry's series (at least the final installment to this date), *Comanche Moon*, picks up the story of Call and Gus in the rangers after the Mexican War, and continues it through the Civil War and up until the point when the two comrades are becoming of a mind to leave the rangers and take up ranching in the little town called Lonesome Dove.

For both James Fenimore Cooper and Larry McMurtry, the sequence of the composition suggests that their novels should be received as meditations on history. Obviously, neither author meant at first to produce a completely linear narration occupying several volumes. Rather, they focused upon separated periods of historical time, developing each novel as a freestanding and coherent representation. Perhaps their meditations proceeded along a continuum of cause and effect, as they asked themselves: What would be the consequences for these characters as America changed historically, and next, what lies in their past to complete the account? When the meditations were completed, so were the imagined histories.

PLOT DEVELOPMENT

Looked upon as a record of fact, history is fixed and complete. Recovery of additional information allows the record to be elaborated, but since "what is past is past," it seems as though history cannot be altered. Considered under the aspect of our consciousness of it, however, history seems changeable, because the past continues as an object of reflection. For example, at one time the immigrant to America may think of her or his past overseas as an experience of oppression or at least limited freedom. At another time, the past can become associated with a distinctive self-validating legacy. We understand our past differently at different times, because occasionally we tell the past as another story. The same factual past, over and done with, reoccurs in many versions. The same simple point describes precisely the relationship of historical novels like McMurtry's four chronicles of Texas to historical fact.

Analysis of McMurtry's writing of historical fiction must begin with the plot, because plot serves to contain and organize events; it provides the story its framework. For example, in keeping with its content of rangers directed by their leaders to journey westward, first to El Paso and then to Santa Fe, *Dead Man's Walk* displays a predominantly sequential construction. Without exception, no chapter in the first three parts of the novel turns to gaze elsewhere than upon the small party of rangers, with Gus and Call featured players. Only in the final section constituting eight chapters and occupying forty-three of the novel's 518 pages is there a break, when Buffalo Hump and Kicking Wolf are assigned three chapters and part of a fourth in alternation with Gus and Call. The effect of this emphasis is to establish the trials of the rangers as the axis of narration.

Movement along the axis is not steady. The first westward expedition of the rangers is aborted, and the second fails of its original purpose; consequently, the sequence of the chapters defies us to read it as a gradual disclosure of progress toward a goal. Indeed, one effect of Mc-

Murtry's adoption of his linear construction is to undercut conventional expectations. Promotional tales might glorify the Texas Rangers by having them successfully achieving their goals, a use of linear plotting which implies that the rangers were a well-integrated team of officers and men. When leadership is questionable, though, the terrain inhospitable, and enemies unforgiving, movement from one point to another will not follow a straight line. So, then, McMurtry furnishes *Dead Man's Walk* with an emphatic direction that through its deflection by climate, topography, and, above all, by the contrary forces of Indians and Mexicans, shows that will, logic, and thoughts of glory do not determine the outcome of history. The variables exceed the control of the champions enlisted in service of Anglo settlement and exceed also, McMurtry surely indicates, the designs of those who would write of the Old West in the unmodified terms of legend.

When the things that the rangers endure in *Dead Man's Walk* are added up, it must be concluded that they have heroic endurance. Even before they are driven on the two-hundred-mile walk that gives the book its title, they experience storms and thirst, fatigue and attacks by a grizzly bear, Apaches, and Comanches. They are subjected to arbitrary betrayal and violent indignity, confront death repeatedly, experience terror, and see companions in arms killed in shocking ways. We can observe two particularly striking qualities about this kind of heroism: One quality is conveyed by the sense that the characters endure events more than they triumph over them. They are portrayed not so much acting upon the world, and certainly not directly changing it; instead, they are like objects in a world that acts upon them. The second striking quality closely relates to the first: Call, Gus, and the other rangers—Matty, too—are decidedly ordinary people. They possess no extraordinary abilities of mind or body. They are all imperfect, and in that respect they attain significance by the accident of their time, place, and occupation. They are passively heroic.

In contrast to this first account of the rangers, *Comanche Moon*, which picks up the story after Texas has become a state, presents a canvas of contrasts and conflicts. At its opening, the narrative introduces Gus and Call once more on an expedition, this time under the command of Captain Inish Scull, an experienced officer who earned approbation in the Mexican War. With the seventh chapter, attention switches to the Comanche chief, Buffalo Hump, and the collection of other figures in the leadership of the Indian warriors, including Kicking Wolf and Buffalo Hump's son, Blue Duck. Buffalo Hump had made a memorable entry in

Dead Man's Walk, where he is seen as a looming presence who puts a lance into Gus MacRae and appears as an apparition to Call. Also, as noted above, Buffalo Hump closes out the narration of *Dead Man's Walk* by returning in the final chapters. In *Comanche Moon*, though, McMurtry elevates him to the position of nemesis (a term originally applied in Greek literature to the personification of the gods' anger at mankind, a manifestation of resentment and punishment, and later coming to refer to a figure in continued opposition to the protagonist or leading figure). In this role, Buffalo Hump becomes the focus of chapters alternating with other chapters that present the rangers. The result is to inform the novel with the leading plot of an Indian-Anglo contest for supremacy. In the contest, Buffalo Hump represents not only the Comanches, the fierce tribe who formed their culture on buffalo hunting and war on the plains, but also traditional Indian ways. For example, despite the efficacy of firearms in battle, Buffalo Hump favors the bow and arrow. In place of accommodation to the arrival of settlers in the territory the Comanches once dominated—a movement of population described in the novel as inexorable—he dreams of, and executes, a great raid designed to drive the settlers forever from the land. The plot of this novel thus attains an archetypal level, that is to say, it suggests that the battle with Buffalo Hump stands for the essential conflict of European American settlers with the indigenous population and represents in one formulation the entire history of the wars mounted to subdue the Indians and remove them as an obstacle to expansion of the American nation.

Subordinate to this master plot lie secondary accounts of contest. Within the Comanche environment appears a contest between Buffalo Hump's conservative integrity, his adherence to tradition, and a debased manner of behavior displayed by Blue Duck, the child of Buffalo Hump's liaison with a Mexican captive, who shows not the slightest sense of an ethic of any sort. Then, too, there are contests between Captain Scull and his wife, Inez. Inish Scull is an eccentric product of the intellectual culture of Cambridge, Massachusetts; Inez is an Alabamian whose nymphomania may be meant to signify the sensual indulgences of the slave-holding society of the South. On one level, their incompatibility seems a commentary of sorts on a marriage; on another they seem to represent a struggling attempt to meld diverse ways of life in the American union. To continue the tally of conflicts inhering in the plot of contestation, there is also the attenuated encounter between Inish Scull and Ahumado, the so-called Black Vaquero, who lives astride the Texas-Mexico border wreaking terror on all. Again, there is the suggestion of an archetypal conflict, this time between Scull as a representative of civilized order and Ahumado, whose milieu is chaos. Significantly in the background of *Co-manche Moon* lies indication of the motion toward civil conflict, the war between North and South that would determine the future direction of the nation.

McMurtry's third volume in his new history of the Old West, *Lonesome Dove*, once again displays a plot functionally related to narrative content. This time, the order of events presents the inception, commission, and completion of the cattle drive, representing the integration of a national economy. The Indian Wars have ended, the rangers reduced to a type of state police, so Call and Gus, whom readers by now have learned to see as an advance guard of historical change, have become ranchers, but ranchers without a purpose until Call conceives the idea of moving cattle to Montana. The subject of the book is nothing short of an account of the creation of the grand American type, the cowboy. Plot, therefore, takes the form of Larry McMurtry's version of the Western genre: a rec-ord of obstacles encountered and overcome. Storm, flood, fatigue, and boredom; disinterested nature and Indian harassment—these are the tribulations. The plot seems as linear as *Dead Man's Walk* in its attentive devotion to the cattle drive, but it presents parallel lives as well—tales of a woman in Indian captivity; a full development of the life of Gus's sweetheart, Clara, and his involvement with Lorena; the abandoned sheriff; the story of how Jake Spoon becomes an outlaw; and on and on, until the canvas is densely filled with renderings of the wide variety of characters who represent the populace of the West in the later nineteenth century. When viewed from afar, inlets and irregularities mark the shore-line of a body of water revealing where streams and rivers flow in to form the lake or sea. Originally diverse, the running waters eventually arrive at a common destination, leaving the pattern of their tracks on the shoreline. The plot of *Lonesome Dove* resembles such a confluence of co-incident stories that eventuate in a panorama of the West in the heyday of the cowboy.

The last installment of the historical fiction of McMurtry's Old West, *Streets of Laredo*, serves to show a process of normalization. When the aging Call is commissioned to pursue Joey Garza, he has assumed a role akin to a Pinkerton detective. The Pinkerton detective agency was founded to squelch commercial fraud and to introduce order into in-dustry, sometimes by undermining labor organizations. In their early years, which coincided with the period of time McMurtry describes in *Streets of Laredo*, the Pinkertons served to make America safe for expanding capitalism. Similarly, Woodrow Call's pursuit of the bandit Garza is meant to protect the railroads that have become crucial to the workings of a national economy which, among other things, requires dependable transportation of beef from the West to the East. The plot of *Streets of Laredo*, constructed as a story of pursuit with an alternating focus on Call and his prey, engenders suspense for the purpose of relating a story whose conclusion is well known. In that respect, the plot offers a return visit to material that has been romanticized in the literature of rogues and outlaws. This time, the view disabuses readers of any tendency to accept glamorous tales of outlaws as guerrillas of righteousness, but at the same time, the plot discourages the idea that agents of order like Call are instruments of morality. Instead, McMurtry's adoption of the age-old plot of pursuit works through its details to confirm that these mortal men and women featured in the new history of the Old West enact history but do not determine it. They are the common people through whom history displays its record.

CHARACTER DEVELOPMENT

Major Characters

The figures populating Larry McMurtry's fiction can be spoken of as common, because they are not given the exaggerated stature of heroes and villains in romance and myth; but this is not to say his portrayals reduce character to a level where it seems ordinary. Inspired, it seems, by an intuitive feeling for the combination of attributes that accord individuals their uniqueness, and equipped, it is certain, by a gift for engrossing personal description, McMurtry mixes the peculiarities illustrative of personality with the typicality that distinguishes a character in its historical time. The result is characterization rendered with the same spirit that moved Mark Twain, William Dean Howells, Stephen Crane, and other authors in the nineteenth century to develop the techniques of literary realism. The realists abandoned romance because they thought it improbable. They filled their narratives with verifiable detail because they intended to write about life as it was actually lived; and they invented characters that would seem to be plausible products of specific times and places. In formulating characters for his new history of the Old West, Larry McMurtry plays a variation on the tradition of realism.

That variation is to be seen through a consideration of the expectations we hold for character development. Often, we determine the realism of characterization from evidence of character change. In stories about coming of age, for instance, the leading figure becomes either wiser in the ways of the world or disillusioned, or both. Stories of emotional trauma usually show a similar alteration, so that a character seems to be a different person at the conclusion of the narrative than he or she was when it began. Such change arises naturally when the narrative centers on a protagonist.,

The selection of Augustus McCrae and Woodrow F. Call as the vehicles for his history illustrates how differently McMurtry has come to think of his Western subject matter since he wrote his first anti-mythic novels. In an interview conducted by Alan F. Crooks in 1971, McMurtry said that he was finished with old men of the West. Roger Wagoner, who leaves his ranch to Patsy and Jim Carpenter in *Moving On*, was, he thought, about the best he could say of westerners, while Danny Deck's Uncle Laredo in *All My Friends Are Going to Be Strangers* was a savagely treated figure of ridicule. At the time, there seemed to McMurtry nowhere to go from there (Crooks in Reynolds 1989, 235). But soon he found a new destination. If they are anything, Gus and Call are representative of the Old West, and their dominance in the *Lonesome Dove* series constitutes powerful evidence of the new depths McMurtry has found in Western history.

McMurtry makes Gus and Call protagonists of each ranger expedition, and although the narration leaves them from time to time to account for events affecting other characters, there is always a return to the two partners. Conversely, other characters are abandoned for long stretches of time—Buffalo Hump is one example, Clara another—while narration sticks by Gus and Call. Then, when they have retired from the Texas Rangers, in *Lonesome Dove*, the account of pacifying Indian territory takes second place to the story of the cattle drive, because Gus and Call bring that story with them into the novel. Even when Gus is gone and, in *Streets of Laredo*, Call is on his own, the memory of the partnership lingers over the narration, serving as contrast of recent past with the present. The nearly continuous presence of Gus and Call thus establishes them as the normative characters of the series of Old West novels, that is, they work as the reader's reference point. Because by their presence they are, for readers, the most familiar characters in the stories, they function as guides to events and analysts of experiences.

To be effective, normative characters must encourage readers to make an identification with them, and for that to occur, they must be amply described and apparently dependable in their observations. Of course, they also must be individualized, but they cannot seem so eccentric as to defy understanding. In the chronologically first novel in the sequence, *Dead Man's Walk*, McMurtry undertakes the task of creating his norma- tive characters by inserting short biographies into the narrative. Gus and Call, the youngest rangers in the troop, are on guard duty. Gus has claimed experience on a riverboat, but Call, remembering all the lies Gus has told him, doubts the story: "I don't believe you was ever on a riv- erboat—why would they hire you?" Gus defends himself, and embel- lishes the story: "I was a top pilot for a dern year—I'm a Tennessee boy. I can run one of them riverboats as well as the next man. I only run aground once, in all the time I worked." Immediately, the third-person narrative voice intrudes upon the scene to explain that Gus had once sneaked aboard a riverboat for two days, but had been discovered and put off on a mud bar near Dubuque: "Shortly after he was put off, the riverboat ran aground—that was the one true fact in the story" (28). Yet, the tale sounds grand to Call, because he "had got no farther in the world than his uncle's scratchy farm near Navasota. Woodrow's parents had been taken by the smallpox, which is why he was raised by the uncle, a tyrant who stropped him so hard that when Woodrow got old enough to follow the road to San Antonio, he ran off." The narrative voice next recounts how Call and Gus had met in San Antonio. Gus, fatigued by a ten-day stagecoach ride, was sleeping "against the wall of a saloon," and Call was on his way to the river to wash off the grime from his work as a blacksmith's helper. Call shared his pallet with Gus, "and the two had been friends ever since." Finally, to complete the biographical insertion, the narrative explains that Gus had decided the two of them should join the Texas Rangers and had convinced Major Chevallie to take them on. Call, we are told, "would never have thought himself worthy of such a position" (29–30).

With this economical exposition—it occupies a little more than a page—McMurtry outlines both the personalities and backgrounds of Gus and Call, suggests a deep bond, and presents an image of a partnership in which the voluble and self-confident Gus is balanced by the taciturn, generous, and realistic Call. Either one alone might be a questionable protagonist; together they promise a balanced view of the history they will experience.

The balance is more than a synthesis of opposite traits, though. For all of their differences in the ways they express themselves, the two men have a similar emotional core. They have practically the same response to the violence of skirmishes with Indians. Having heard stories of Indian brutalities, "Call had long known in his head that Indian fighting on the raw frontier between the Brazos and the Pecos was bloody and violent. But hearing about it and seeing it were two different things. Rangering was supposed to be adventure, but this was not just adventure. This was struggle and death, both violent" (*Dead Man's Walk*, 73). Gus's response is more visceral, his stomach churns, and it weighs on his mind that the terrifying encounter he has had with one Indian will be all the worse when the rangers meet the hundreds of Comanches they have heard are on their way toward them (74). The inglorious feelings of the two men are preparation for later emotional reflections. When harsh episodes mount in number, Call is overtaken by an existential sadness, not for any one thing, the narrative explains, but for human vulnerability: "They were small, and the world was large and violent. They were alive and, for the moment, well enough fed; but the very next day another storm might come, or an Indian party, and then they wouldn't be" (104). Gus's extroverted manner gives him some apparent protection during the course of their fighting the Indians and their captivity by Mexican cavalry, but when mutual panic results in the cavalry slaughtering his ranger comrades, he, too, is deeply affected. The death of a boy he cheated at cards becomes too much. Gus cries uncontrollably, and it seems that existential sadness has claimed him also (428).

With *Comanche Moon* and *Lonesome Dove*, the second and third novels in chronology, Gus and Call are shown developing their individual ways of handling personal feelings. Both men seem to take sex when and where they can find it, usually with one of the always-available prostitutes, but each also has a special woman. For Gus it is Clara Forsythe, the daughter of a store owner whom he meets first in *Dead Man's Walk* and for whom by the time of events in *Lonesome Dove* he has formed an enduring but frustrated attraction. To Gus's conscious mind, it is inexplicable that she would marry the horse dealer Bob Allen, as she does in *Comanche Moon* (212). On the other hand, it appears evident that as deep as his affection may be, it is not accompanied by commitment to domesticity. He is a talker and a wanderer, good to have for a friend, and the sort of man Clara hopes her children will someday meet, but this man's life has no room in it suitable to share with a woman. Clara expresses the point this way to Call near the end of *Lonesome Dove*: "I'm sorry you and Gus McCrae ever met. All you two done was ruin one another, not to mention those close to you. Another reason I didn't marry him was because I didn't want to fight you for him every day of my life" (931). That, of course, is just Clara's perspective on the matter. Even though Gus did eventually marry, and more than once, his wives are negligible in his story. For Gus, Call's companionship was the most satisfactory experience of his life, unequaled by any other association. So, while Gus feels nostalgia about the moments of affection he shared with Clara, even to the point of commissioning Call to carry his body back to the orchard where he had happy picnics with her, it is, after all, Call whom he calls upon in *Lonesome Dove* to undertake the remarkable act of devotion encumbered in the transport of his body on a reverse trip from the new cattle country where he meets his death back to the land where Gus and Call began their partnership as Texas Rangers and ranchers.

Gus's incapacity for more than one emotional commitment has its match in Call's own determinedly masculinist affinity for Gus. Call actually has a fruitful heterosexual relationship with Maggie Tilton. They have a child, Newt, together, but while he shows no interest in other women, Call cannot admit an attachment to Maggie, and remains perversely resistant to acknowledging their kinship in the child. When Maggie, like Clara, takes another man for companionship, Call feels as morose and jealous as Gus had felt. Still, he will claim no affection other than Gus's.

In describing McCrae and Call as he has, Larry McMurtry plumbs the significance of male bonding in American culture. The examples in literature are many—James Fenimore Cooper's leather stocking and Chingachgook, Herman Melville's Ishamel and Queequeg in *Moby Dick*, Huck Finn and Jim—and they abound in popular films. A world of seafaring, frontier exploration, and martial combat was the historical source of narratives, with women in only minor roles. In literary enactment of analogues with those realms of experience that were nearly exclusively male, writers have found that if their characters are to be realistically complex, multidimensional, and representative of the feelings along with the physical power of which men are capable, then male characters must be shown in more than their functional relationships. When women can realistically appear as characters in fiction, there is a range of convention about flirtation, courtship, and marriage allowing the release of male devotion and tenderness. When fidelity to the historical record seems to bar women from lead roles in narrative, then men become the object as well as subject of amity and fondness. Writers will handle intense male relationships carefully because, of course, they will be wary of evoking stereotypical notions about homosexuality that can result in their work being categorized as merely lifestyle advocacy. Still, if they are honest in character portrayal and lay a claim to realism, they must do as Larry McMurtry does in his stories of the Old West and construct characters in the knowledge that historically there were two quite distinct worlds separated by sex and gender.

In texts other than McMurtry's, the experiences of Gus and Call in their masculine world might be presented as capital A adventures, extraordinary occurrences that break into the continuity of an otherwise routine existence. For McMurtry's protagonists, though, struggle is the routine. The novels emphasize the routine of hardship in several ways. One such way lies in the construction of narrative plots, as we have discussed them. In the books about their lives as Texas Rangers, the repetitive expeditions, each involving mortal risk and a daily dose of violence, depict Gus and Call facing such unrelenting difficulties that there is scarcely any relief for them from stress and no escape, unless it is to be found in drink and sex, and that more for Gus than Call. *Lonesome Dove*, with its attenuated confrontation of inhospitable nature and inevitable meetings with hostile Indians and outlaws similarly conveys the impression of unrelieved conflict. Then Call, at the time in his life presented in *Streets of Laredo*, when as a survivor of the travails that killed his partner, Gus, he might be conventionally expected to lapse into the role of the wizened monument of past times, full of tales about glory days, he follows instead the path of a bounty hunter routinely living a life of privation and rigor.

Another indicator of McMurtry writing against the grain of conventions about adventure can be seen in his deliberate refusal to allow his protagonists to participate in celebrated historical events. When news of the Civil War reaches Gus and Call in *Comanche Moon*, they resist the urging that they declare themselves Yank or Reb, just as they resist the propaganda of war fever, and agree instead to the governor's plea that they stay on as rangers (555–64). A scene in *Lonesome Dove* set in San Antonio provides yet another opportunity to place the protagonists at a distance from celebrated events. When they had arrived in Texas during the 1840s, the narrative voice tells readers, the talk had been all about the famous battle at the Alamo, but now "the battle had mostly been forgotten" (357). So much for the war cry, "Remember the Alamo." In the same scene, Gus sardonically remarks about another celebrated historic event that, "If a thousand Comanches had cornered us in some gully and wiped us out, like the Sioux just done Custer, they'd write songs about us for a hundred years," to which Call characteristically replies, "I doubt there was ever a thousand Comanches in one bunch . . . If there had been they would have taken Washington, D.C." (357). As these scenes show us, McMurtry is not only keeping his characters physically distant from the artifice of adventures, he is also demonstrating their mental and emotional distance.

In view of McMurtry's withholding the sheen of adventures from Gus and Call, it seems completely consistent that he also employs techniques that strip away from occurrences of plot any possibility of their inflation into symbol-laden passages of rhetorical nostalgia. *Comanche Moon*, a novel given over for long stretches to pursuit of Buffalo Hump, Kicking Wolf, and Blue Duck, concludes ironically. Buffalo Hump has been killed, but by his own sociopathic son rather than by the rangers. When they come upon his body, Call says, "I thought he was bigger" (775). Four chapters later, in the final scene of the novel, the men awaken and see that Kicking Wolf had been to their camp in the night and had not stolen their remaining stock, an old mule, because he habitually stole only good horses. Gus finds the situation absurd and amusing; Call feels its frustration, "because once again he had to carry with him, on a long trip home, a sense of incompletion." What a scandal, Gus says, "We didn't get our man, and now we've sunk so low that a Comanche won't even steal our mule. I guess that means the fun's over." "It may be over but it wasn't fun," Call says, as he looks "at the long dry distance that still waited to be crossed" (802–3). In keeping with this inglorious conclusion to the Indian wars, the cattle drive north, and the founding of a Montana ranch in *Lonesome Dove* also show diminished returns. Gus is killed and the ranch soon fails.

A good way to understand the development of McMurtry's lead characters is to take them as agents of interpretation. Aside from the inherent interest they generate because they are so vividly particularized, Augustus McCrae and Woodrow Call function to register adaptation to the reality of the experience of settling the West. Completely implicated in their routine of hardship, and, like all the other common people whose stories they represent in their own, without the option of either mental or physical escape, the normative characters of Gus and Call present a philosophy of endurance. Mostly, that philosophy is enacted rather than explained, but there are two exchanges of dialogue in *Lonesome Dove* that can illustrate all that is otherwise unsaid.

In the first exchange, Gus and Call are estimating the distance from their Texas ranch to Montana. Call says the Indian, Black Beaver, could

tell them how far it is, because he has been all over the West. "Well,"
Gus replies, "he was an Indian. He didn't have to go along establishing
law and order and making it safe for bankers and Sunday-school teachers, like we done . . . That's what we done, you know. Kilt the dern Indians so they wouldn't bother the bankers." Call seems to disagree,
saying the Indians bothered more than bankers, women, and children,
"not to mention plain settlers" (*Lonesome Dove*, 83). The discussion remains inconclusive until a time when they are well into the cattle drive.
"I hope this is hard enough for you, Call," says Gus, "I hope it makes
you happy. If it don't, I give up. Driving all these skinny cattle all that
way is a funny way to maintain an interest in life, if you ask me . . . You
should have died in the line of duty, Woodrow. You'd know how to do
that fine. The problem is you don't know how to live." Call retorts,
"Whereas you do?" Blabbermouth that he is, Gus insists that he has
indeed lived a full life, but this new jaunt of theirs is "just fortune hunting." The last word is Call's: "Well, we wasn't finding one in Lonesome
Dove" (242).

Between the two of them, they have it about right. Looked at one way,
they have been tools for the designs of others with plans to open the
West to exploitation, but they had put all of their energies into the work
anyway, finding satisfaction in doing the job as well as they could. And,
yes, an interest in life is necessary, as Gus demonstrates by going along
on the cattle drive despite his talk. How is that interest and satisfaction
achieved? Evidently it takes an act of will, a more or less free choice to
make of circumstances what you can. Professional historians aggregate
the experiences of individuals into exposition of large patterns. Creators
of myth will absorb those large patterns into larger-than-life accounts of
heroes whose tales advance an agenda. But McMurtry's fiction provides
what neither the genres of professional historians nor the inventions of
mythmakers do, a close-up view of individuals *in* history. On that level
of reality, motivation naturally, is as personal as it is for Gus and Call,
values are developed in action, and life most of the time is routine,
whether in hardship or comfort. To convey this view of reality in a historical setting is the purpose underlying the creation of Augustus Mc-
Crae and Woodrow F. Call.

Secondary Characters

With Gus and Call established as the primary characters of the series
of novels, remaining characters fall into relationship with them. The most

immediately striking group of these secondary characters is the set of oppositional figures who serve as nemeses. The term nemesis comes from the name of the Classical goddess of retribution and has come to mean an opponent and sometimes a figure over whom the protagonist will never triumph. Professor Moriarty in the stories of Sherlock Holmes is an example. In Larry McMurtry's Western series, the characters most deserving the appellation nemeses are Buffalo Hump, Blue Duck, and Kicking Wolf, because one or more of them pursues the lead figures through the plots of most of these novels, and because, as Indians, they assume representation for the native people who stand in the way of European-American settlement.

McMurtry enters Buffalo Hump into his history in a dramatically revealing scene early in *Dead Man's Walk*. Gus, on foot and separated from the ranger troop on a dark, stormy night, observes what he fears most—the legendary Comanche chief, "the most feared man on the frontier," illuminated by a flash of lightning. In another flash, Call approaching from another direction sees Buffalo Hump throwing a lance at the fleeing figure of Gus (39–41). In the subsequent darkness, Call loses sight of the Indian, but his presence is established on the material scene and in the minds of the protagonists.

Following scenes show Buffalo Hump deceiving the rangers into ambush, shooting one ranger to death with an arrow, scalping another, and generally terrorizing the troop. Before Buffalo Hump and his band disappear, the opposition of rangers and Comanches is underlined by comment on their irreconcilable differences. While Gus and Call are watching a "party of fighting Comanches, riding at ease through the country that was theirs," the narrative observes how different they seemed from any men the rangers had seen before. They were wild, but skilled, and their actions (they have just scalped some of the rangers' party) seem to show that "their rules were not white rules, and their thinking was not white thinking" (*Dead Man's Walk*, 79).

Comanche Moon, the novel that takes its name from reference to seasonal Indian raids, takes up the story of Indian wars about two decades after the first appearance of Buffalo Hump. In contrast to the protagonists of the stories—Gus and Call—Buffalo Hump does alter in his character. Though in his age he remains an obstacle to White settlements and, thus, quarry for the rangers, he is also a relic of traditional warrior ways, intent on maintaining the discipline associated with use of the old weapons of bow and arrow and lance. A massive raid on Austin organized and led by Buffalo Hump stands as a major engagement of the two civilizations in battle. Buffalo Hump means to make sure that the Texans will have something to remember him by (277). Despite the carnage, though, Buffalo Hump's sorties are the final act of his drama of resistance. He becomes ill, but even worse, he is afflicted with a son, Blue Duck, without respect for the old ways and eager to supplant his father's leadership, which has been described in the fiction as possessing the integrity of "Indian ways," with a purely opportunistic indulgence of mayhem and terror. With the same resignation that McMurtry assigns to Crazy Horse in his recent short biography of the Sioux, *Crazy Horse*, Buffalo Hump is brought to a realization that his struggle has been lost. In a dialogue with Kicking Wolf about the evident paucity of buffalo on the plains, he says, "The Buffalo won't return, because they are dead. The whites have killed them. When you go north you will only find their bones." Kicking Wolf begins to protest that they will beat the Whites yet, "but, as he was speaking, Kicking Wolf suddenly lost heart. He realized that Buffalo Hump was right" (*Comanche Moon*, 713). Shortly thereafter, Blue Duck kills his father. He does so clumsily, without skill, but that is entirely appropriate to the scene marking the end of Comanche tradition (771). A nemesis is dead, but he was not bested by the ranger protagonists. In memory, at least, he remains their worthy opposition.

Due to his random and merciless killings, his expertise "at working the line between the wild country and the settled" (*Comanche Moon*, 582), Blue Duck becomes more famous than his father. He is the consummate villain, representing nothing greater than his own restlessness, conducting raids in defense of nothing and for purposes only of satisfying his lusts and greed. A nemesis need not be a character of worth and quality to occupy an oppositional position in narrative, though. In *Lonesome Dove*, Blue Duck serves as an embodiment of sadistic violence that is given full play in the subplot of the captivity of Lorena. By word and deed he horrifies the woman and leads her on a traumatizing journey to nowhere. After a long chase and capture, Blue Duck finally eludes the law. Instead of submitting to a hanging, he leaps through a window, flying he calls it, and, as though his lawlessness is uncontrollable by others, dashes himself to death (937).

One more villain, this one in a class beneath nemesis, is Joey Garza, who shows McMurtry's ability to create a dehumanized character for his historical purpose. Denying every expectation about there being an innate sense of respect for life and kin in a human being, Joey abuses his mother, seizes his siblings, and wantonly ranges about the landscape, killing and pillaging. That he becomes the prey of Call in his late occupation of bounty hunter illustrates that the conclusion of the Indian wars and the planting of settlements were no guarantee of the arrival of civilization.

Another grouping of secondary characters is the close companions of Gus and Call. These include Newt, Call's unacknowledged son, whose consciousness is briefly entered by the narration of *Lonesome Dove* to illustrate his psychic insecurity (e.g., 695, 764), and Deets, an escaped slave who is the one man Call "could have a comfortable word with from time to time" (389). Deets is a gentle man, affectionate, and the only person whose death is marked by the rite of a funeral (806). Many others also ride with Gus and Call—Bigfoot in *Dead Man's Walk*; the helpless Irishmen in *Lonesome Dove*; and the historical Charles Goodnight, who makes cameo appearances in both of those novels. What is remarkable about their portrayal is that not a one is flat. Each has individual peculiarities, and each is provided sufficient biography to indicate how he might have become the person he is.

Military characters form another distinguishable group. Inish Scull is outstanding among these. A college-trained officer who greets one of his captors, "Hello from Harvard," Inish Scull, and his nymphomaniac wife, Inez, do little to advance the plot of *Comanche Moon* and are portrayed with such detailed peculiarity as to appear like excursions for the display of McMurtry's ability to draw absorbing characters. On the other hand, Caleb Cobb in *Dead Man's Walk* is a military officer seeming to represent an incompetent contrast to the protagonists Gus and Call. While they create for themselves a situational code of fidelity and respect toward their companions, always keeping in mind whose side they are on, Cobb abandons his leadership responsibility.

Although the study of the protagonists has indicated that these novels take place in a masculine environment, there is a body of women in the narratives, all of them appendages to the male world. There are the whores. They can be affectionate and caring, like Matty Roberts who assumes the role of spouse to Shadrach in *Dead Man's Walk*, or Maggie Tilton who bears Call's son, and Lorena whose fondness for Gus is shown in *Lonesome Dove*, but their designation as sexual objects puts them in subordinate positions. The one exception is not Inez Scull, whose identity depends entirely on male sexuality, but Clara Forsythe Allen, Gus's sweetheart. All of the women are portrayed sympathetically and allowed complexity that assures us they are more than just whores, but it is Clara alone who furnishes a world for herself. She becomes a capable horsewoman and dealer, a self-determining person who knows who she should *not* marry, a caring mother, the executive of a farm household, a counselor, and a woman who has selected, rather than fallen into, her life. If Gus and Call are the normative men in these novels, then

Clara must be the normative woman, a person readers can identify with when they grow tired of the limitations set by the male world of the Old West.

Discussion of the characters in McMurtry's novels will always seem incomplete, so interesting are they all. If, however, we keep in mind that for purposes of analysis it is the means of characterization and the functions that characters perform for the dynamics of the narrative that is important, then a selective treatment such as we have here can suffice. All of the characterizations occur through the voice of the third-person narration. When dialogue interrupts exposition, it is prepared and selected by the dominant presence of the unnamed narrator, who also manages the appearance and disappearance of characters, arranges the parallels of their lives and the chronology of their experiences, and by the insinuations of descriptive language directs readers toward a predetermined interpretation of the characters in their stories. That controlling narrative voice is a great deal more than a channel for facts, and nothing less than Larry McMurtry working as historian.

THEMATIC ISSUES

While the theme of character in struggle with the environment and the theme of social change resulting from "pacification" of the indigenous peoples and subsequent Anglo settlement inhere in all the elements of composition so far discussed, there are three motifs requiring further notice, because they convey the depth of thematic concerns in this series of Western novels.

Physical landscape and geography produce the first motif. Setting is always more than a location for events. It always has presence, as when the earth and sky seem to widen when the rangers arrive at the Llano Estacado in *Dead Man's Walk*. "The meaning of distance seemed changed." The world has become nothing but the "silent and endless" and the "smaller world" of towns and woodlands "seemed difficult to remember" (227–28). Accompanying the lay of the land in canyon and plain are the evidences of nature's force as they are shown beleaguering the trail drive in *Lonesome Dove*. When the drive reaches Montana and the cowboys view the cloud-topped Bighorn Mountains, "it seemed to all of them that they were leaving behind not only heat and drought but ugliness and danger too" (829). Before such presences, it becomes easy to accept a materialist view of history declaring, as the narratives of McMurtry's tetralogy do, that physical environment shapes the fate of human enterprise and culture.

A further image of forces that make history occurs in McMurtry's treatment of the motif of settlement, which can be capsulized in a passage from *Comanche Moon*. The perspective is Slow Tree's, a warrior with Buffalo Hump: "Slow Tree . . . saw what any man of sense could see: that it was the whites, not the People who were growing more numerous. For every white that died, three arrived to take his place . . . Soon there would be so many that no chief could hope to kill them all in war or drive them away" (194). Slow Tree's prophetic sense of inevitability suggests a force more powerful than even collective will, a force without a guiding intelligence that arises from a confluence and sweeps onto the plains to alter life so irremediably that all one might hope to do is adapt.

Streets of Laredo adds to the impression of inexorable historical change by the simple inclusion of the railroad in the story line. The greenhorn Brookshire arrives in Texas to engage Call's services, because the bandit Joey Garza is impeding commerce by holding up trains. The situation evokes the well-known associations of gunmen like Jesse and Frank James, but like the observations attributed to Slow Tree, it also manifests in its way the irrevocable power of historical change.

These thematic motifs may be taken to be the historical backbone of McMurtry's series of novels. In conjunction with the evident timeline of events, beginning around the Mexican War and running through the narratives until the last quarter of the nineteenth century, the theme of history as material development creates the context for the stories of individuals. The significance of McMurtry's formulation will be seen if it is contrasted with the mythic treatments of the Old West that his fiction implicitly criticizes. In the myths, whether they are about General Custer or an unbeatable lawman, the power of will and consciousness of the character's importance is immense. The mythic heroes know they are champions of civilization (White and European in origin). They are aware their cause is righteous and, because of that, they are ultimately invincible. They dominate, rather than are dominated by, their environment. They may suffer defeat, but they die as ennobled prophets. Immediately, one sees a difference in scale between the heroes of made-up myths and the figures in McMurtry's realist novels. Gus, Call, and the other characters are more like objects of history than its commanders. They avoid being victims only by grit and application of their humanly limited vision to the experiences that routinely confront them. In short, the mythic characters live as nobody can, while McMurtry's people live as we all do.

A MARXIST READING OF THE NEW HISTORY

The theory of Marxist literary criticism derives from the writing of Karl Marx and Friedrich Engels. Their most famous collaborative work was *The Communist Manifesto*, while the most influential production of Marxist study is *Das Kapital*. Marx and Engels wrote incidentally about literature—Marx's comments being notable for his interest in Classical literature that enjoyed "staying power," despite the historical changes that altered the social environment of its origin—but it has been followers of Marx who are mostly responsible for development of a Marxist theory of literature.

That theory depends upon the conviction that an understanding of the laws and forces adduced in *Das Kapital* and other economic and historical writings by Marx and Engels provide a scientific method for analysis and prediction of history. The premise is that material conditions for production of the necessities of life, such as food and shelter, and the reproduction of social life from one generation to the next are the processes that determine the reality of human life, although there are many things—religious explanations of reality, for one—that obscure people's understanding of what actually determines how they live—the social class to which they belong, the powerlessness they may feel, the poverty they might experience. Extending the premise, Marxist analysis proceeds to identify the forms of organization human beings have employed for production and social reproduction. The forms are categorically labeled socioeconomic classes, and historical periods are distinguished by the manner in which a dominant class arranged for production; thus, in the European Middle Ages, the nobility exercised their power of control over land and its products in a system of feudalism. Feudalism gradually gave way to the emergence of national states, as centralized governments took dominion over the wealth generated from the land. The economic relationships underlying feudalism and successor establishments are viewed in Marxism as the base of history. On the other hand such constructions as legal systems, religious practices, customs, and culture arise out of the base forming a superstructure. It is to the advantage of a dominant class to generate a belief that the superstructure, through which they assert power, is not a consequence of the basic material relations, so typically a ruling group will encourage belief that its power is in the "nature of things." To dispel the mystery of such claims and to reveal the actuality of history's workings is the aim of Marxist historical interpretation.

Marxist study of history, however, is centered upon Europe, where the scheme of modern historical change is said by Marxists to begin with a shift from feudalism (during which hereditary land holders known as the aristocracy are the dominant class) to capitalism, when the middle class or *bourgeoisie* that owns the means of industrial production becomes supreme, that was the revolutionary upheaval that created the modern world. Marxism declares that the theme or explanatory concept of this revolutionary change must be seen as class struggle, that is, the exercise of conclusive power by one class that recognizes itself in contest with a competing class. The *bourgeoisie* saw itself in a struggle to usurp the power once exercised by the aristocracy, and, so Marxism predicts, an entirely new class created in the cauldron of industrialism—the class of propertyless workers known as the proletariat—enters into conflict with the reigning *bourgeoisie* for dominance.

Application of Marxism to localities outside of Europe requires some revision of the core theory; nevertheless, when one encounters an extended historical project such as Larry McMurtry's *Lonesome Dove* series it can serve to frame the broad changes described in the novels. For instance, the Marxist lens for viewing history will suggest that the careers of the Texas Rangers represented in these novels shows them as an advance guard in the geographical expansion that followed upon the establishment of the middle class in the United States. Marxism will then explain that the Indian wars amounted to forced relocation, or attempted extermination, of an indigenous population in order to secure territory needed to feed the industrial workers that were the foundation of Euro-American capitalism.

An apparent problem with applying this analysis to McMurtry's historical novels is that the interpretation is at once both obvious and reductive. Obviously, the historical changes related in the novels are connected with the development of America's capitalist economy. As for the reductiveness of an analysis that describes Gus, Call, and their associates as soldiers of capitalism, Marxism will defend the analysis with the observation that literature is like a code. On one level, fiction such as McMurtry's Western novels functions to present characters, events, and themes as they have been discussed earlier in this chapter, but underlying all of that—or as Marxism typically puts it, *in the final analysis—*

expansion of capitalism is the historical theme captured by the novels. If one understands literature to be a system that encodes history, then Marxism is not reducing the richly detailed stories of Gus and Call to some kind of allegory, but is instead bent upon simply uncovering the historical infrastructure or background reference upon which fictional event and character has been built.

Returning to the charge that the Marxist interpretation of the history in these novels as a fictional record of capitalist development in the United States is perfectly obvious, a Marxist critic can reply that the perceptibility of the interpretation indicates why the *Lonesome Dove* series should be associated with Marxism. In undercutting the myths of the Old West, as has been shown in the discussion of character, plot, and theme above, McMurtry has stripped away the misrepresentations of history that obscure its true pattern. The conventional views of heroism found in dime novels and Western movies convey the idea that in "the making of the West," extraordinary deeds of valor by unusual men are more important than influences such as the flood of White settlers, the invasion of the territory by military units, the promotion of the dream of free land in the East, and other instances of the concerted campaign to seize the West as land for exploitation by the national economy. In the reckoning of Marxism, these older renditions of Western history do more than exaggerate. They create the illusion that Western settlement was something like a moral crusade when, in fact, the campaign to take the West for Euro-American use was motivated by the economic interests of the class that profited most from capitalism.

Although he does not employ the language of Marxism and refuses to belabor any single theme in his novels (even his antiheroic, "realistic" view of character is more implied than overt), embedded in the texture of his fiction is a version of history that McMurtry claims will dispel illusions and that in turn Marxist criticism can claim squares with its vision of the truth about the West.

7

Heroes in Reality and Legend
Anything for Billy (1988)
Buffalo Girls (1990)

Turning again to the subject of the Old West in *Anything for Billy* and *Buffalo Girls*, Larry McMurtry executes a significant shift in his narrative strategy. Where *Lonesome Dove* and the subsequent novels making up his "new history" employ fictional characters as illustrative figures in a panorama of the developing and changing West, in these two additions to his project of reexamining Western legends, McMurtry directly targets the processes by which history is written as distinct from the way it was lived.

To create conviction in readers, the presentation of history being lived, as McMurtry undertakes it in *Lonesome Dove*, its sequel and prequels, requires an objective manner of narration. While the author is hypothesizing a "truth" about events, the construction of that "truth" must be concealed. The author's selection of episodes to relate, attributes to be assigned the characters, and a plot to be embedded in the story are submerged beneath the simulation of a plausible reality. Readers are shut out of the writer's workshop, leaving them just the power of their own inferences to detect how the writer designed the story. By contrast, when a narrative introduces contradictory truths or ambiguity, the doors of the workshop can be opened. The historical record is cast into doubt, and the reader is asked to consider not just what experience has been lived, but also how it has come to be written in the way that it has. Literary critics classify writing that reveals its artifice as reflexive, meaning that by devices drawing attention to how stories are told, such works lay open the fact that we are reading a deliberately constructed piece of writing. If the revelations concern the text before us, critics term it self-reflexive. An early example is the British author Laurence Sterne's novel, *Tristram Shandy* (1759–67), which comically interrupts the narration so that the narrating voice can tell the audience that memory is faulty. However, when the references are to literature other than the text in hand, the variety of literary awareness may be termed simply reflexive. Illustrative examples of the composition of a simply reflexive work appear throughout Larry McMurtry's *Anything for Billy* and *Buffalo Girls*.

The trail to reflexivity in *Anything for Billy* and *Buffalo Girls* follows upon Larry McMurtry's selection of well-known historical figures for leading characters. The title of the first novel alludes to the notorious outlaw Billy the Kid, who stands at the center throughout the novel. The most prominent of the "girls" in the second novel is Calamity Jane, who contributes her own version of events to the tale. In each novel, other historically identifiable persons fill out the cast—for example, Pat Garrett in *Anything for Billy*; Buffalo Bill Cody, Annie Oakley, and Sitting Bull, among others in *Buffalo Girls*. Not only are these characters historical, but more to the point of McMurtry's project, they also have stimulated production of a huge body of written commentary, interpretation, and controversy. Opening an internet address (*http://www.mysteries-megasite.com/main/bigsearch/billy-1.htm*) will lead to three hundred links related to Billy the Kid, including: a compilation of "Myths and Facts About Billy the Kid," a list of twenty-four books about him, brief biographies (not all in agreement on the facts), an account of an art installation devoted to *The Death(s) of Billy the Kid*, even a solicitation for membership in the Billy the Kid Outlaw Gang. Moreover, at least three films have presented his story: Arthur Penn's *The Left Handed Gun* (1958) starring Paul Newman, Sam Peckinpah's *Pat Garrett and Billy the Kid* (1973) with Kris Kristofferson, and Gore Vidal's *Billy the Kid* (1989). An autobiography of Calamity Jane was attributed to her by Robert J. Casey in *The Black Hills and Their Incredible Characters* (1949), and she, too, has a web page. Of course, Buffalo Bill's fame has been widespread for generations. His exploits were celebrated and expanded upon by Ned Buntline in a series of dime novels beginning in 1869 and then continued by other hands until they reached an output estimated to be 1,700 (*PBS The West*). Cody personally appeared in the starring role of a play called *The Scouts of the Plains* (1872); released an autobiography in 1879; and in 1883, began production of the pageant known as *Buffalo Bill's Wild West*, which presented Annie Oakley and Sitting Bull, among others, in dramatization of a buffalo hunt, Indian fights, a Pony Express ride, and a tableau of Custer's last stand at Little Big Horn. In short, these historical personages, as McMurtry puts it in *Buffalo Girls*, have outgrown their lives (345) and become the raw material for a cultural industry. The differences between the product of the cultural industry and the likely reality of the characters' lives as they probably lived them provide McMurtry his focus in these treatments of Western heroes, real and legendary.

NARRATIVE VIEWPOINT

The second important decision McMurtry made in constructing these reflexive novels was his selection of narrative viewpoint. In *Anything for Billy*, the narrative is presented through the words of Ben Sippi, a dime novel writer. Accommodating to the style of his genre, Ben tells about Billy in brief chapters that rapidly set a scene and move almost at once to a crisis moment. The effect of the rapid-fire narration resembles, in its brevity, a telegram or perhaps E-mail message. Through regular foreshadowing, though, it becomes evident that Ben Sippi has no intention of recreating the adventures of Billy the Kid by using the illusion of a linear unfolding of events. At one point he writes, "If I had realized that still morning how fast the old wheel of fate was spinning, I would have wired for some money" (32). Later, when writing about Billy and his love, Katie Garza, he states, "I guess I didn't realize how deeply Katie Garza loved Billy Bone until that dark morning in Chavez County" (159). Here, the reference is to an occurrence that will not appear in the text until its end. Again, in chapter 10 of the third book of the novel, Ben writes about a conversation he holds with Billy Roebuck "years later" and concludes the memory with the remark that "Scarcely a month after our conversation Tully himself was ambushed by Brushy Bob Wade, leaving the little blind daughter, for whom he grieved so deeply, to be raised by a sister in Oklahoma" (182–83). These comments establish a chronology independent of the recalled events. Ben Sippi already knows the outcome of Billy's career. As a result, there is none of the contrivance of suspense that ordinarily would appear if the narration were bent upon reanimating Billy the Kid's story. And what is more important, as the narration by Ben Sippi registers his retrospective sense of his engagement of Billy's outlaw career, it supplants the story of Billy as he lived his life, with Ben's thoughts upon the distinction between history and legend.

In *Buffalo Girls*, McMurtry constructs the narrative through a counter-point of voices: Calamity Jane's personal letters to her daughter, an omniscient third-person point of view relating the broad events that occupy the characters in addition to and including Jane, and a version of free indirect discourse dedicated to the reflective consciousness of No Ears, a fifty-year-old Indian who acquired his name after an attack by French traders who cut off his ears when he was a boy.

By the insertion of twenty-seven letters written by Calamity Jane into the narrative, McMurtry echoes the epistolary novel, the type of fiction pioneered by Samuel Richardson in *Pamela, or, Virtue Rewarded* (1740) and *Clarissa* (1747–48). Richardson confined his narratives entirely to an exchange of letters and thus found a way to create a tight first-person point of view that would serve to reveal character psychology. While the story of *Buffalo Girls* is not conducted exclusively through letters, the epistolary device serves a purpose for McMurtry similar to Richardson's. This is particularly so in the fourth book of the novel, which is comprised only of thirteen letters by Jane that gradually disclose her motives for writing *and* for inventing the daughter to whom all the letters throughout the novel have been addressed.

It is important to observe how the genre of the letter differs from the more familiar first-person point of view used in *Anything for Billy*. Letters are understood to be composed. They are personal writings displaying an intimacy of feeling not always present in the simulations of a narrator whose audience is understood to be unlimited. In this respect, they are both literature, that is, obviously written language, and self-disclosures. By employing Calamity Jane's letters as he does, McMurtry produces a unique type of historical writing. Some of these letters advance the story, telling how circumstances previously stated by the third-person voice work themselves out. In this sense, they are accounts written by a participant with an observing eye. Always, though, the letters are also projections of the subjective consciousness of their author, her failings of self-esteem, her pathetic loves, her loneliness, her illusions.

Calamity Jane's letters proceed through her personal time frame, which is then enclosed within the chronology of a third-person narrator gifted with a bird's-eye view of the characters together and apart. Although this narrator has full access to the details of the lives and times recorded, the voice is restrained in interpretation. Preferring to relate the story incident by incident, rather than by announcing and then insistently demonstrating a grand theme, the third-person portions of *Buffalo Girls* attempt to convey the realism of the immediate experiences—the sad behavior of beaver trappers who have lost their occupation when their game was depleted, the curious courtships of a whorehouse madam who seems to know all the famous Western figures of her time, the rising sense of a messianic mission in a provincial Indian who travels beyond his traditional lands.

With this latter character, McMurtry introduces a third narrative variation into the novel. When No Ears observes the cranes who are spirit messengers (*Buffalo Girls*, 18), the narrative voice enters deeply into his thoughts. By the use of what is termed free indirect discourse, the narration proceeds to translate otherwise inaccessible feelings into statement. Because the passages that do this are not spoken by No Ears, they are indirect; yet, they are nonetheless discourse. We only have to understand that in this case the third-person point of view shifts into a subjective mode intended to simulate No Ears speaking for himself. The same is true when, on the journey to Europe with the Wild West Show, No Ears encounters the wide water of the Atlantic, a whale, and then London. By relating his feeling of awe at the sights and his internal reflections upon the errors of traditional learning, the narration establishes No Ears as the sensitive observer of the passing of old ways.

The alternate voicings enter complexity into *Buffalo Girls*. While the third-person voice dominates with its unglamorous rendition of the episodes of the novel, Calamity Jane and No Ears offer personalized perspectives that may not contradict the remainder of the novel, but do cause us to wonder what, after all, is the West. Is it the West marketed by Ned Buntline and Buffalo Bill? Is it the terrain of emptiness and loneliness where Calamity Jane, Ragg, and Bone wander? As readers recognize that these are the questions Larry McMurtry is posing, they see, too, that his selection of narrative techniques for this novel make it another example of a reflexive work about how history is written.

PLOT DEVELOPMENT

The data of the world and the stimuli to our senses that flood our awareness rival the sky in breadth and width. Unlike our fellow creatures, the animals, we have the capacity to retard our responses and to hold records of several sets of data in our awareness at once. But this only complicates matters by multiplying the causes for thought and behavior. Were we not equipped with screening devices, human beings might be immobilized by each day's reception of information, never able to decide if we should eat now or mate, sleep or flee. We are, however, so equipped, partly through the construction of our nervous system that allows us to designate what is immediately important and to disregard seeming irrelevancies. Also, though, through culture we have equipped ourselves with techniques to determine the relative importance of data streaming into our brains. Above the level of techniques that give us the means of survival, we have devised intricate conceptual arrangements to classify information about the world according to what we think of as values.

All referential art mimics these selective procedures. The painter daubing oil on a canvas frames a landscape so as to include haystacks, giving them a glowing color and irregular shape against an eerily dark sky. The village that may lie over the hill does not appear in the picture. Another painter, following a different purpose, will trace power lines crossing a meadow and hillside, thus suggesting a presence unseen in the other artist's painting. Among the most powerful means of framing available to writers of fiction is plot or the arrangement of events and actions. Although plots may take various forms, they are surprisingly familiar to experienced readers in whatever shape they take, for among the techniques of data selection instilled in us by our cultures is the collection of plots we learn from stories. Our knowledge of these plots constitutes a significant portion of cultural literacy.

In simplest form, literary plots tend to sketch an arc. After characters are introduced, and the scene set, the action becomes more and more complicated, characters more and more engaged in struggles to achieve some goal. The action proceeds, then, to a climax, followed by a decline in the energy of the story that will be marked perhaps by a reversal of the hero's fortunes or some other alteration that confirms the awareness of the audience that the chief actor in the story has undergone change.

Despite nearly limitless improvisations on the arc of the plot, audiences are generally conditioned to hold in mind an expectation that they will witness a rise and fall. This is the baseline against which the writer can play variation. *Anything for Billy* can serve as a lucid illustration. Ben Sippi encounters a youth of uncertain background. The youth's fame has preceded him, and because of his inexplicable charisma, Ben hooks up with the youth and follows him in travel and adventures. Through Billy's unpredictable and notorious actions such as: a fight in the China Pond Bar, when he disputes a companion's plan to kill Wyatt Earp, inexplicably viewing the idea as cowardly (129–30); his killing of Elmer Fay when he mistakes him for someone else (177); his braining a bystander with his rifle stock when he is provoked by Doc Holladay's seeming disrespect in calling him "little Bill" (204); his violation of a truce during a gunfight when he shoots the other Fay brother (221); his unmotivated killing of two mute shepherds (320); and his shooting of a ten-year-old Apache boy—the youth's reputation rises and inevitably generates antipathy. After being imprisoned, Billy is helped to escape through the nearly perfect intervention of a female desperado and her gang (347–48). The narrative then proceeds to take the young man to his ignominious death, adding notice that through celebratory stories told and retold, he gains a kind of immortality. Laid out in this way, the plot of *Anything for Billy* may be seen to resemble an ironic version of the archetypal story of a culture hero. But this hero is a destroyer, so his tale transforms into a parody, emerging from McMurtry's workshop repeating the serious features of other well-known compositions, but applying those features to an inappropriate subject. In addition, the parodic nature of the novel's plot contributes to our recognition of *Anything for Billy* as a reflexive text freighted with themes about the writing of history.

Although equally concerned to comment on the composition of historical story and legend, *Buffalo Girls* does not exhibit a clear tracing of an arc in its plot. Instead, this novel is composed of linear episodes interrelating the lives of the characters as they become caught up in the production of Buffalo Bill Cody's pageant of the West. The plot gives the novel a resemblance to McMurtry's favored form of a journey novel, except that here, practically the entire cast of characters—Calamity Jane, Sitting Bull, No Ears, Annie Oakley, the trappers Ragg and Bone, and Buffalo Bill—participates in traveling to London and back to the American West. Again, as in *Moving On* and *Cadillac Jack*, among other McMurtry novels, the physical travel becomes occasion for some of the characters to journey within themselves. Ragg and Bone pursue a lost past when beaver were plentiful in America. Calamity undergoes the misery of loneliness. No Ears finds a mission to tell his people what the future holds.

The greater utility of the foundational journey plot lies in the unity it gives to the diversity among the characters' stories. The episode of Annie Oakley's shooting match with Lord Windhouveren (*Buffalo Girls*, 178–85) provides the satisfaction of showing the landed aristocrat beaten by the upstart American, but it fits into the novel not so much for its theme as because Annie is part of Buffalo Bill's traveling troupe. Bartle Bone's romance with the Englishwoman Pansy Clowes, who then calculatedly leaves him in America for another man, adds a poignancy to a story of a man who has lost his occupation when settlement of the West renders impossible the life of a free mountain man; yet, despite its thematic pertinence in *Buffalo Girls*, it would be out of place if the basic plot did not justify including Bone in the traveling troupe. Moreover, the linkage accorded to diverse stories by this plot even allows for the introduction of characters and episodes only tangentially connected to the traveling band. This is how Dora Du Fran, friend of Calamity Jane and beloved by Buffalo Bill, gains her place in the novel.

McMurtry's purpose in selecting the form for his plots in *Anything for Billy* and *Buffalo Girls* was to find effective means of constructing narratives that would allow a contrast between false history and reality. *Anything for Billy*, using for its plot a model of events arranged in conclusive order, permits McMurtry to parody the hero story and thus undercut the manufactured myths of Western glory. In *Buffalo Girls*, McMurtry takes another tack. Opting to use the least rigid of plot constructions, he offers the implied opinion that the reality of the Old West will not conform to the false designs of triumphal history. Together, *Anything for Billy* and *Buffalo Girls* continue the author's career-long search for ways to repeat the message that the West was not what popular culture reports it to have been.

CHARACTER DEVELOPMENT

A curious tension between romance and realism arises from the narrative point of view in *Anything for Billy*. Ben Sippi, the fifty-year-old author of extraordinarily popular "half-dimers," follows a career as a writer who helps to construct the imaginary West of bold adventure and outsized characters, but in the story he relates firsthand about Billy the Kid, Ben fixes upon facts about Billy and the West that cannot be processed into noble myth. As a result, Ben Sippi serves a doubly normative function in the novel.

Normative characters, as the term implies, work as stand-ins for the reader. Other characters in a story may conceal their motives or behave deceptively, but a normative character offers the reader opportunity to identify with someone who steers a clear course through the events of the plot. When normative characters narrate the story, they seem to possess clarity of vision and hold values sufficiently like the reader's to make them dependable reporters. When they are actors within a story recounted in third-person narration, normative characters display traits meant to resemble similar ones readers find in themselves. Again, they give readers a fixed point of reference.

Through the autobiographical exposition McMurtry assigns to Ben Sippi in order to explain how he came to be in the West, we learn that Ben has a boundless thirst for fiction. Dime novels, he explains to the illiterate Billy Bone and Joe Lovelady, brought him out West (*Anything for Billy*, 15). Turning, then, to literate auditors, namely, the audience reading this account, Ben proceeds to tell a tale of how literature became his fate. Because he "chanced upon" *Hurricane Nell, Queen of Saddle and Lasso*, he left his comfortable but boring life in Philadelphia. Excited by the tale of Nell, he searched out and read more and more dime novels. When his favorite series heroes did not make timely new appearances, he began to write adventures himself. He became possessed: "The more I read and wrote, the more I burned. For hours each day—having read all the available adventures and written till my hand stiffened and my arm cramped—I would sit in a kind of agitated lethargy . . . seeing in my mind a horde of gaudy figures streaming across an endless plain. Cowboys, Indians, buffalo, stage coaches blew through my vision like leaves" (19–20). Although *Buffalo Girls* is the novel more akin to the picaresque in form, Ben's testimony to his literary mania in *Anything for Billy* marks his relationship to the picaro Don Quixote, for, like his Spanish predecessor, Ben has set forth to live out in reality the conventions belonging to romance. Like Quixote, Ben tilts at windmills, only in Ben's case the humorous irony applies to misreading the realities of train robbery (12–14).

McMurtry exaggerates Ben Sippi's manic possession by an imaginary West for comic effect, but Ben's testimony to his captivation by literature has the serious purpose of establishing the appeal of fictitiously written adventures. Ben Sippi uses both reading and writing to find his sufficient reality, and the development of his character in *Anything for Billy* demonstrates how his taste in storytelling becomes increasingly tempered by the mystery found in lived reality. We read that Ben undertakes the first leg of his journey to the West alert to potential differences between dime-novel illusion and reality: "Why would I need cheap tales, once I was bound for the real—even, by some standards, the mighty real—West? I had jettisoned my sedate habits; why not also jettison my gaudy dreams?" (41). Train robbery represents Ben's attempt at direct transference of episodes from story to reality, and his failure as a hold-up man shows that when he arrived in the West he still held a mistaken belief that dime novels and actuality are equivalent experiences. Billy the Kid, however, teaches Ben that while the materials of life and fiction are similar, their end products are substantially different.

Billy Bone (his surname is McMurtry's adaptation of Bonney, the name assigned the outlaw in most historical accounts) enters Ben's narration "walking out of a cloud," but any mythic suggestions of a young god made by the manner of his arrival in the story are immediately undercut by the "scared look on [Billy's] rough young face" and a natural explanation of the cloud as an atmospheric phenomenon of the plains (*Anything for Billy*, 3). With Billy's figure before him, Ben, like a good normative reporter, must describe the actuality. Billy is short, ugly, chip-toothed, ill-dressed, and silly with a yet-unfounded reputation as a cool killer, but he was "a winning kid" (4–5). This opening scene thus introduces the formulation of character that will remain evident throughout the story of Billy the Kid. Billy is terrorized in a storm (44), superstitious about a Death Dog prophecy he has heard (49), a poor shot with a gun (180)—he is anything but a prepossessing hero. Still, he fashions a reputation in a manner suggestive of gangsters and youth gangs whose culture awards status for cold ruthlessness, and the course of his development in the novel records Billy's filling out such a reputation.

The acme of his growth is reached when Billy explains his cold-blooded shooting of Jody Fay, who was carrying a flag of truce at the time, as an act that "just seemed fun at the time" (*Anything for Billy*, 221). Ben's narration drives home the point: "Four days ago his reputation had only been built on gossip and exaggeration: but Jody Fay lay dead outside the cabin, and that was not gossip" (222). Is the individual's reputation identical to the person, though? That seems to be the question Ben's narration is meant to explore. Ben states at the opening of the novel that once "I would have done anything for Billy" (4). Katie Garza falls deeply in love with him, pledging herself also willing to do anything for Billy, a pledge she redeems when she assists him in escaping from jail. Lady Cecily Snow, "the tall, brilliant, beautiful daughter of the Cavendishes and the Montstuarts" takes the "young, short, dirty, ugly, and violent—and American . . . boy with no grace and no learning" as her paramour (288). Adored by others, he laments at one time that nobody knows what he is like (174), and at another time miserably states through his sobs that "nobody likes a person like me . . . I'm just alone. I was always alone. There ain't really no place for me. I wish they'd just let me fall" (313). Sought as an object of love by Cecily and Katie, he is diminished in their more masterful presence (301). Viewed by his contemporaries as decisive in action, he displays no sense of right or wrong on which to base actions. The contradictions between the person revealed by his actions and the impression his presence creates in others receive no explanation; the "lonely eyes" generating such fondness in Ben and others (292) are windows into a vacancy. Ultimately, the conventions of humanistic characterization (plausible motive and probable behavior) offer no help in comprehending Billy. The explanation for his character lies instead in the pathology of a socially dysfunctional ego, making Billy the consummate antihero.

Secondary characters in *Anything for Billy* show less development than Ben and Billy, but their rich portrayals convey McMurtry's idea that the actual West was fertile enough to require no falsification. The Whiskey Glass War (McMurtry's version of the historical New Mexican Lincoln County War of 1878) brings into the story Will Isinglass, the autocratic owner of a huge ranch and father of Katie Garza, as well as several of Billy's victims. His right-hand man is Mesty-Woolah, a transplanted African, and his consort is Cecily. Within the story, such figures meet the narrative requirements for there to be human agency to move the plot, but in McMurtry's hands, the secondary characters acquire intrinsic interest that elevates them above merely technical convenience. A modest exception can be found in Joe Lovelady, described by Ben Sippi as "the perfect cowboy" (31). Where Billy is a skeptic about happiness, and Ben agnostic, Joe has ideals, including the belief that "life would yield its ripe sweet fruits to competence and application" (40). In that respect, Joe appears to be a hopeful norm, the figure reassuring us that in the blighted social conditions where violence flourishes, some men still are good.

The interesting thing about character development in *Buffalo Girls* is the indication that rather than possessing an inborn essence, the characters are viewed as conditioned and changeable creatures. The circumstances they experienced in early years formed their characters, and in the liminal period of the narrative's present, when the Old West is passing from historical actuality into nostalgic recreation as entertainment and legend, they live with a feeling of displacement. Some characters have no means to alleviate the displacement. For instance, the mountain men Jim Ragg and Bartle Bone (whose last names echo a line from William Butler Yeats about a man being a rag, a bone, a hank of hair) were with the Sioux at the time of Custer's last stand at Little Big Horn (1876) and harbor a durable memory of the great leaving by thousands of Indians from the battle site (70). Now, after a quarter century, neither has ever held a job in town or in any other way joined the economy of settlements. Consistent with the episodic plotting of the novel, they move along a more or less aimless path of physical events showing no particular causal linkage, while psychologically they proceed on a downward pitch.

Because Calamity Jane is a primary figure in the novel, her passage through its pages is more complex. While she experiences a sense of displacement similar to Ragg and Bone, the letters she writes to her imaginary daughter trace the inner life she has created to compensate for the recognition that her biological oddity (she is a hermaphrodite [possessing both female and male genitals]) has rendered her a social misfit. Outwardly, she dramatizes her rejection of gender definition by cross-dressing, the pursuit of typically male work, and adoption of common male behavior such as binge drinking. Subjectively, though, she creates an imagined feminine plot for her life: a torrid love affair with the famous Wild Bill Hickok and a love child borne of their union, to whom she devotedly addresses affectionate letters of self-revelation. Her course is also downward, though, as the compensatory fantasy erodes until, left with nothing to restore her psychic energy, Calamity Jane confesses to a hopeless loneliness.

Dora Du Fran indicates by her own handling of fantasy another variety of displacement. Teddy Blue is her ideal lover, but he short-circuits the possibility of their permanent attachment by marrying someone else. Buffalo Bill Cody would marry her in an instant, but inexplicably she consistently refuses him, as though waiting for the man of her dreams. When Dora does marry, it is an unlikely match to Ogden, a naïve boy-giant, whose main attraction seems to be that he is such an unlikely lover for a whorehouse madam. After a momentary upswing, when she takes over a fine hotel and becomes pregnant, Dora's life also runs downward so that the logic of the novel makes it necessary that she die just when it might conventionally be expected that the hopes of "a starved girl wearing her dead father's shoes," as she walked into Abilene many years before, might be realized (*Buffalo Girls*, 297).

Against all of this displacement and failure by characters without means to adapt to change, the development of Buffalo Bill Cody's character provides a purposeful contrast. Buffalo Bill, who earned his name by feats of excessive carnage as a hunter employed by the railroad to slaughter the meat to feed construction crews, knows the Old West is gone. He may even know that the heroes of the old time like Custer were, as Calamity Jane writes, cold and careless (*Buffalo Girls*, 90). Probably, he knows his own reputation is misplaced (he states his regret for killing so many buffalo and his resolve to regrow the herds), but Buffalo Bill suffers no sense of displacement, because he knows that as conditions forming the person alter, the person must change too. He has a strong sense of historical change that he seeks to explain to the recruits for his Wild West Show. Addressing Bartle and Bone, he says, "Boys, you've got to look at it from the point of view of younger generations ... The whole eastern part of the country is civilized now, and the plains are filling up with towns ... It won't be long before the only chance people have to see riding and shooting will be in a show." In confirmation of Cody's genius and character adaptability, we learn from one of Calamity Jane's letters that she considers him "the most successful person ever to come out of the west" (333), and we learn, also, that Cody's show has fostered another sort of entertainment consisting of roping contests and the riding of pitching horses (327). What McMurtry elsewhere describes as stylized lies (*Rodeo*, 83) have risen from the ruins and failures, and by the development of the character of that gifted entrepreneur Buffalo Bill, we are led to believe that the succession from an actual West to an imaginary West was the preferred choice over ignominious death.

THEMATIC ISSUES

Ben Sippi is responsible for the scene setting in *Anything for Billy*, which, in turn, introduces the theme of the *real West* at odds with the made-up West of romance. Opening the eleventh chapter of the first book of the novel, Ben's voice tells of riding all day at a fast clip and getting "nowhere that one could rightly call anywhere." There was "such an immensity of sky and grass! And when you've said sky and grass, you've said it all." For this city emigrant, the distances make him feel he might never get across the plains. His mind tells him there are places across the distance, Philadelphia, St. Louis, and other cities, "but so endless were the plains that it seemed I would be lucky to arrive at any of those cities much before the hour of my death" (33–34). This sardonic description of landscape is matched by Ben's discovery that bugs are a greater bother in the West than Apaches and bandits. Books never mention bugs. Dime novels take no account of insects. Sleeping in prairie grass, Hurricane Nell never complains of chiggers, but Ben complains, "I had not been on the Texas shore twenty-four hours before I had to contend with lice, chiggers, mosquitoes, nits, ticks, houseflies, horseflies, bedbugs, beetles, ants, spiders, roaches, centipedes, scorpions, and gnats. And so it was to be in all my Western jaunts" (*Anything for Billy*, 48).

It is hard to feel visionary or inspired by grandeur when the environment seems to harbor no life but pests. Equally resistant to glorification is a trip in that omnipresent vehicle of Western romance, the stagecoach. Nothing less than two chapters will do for Ben to present his description of the discomfort of bumping across stone-hard terrain, bracing oneself to resist falling forward onto other passengers, and suffering the intrusions of the retching, flatulence, and drunkenness of the companions on the journey. Although the famous writer "splashes color on his story," Billy and Joe Lovelady are more amused than impressed by Ben's lavish description of his journey's hardship and the stupor into which he sank on a saloon floor in El Paso (*Anything for Billy*, 51–58). Ben Sippi discovers that there is something about the West and the people who inhabit it that discourages romance. Time and again, reality fails to live up to expectation. The famous gunman Hill Coe practices his shooting daily, expending by Ben's calculations 18,250 bullets a year sharpening his aim; yet, when Katie Garza challenged him to a match, he lifted his pistol and "missed clean with his first and only shot." So shocked is Coe by the failure of reality to respect his reputation that he falls into depression (89–97). In emphasis of the gap between the expectations of legend and reality, Billy takes up the challenge of the shooting match and misses his targets eighteen times, while Sippi hits seventeen straight bulls-eyes on the target bottles.

As the narrative point of view of the novel and such incidents as those just related suggest, the thematic burden of *Anything for Billy* is the sharp difference between imagined story and real experience. At one point, after seeing men killed and the West revealed in its barrenness and disappointing reality, Ben loses his ability to write dime novels (156–57). What has happened is that he has become the eye witness to events more shocking, and also more real, than any he could imagine. That point being made, Ben becomes concerned with the process of writing the history of actual events.

Because Ben is the only living witness to the love affair of Katie and Billy, historians come to see him for the facts. Invariably they go away annoyed, because what Ben remembers is how sad he felt during that time. Details of the love story are lost to him, because he was living then, not collecting data. Newspapermen and historians distrust his accounts of the Old West, because while "they have made a study of it," he "was just there" (*Anything for Billy*, 229). Apparently, history, as written by the experts who never saw Billy in person and participated in none of the events marking his fall, owes little fidelity to primary sources. Instead, it derives from the body of *a priori* assumptions of an ideal history.

Once more, the point is not the simple one, that actuality as lived is true and made-up stories false. Rather the distinction is between two kinds of experience. When Ben Sippi identifies himself to Sister Blandina, another character fondly devoted to Billy, she offers "sharp criticisms of [Ben's novel] *Wedded but Not Won*." Speaking of the wife in the story, as though she were a living person, the Sister tells him she only wanted attention, and had she "got her due, she soon *would* have been won." Sister Blandina is a well-read person, fit to talk about the novelists Scott and Thackeray, not an innocent, unable to discern the difference between fact and fiction. As McMurtry makes Ben realize, Sister Blandina is like all of us, dreaming "of a life other than the one we actually live on this indifferent earth" (*Anything for Billy*, 199–200). Old Man Isinglass is another character devoted to the imaginary life found in literature, so much so that he makes Ben Sippi into a Scheharazade (the wife of the Sultan in *Arabian Nights Entertainments* who postpones her execution by telling him engrossing stories night after night) by delaying his hanging so long as Ben tells him stories that will keep him awake each night long enough for him to digest his dinner (241). Clearly, Isinglass also relishes the alternate reality of literature.

The final twist of the ironic theme of literature in contest with actuality comes with the triumph of fiction in the subject area of the novel where it is most frail, namely, in the histories written about Billy the Kid. Late in the novel, after Billy has killed a ten-year-old Apache, Ben explains that there is a school of historians bent upon whittling down the number of Billy's killings, starting with this murder of an unarmed child. The action does not fit the template of the Western hero, so those historians raise doubts about the veracity of Ben's witness to the killing. Inventing an entirely different version of events, they claim that Ben could not have been present (*Anything for Billy*, 333–34). Those historians who write of Billy's death prove themselves just as ingenious in dodging the facts that Ben saw with his own eyes; one is described as smiling knowingly at Ben's unmannerly assertion of what he actually saw as though certain Ben is lying. But another historical personage takes the award for brassiest rewriting of Billy's end. That is Tully Roebuck, who somehow has convinced himself that he, not Katie, shot Billy dead. Not surprisingly in a novel whose theme is revisions of historical reality, Tully's book becomes more popular, and is taken as more authoritative than *Billy the*

Kid or *The Wandering Boy's Doom*, the book Ben Sippi himself wrote immediately after Billy's death in the hope and expectation that it would finally assure his glory and income as a writer of "true" Western tales (*Anything for Billy*, 396). Compelling illusion has bested depressing actuality, and to complete the comic turn in the novel we hear from Ben that his abortive career as a holdup man has inspired a motion picture called *The Great Train Robbery*, a work whose classic status announces the arrival of Western legend into the newest genre of popular narrative entertainment.

Thematically, *Buffalo Girls* also concerns the emergence of Western legend and repeats the description of variance between actuality and imagined reality. By introduction of Buffalo Bill's Wild West Show, this novel covers the larger canvas of spectacle that extends beyond literature. Moreover, it adds to the mix a consideration of the motives for participation in the simulated, inauthentic West. Americans yearn for portrayal of their country's rise to greatness, while other peoples wish for accounts of the times when the new American empire was forming. When Frederick Jackson Turner argued that the frontier explained the unique experience and values of the nation, he found a responsive chord in the nationalism developed by our continuing emphasis of American exceptionalism. America is fresh and innocent, it is claimed, or America represents fulfillment of a modern conception of the individual—and both freshness and individualism can be seen in the anarchic days before settlement and institutional law took over the West. Those times, it is believed, mark the nativity of new people, Adam and Eve returned to their paradise. It hardly matters that the Western past cannot be recovered, because it can be simulated in pageants like Buffalo Bill's, refelt in the plots of hundreds of stories about lone men in struggle, and admired in the dance of characters in rodeo and films making display of activities that once were merely the ways horsemen and ranchers did their work.

The American cultural love affair with a revision of Western experience explains the success that Buffalo Bill foresaw and that Calamity Jane despaired of achieving. A wish for acclaim explains the participation of characters such as Annie Oakley, Sitting Bull, and the other characters of *Buffalo Girls* in the production of a simulation of the West. American merchandising practices explain the mechanism by which the fictitious West of legend penetrated American culture to influence the games children play (cowboys and Indians), the roles many youths seek to play as individualists defiant of authority, the icons that market tobacco (the Marlboro man), regional dress, and vernacular language (fast drivers, surgeons, and other macho figures are called cowboys). The achievement of Larry McMurtry's *Buffalo Girls* is to expose the selling of the West.

A NEW HISTORICIST READING

Historical study of literature developed into a sturdy academic enterprise during the nineteenth century by analogy with the practices of science. Everything in nature and social reality was subjected to rigorous standards of objective inquiry, literature as much as anything else. Influenced by the French critic and historian Hippolyte Taine (1828–93), students of written texts came to view literature as an assemblage of cultural artifacts similar in its possibilities for analysis to the material evidence from which archaeologists derive their knowledge of past communities. Philosophically, the nineteenth-century historical investigations into literature continued the scientific analogy by the adoption of a similar idea that literature can be explained by reference to its environment. As Taine sought to explain in such works as *Histoire de la litterature anglaise* (1864; English translation as *History of English Literature*, 1871–72), literature must be recognized as the product and consequence of a particular social and temporal environment, just as the organisms examined in biological science demonstrably evolve through the interaction of environment and heredity. Studied in the manner recommended by Taine and his followers, literature should be expected to reveal to an inductive examination, markers of its origin within a historical time and its authorship by a representative of a specific "race" or people. The effective result of this method and its underlying philosophy was to encourage the belief that literature reflects or documents history and society.

Suppose, however, that the markers discernible in the language of literary texts were inscribed by authors in no substantive way representative of the majority of people who lived in their time and place. Suppose also that in the passage of time, we have lost the capacity to recover the full set of references surrounding the language in the document. Then, to complicate matters further, consider that when a writer drafts a narrative (or poem or play), she or he makes dozens of seemingly free decisions about the plot, characterization, and style employed in the "telling" of the story. With these thoughts in mind, can a critic comfortably conclude that a work of literature simply reflects actuality?

A school of criticism giving an emphatic "No" in answer to this question has come to be known as New Historicism. It is historicist because it carries on the belief that literature arises in social experience, but it is "New" because this school of critics finds that rather than conveying what might be thought of as the consensus of attitudes from the past, literature more likely records in peculiar ways the controversies of the past. Even the "facts" in literature often appear disputable to the student of New Historicism. Are not Shakespeare's history plays partisan toward the Tudors, who ruled England when he began his writing career? Of course they are. Is it not plausible, therefore, knowing what we do about patronage in English Renaissance times, to conclude that Shakespeare's history plays "reflect" the so-called facts, not as they might have actually been, but instead as they were viewed to the convenience of the ruling party?

Applying New Historicism to Larry McMurtry's *Anything for Billy* and *Buffalo Girls* becomes a simple task, since it seems that if McMurtry is not a conscious adherent to the school of New Historicism, he is at least an intuitive new historicist. Each of the novels is constructed to present differing views of events, and both novels thematically enforce the point that the history of the Old West retailed by American culture is an invention, not a record.

A cautionary word is in order now. New Historicism, either as it is practiced by literary critics or by Larry McMurtry, is not the same thing as exposé or attack on cherished beliefs. Those breakers of religious images from whose action we get the term "iconoclast" were motivated by the conviction that images of false gods must be destroyed so that the true gods may prevail. Iconoclasts may be as dedicated to an absolute truth as the false believers. They just want to set things straight. The works of New Historicism are more skeptical than that. Objective, conclusive evidence of the true reality, New Historicists contend, is impossible to obtain, because all communications from or about the past are mediated, which is to say, filtered by a selective point of view. Consequently, when we study literature with the methods of New Historicism, we are studying the conditions and sources of mediation as they can be identified through a study of information about authors' biography, audience wishes and expectations, the cultural milieu, politics, and literary traditions.

Again, McMurtry seems to be working in the mode of New Historicism. Although his sharpest jabs are directed at other historians, McMurtry's reflexive textual constructions insistently direct the reader's attention to the ways reality is being mediated. It is no stretch at all to see his implicit argument that history is subjective invention applying equally well to the novels *Anything for Billy* and *Buffalo Girls*.

8

The Matter of Sequels
Some Can Whistle (1989)
The Evening Star (1992)
The Late Child (1995)

Writing for the *Detroit News*, H. H. Harriman observed that "more than any other writer I know of, McMurtry is inclined to return to his earlier books and spin off sequels." Twenty years after the apparent completion of his "Hometown Project" (discussed in chapter 3) with *The Last Picture Show* (1966), he reprised his exploration of the mores of Thalia in *Texasville* (1987), and, twelve years after that, again continued the story in a novel centered on the mental crisis endured by the middle-aged Duane Moore (*Duane's Depressed*, 1999). Similarly, McMurtry's development of a new history of the Old West (discussed in chapter 6) occurred through repeated appearances of the characters introduced in *Lonesome Dove* (1985) in three subsequent novels, published over a period of twelve years, that eventually complete the life cycle of Gus McCrae, Woodrow Call, and their historical period. Harriman thinks it is "hard to say exactly what the motivation is here—genuine and fond nostalgia, what could pass for a genuine preoccupation with unfinished business, or more darkly, the less than genuine and never gentle persuasion of a publisher's greed" (quoted in Metzger 1987).

Reviews of McMurtry's sequels show other writers sharing Harriman's unease about the purpose and value of his continuing stories once well-told. Novelist Louise Erdrich finds "the leisurely, lyrical character development, description and complexity that distinguished [*The Last Picture Show*] absent from [*Texasville*]" (*New York Times Book Review* in Reynolds 1989, 338). Critic Noel Perrin greeted the appearance of *Streets of Laredo* by stating "it turns out that the person who can write the best parody of Larry McMurtry is Larry McMurtry" (*New York Times Book Review*, 25 July 1993). And when *Comanche Moon* was issued, book reviewer Steve Duin announced in the *Portland Oregonian* that "at long last, Larry McMurtry has beaten the life out of Gus McCrae and Woodrow Call. He has bled the Texas Rangers dry. Smothered them beneath a million words. Told us more than we ever needed to know" (3 November 1997).

The interesting thing about the negative and mixed reviews given to McMurtry's sequels is that even while they refer to the earlier works for purposes of comparison, the reviews also treat these additional novels as independent, freestanding compositions to which are applied the usual expectations for originality and completeness of design. This is natural, because reviews, after all, are meant to serve as appraisals of new commodities on the literary market. Normally, book reviews do not have time for the long view of either literary history or criticism of the evolving body of an author's output. Repetition becomes problematic for reviewers; since a return to characters and scenes from earlier books can never result in entirely original work and will always provoke contrast with what was once new and presented for reading as a conclusive narrative. In the short term view of the marketplace, represented in the speculation of H. H. Harriman above, sequels must be born of a writer's feeling that the characters are like real people, in which case fond nostalgia explains their return, or alternatively their cause lies in collusion of the writer and publisher in an effort to repackage a familiar commodity. In other words, a writer of sequels like Larry McMurtry must be so forgetful of his technical inventions that he succumbs to the power of his realism while also having a publisher indulgent of an author on automatic pilot, or, in complete contradiction to this scenario, the sequel writer and his publisher are fully conscious manipulators of literary tricks.

The longer term view of literary criticism, rather than considering sequels an issue for the marketplace of publishing, examines them as products from the writer's workshop. Once invented, characters and settings become a writer's materials—like Wessex, Tess of the D'urbervilles, and Jude did for Thomas Hardy; Yoknapatawpha County, the Compsons, and the Snopes became reusable material for William Faulkner; and Dawson's Landing, Huck, and Tom became returning subjects for Mark Twain. In their reappearances, the materials of character and setting continue as established references due to their prior use, suggesting that as a suprareality generated by the writer's imagination they are uncontainable within the form of a single story. Providing in sequels the opportunity for different applications through different constructions of plot, the already created materials of first works convert into instruments for analysis of additional topics. For one example, analysis of McMurtry's project of drafting a new history of the Old West allows us to see that the characters and settings he uses to trace the historical beginnings of cattle drives in the plot of *Lonesome Dove* are reanimated in *Dead Man's Walk* and *Comanche Moon* for treatment of the early settlement and Indian fighting that occupy earlier history, and revived again in *Streets of Laredo* to describe the history of late settlement days. Because the periods of time differ in terms of the points at issue between Anglos and Native Americans, settlers and the lawless, the novels require different plots and result in different thematic messages. For another example, in reusing characters and the small-town setting in the Thalia novels, McMurtry is not only continuing his story, but is adopting different thematic perspectives. Where *Horseman, Pass By* works as a coming-of-age story commenting on the limited resources for maturity, and *Leaving Cheyenne* portrays a conflict between erotic impulse and social convention, later additions to the series offer social satire in *The Last Picture Show* and *Texasville* and a probing of a protagonist's psyche in *Duane's Depressed*.

The novels discussed in this chapter illustrate yet another possibility open to the writer of sequels. The first novel, *Some Can Whistle*, takes up the story of Danny Deck, the writer who figures prominently in *All My Friends Are Going to Be Strangers* where he meets disillusion in the literature game, when he is fifty-one years of age and gains a last chance for a normally affectionate life. Danny receives mention also in *Somebody's Darling* as a one-time lover of Jill Peel, and before that in *Texasville* where he is ensconced in a mansion outside of town. The second novel, *The Evening Star*, recalls Aurora Greenway, the mother of Emma Horton, whose death is recorded in *Terms of Endearment* and whose children Aurora has taken to raise. Also figuring in the story is Patsy Carpenter, who first entered McMurtry's fiction as one of the young people around the Rice University English Department in *Moving On*. The third novel recovers Harmony, the protagonist of *Desert Rose*, for a story about grief over a lost child.

For almost thirty years, then, McMurtry has been seasoning these characters and making use of their home settings of Houston and Las Vegas. On the level best appreciated by book reviewers, these three sequels are simply reappearances of characters previously established, a chance to see how their careers have turned out. In the broader view of literary criticism, however, sequels offer a new vantage point. Even though the novels incorporate some of the materials he earlier wrought for examination of contemporary life, McMurtry's newly constructed narratives provide a distanced and differing vantage point of considerable interest to literary criticism, because the new view of Danny, Aurora, Patsy, Harmony, and others who reappear in these sequels represent McMurtry's more recent thinking about the content and craft of characterization and fictional plotting. These sequels are windows upon the thought of a celebrated and fully mature author about the fundamental and invariable elements constituting American character and lives.

These sequels derive from distinct periods of McMurtry development and interest, but having been published over a period of just six years they seem also to reveal a common viewpoint cutting across the differences once evident in the original appearances of the characters and their native places. That viewpoint can be summed up as seriocomic, part serious and part humorous. More than that, all three novels also show a fixation by the author on clinical depression that directs the story in each novel toward the detailing of symptoms of psychological desperation. Taken together with McMurtry's other important sequel from the 1990s, *Duane's Depressed*, these works mark a switch from the broad-brushed canvases of social criticism making up the original Thalia and Houston novels to intensely personalized portraits of subjective crisis. To literary critics and historians, if not to book reviewers, these works are evidence of a distinct and different period in Larry McMurtry's career.

PLOT DEVELOPMENT

Some Can Whistle achieves its comic tone through contrasts and exaggerations. The rough, untutored Tyler Rose (known as TR) set against her deracinated, withdrawn father, Danny Deck, presents the sharpest contrast in that neither has any idea how to deal with the other. TR turns toward the world in a brash manner, meant to conceal the insecurity she has acquired from her grandparents' abusive treatment. Danny, who has been experiencing immovable writer's block and migraine headaches since turning back to novel writing after the suspension of his hit television sitcom, *Al and Sal*, takes recourse in the belief that females are inscrutable. Inevitably, misunderstandings and mistaken feelings fill the conversations between the two. For comic exaggeration there is the behavior of Lloyd Jons Godwin, another import from *All My Friends Are Going to Be Strangers* and a permanent houseguest of Danny's, who turns alternately lustful as a satyr looking for sex with any other human being, male or female, he can seduce and effete in his pedantic statements on culture and literature. Meanwhile, a woman named Gladys plays the part of the brusque and controlling, but dedicated housekeeper. The contrasts are heightened when TR brings into Danny's home her workmates from the Mr. Burger in Houston and Muddy, the father of one of her two children.

The strain of seriousness within the account of the failures in their relationship flows from the deep importance that the meeting of TR and Danny holds. She is a child-woman denied affectionate parenting. He is a withdrawn, self-absorbed man, so fearful of commitment to another human being that even his inexperienced daughter can intuit that a man who maintains relationships with women by leaving messages on their answering machines is a troubled case. The plot of the novel toys with an audience's expectation that TR and Danny will be able to give each other what they need to open up, by demonstrating a rising fondness in Danny when he tells his grandchildren stories and witnesses TR's sobbing responses to the gifts he has saved for her through the years when his ex-wife and her parents forbade him to communicate with the girl. At the same time, though, the narrative repeatedly illustrates Danny's isolation from colleagues and friends, while also recording eruptions of his symptoms of depression. As the first-person narrator of the novel, he has reason to relate information about his past as well as his present, so thinking back over his TV career, he states that where once success had seemed as natural as sunlight and energized him, it came in time to enervate him instead: "For months at a stretch I awoke lethargic, paralyzed by the knowledge that there was no longer any need to rise" (*Some Can Whistle*, 113). In personal hygiene, he exhibits the compulsive need to wash his hair constantly, sometimes twice a day (155). When the children move into his house, "the human emanations all around me, of which the most extreme manifestation was [his grandson's] screaming, began to make my temples throb alarmingly" (166). Migraine headaches incapacitate him, so that journeys he takes with TR and the children have to be broken up while he retreats to a dark room. The plot thus pulls in two directions. One direction calls for a happy ending, and at one moment, when Danny goes dancing with TR, such an ending seems possible. Pulling in another direction, though, is the evidence of Danny's depression, making a feeling of happiness for him unlikely. With the contrary forces of promising happiness and disabling depression set forth, McMurtry brings the plot to its climax with the vicious and mind- less murder of TR by the estranged father of her other child. The feelings of incapacity that Danny's narrative tells us flood him may be, as they say, all in his mind, but events in the objective world validate the sub- jective feelings. He truly does seem to be powerless.

Danny is not tragic, however, because the cause of the painful climax lies not in the excess of a human trait that critics call a tragic flaw, but in the fevered brain of the congenitally criminal Earl Dee. In the world that McMurtry has sketched, the climax of violent death lacks any hu- manistic explanation. It simply is an absurd event, a happening carrying no inherent meaning. Recovery from loss and depression in such a world follows no rational path and may not happen at all, because states of mind have no clear origin in deeds or influences. A state of mind and, consequently, character comes unbidden, its sources hidden in biochem- istry. Danny wraps up his narrative with updates. Earl Dee is killed in prison; Muddy, who overcomes his despair, meets a chance death in traffic; and the children of TR turn out to be inexplicably different. Nobody likes her son, Bo, while her daughter, Jessie, is delightfully en- ergetic, intellectually curious, and a very satisfying telephonic compan- ion to her grandfather. Danny tells, too, that his writer's block is gone and the novel he wrote afterwards was not about the women he once had planned to memorialize, but is instead about the character of a crim- inal old preacher based on his father-in-law, TR's grandfather. This in- formation is not to be mistaken as a sign of character change. As Danny sees it, there are just two kinds of people: the happy ones, whose lives are dense and active; and the sorrowing, who "are nomads, on a plain with few landmarks and no boundaries" (*Some Can Whistle*, 368). In Danny's life and in the plot of this sequel there is nothing more to learn.

The first-person narration of *Some Can Whistle* functions to reinforce a plot dedicated to recording the state of Danny Deck's consciousness, but in *Evening Star*, a novel equally concerned with delineation of a character from an earlier work, McMurtry relinquishes the economy of the first person to gain the panoramic effects of an omniscient third-person nar- ration. Aurora Greenway is the cynosure of the story, the Polaris com- pleting the constellation of characters and serving as direction for events in the novel. Each character takes a place in a pattern relating to Aurora; all of the numberless incidents in the novel are in some way occurrences in her presence, taking place with Aurora on the scene, or reported to her. One of her grandchildren runs off to Los Angeles, but telephone calls filter all that we know of her adventures through conversations she holds with Aurora. Rosie, her companion-housekeeper, apparently has a love life, but it is not at all private, since Rosie, too, relates everything about her personal feelings and behavior in overheard conversations with Aurora. Yet, while constructing the narrative on the model of *Ursa Minor* (the configuration in which Polaris is the outermost star and navigational point for mariners), McMurtry also takes advantage of the limitless third-person narration point of view for lengthy passages of indirect discourse, relating what every character thinks and feels in lavish detail. The result is a sprawling work of fiction requiring either strong characterization or an absorbing plot to prevent it from falling to pieces.

McMurtry opts for the former to give shape to this novel. The episodes presenting Aurora dallying with her several suitors enact mating rituals. The contention between Aurora and Patsy Carpenter for sexual possession of Dr. Bruckner raises the stakes in the carnal game, but otherwise repeats the notion that erotic desire is the agency of life. Generally, the sexual play is inscribed as farce, the mode of presentation that through distanced observation and exploitation of indignity reduces behavior to ridiculousness. For example, Aurora's stalled seduction of Pascal on a couch (Book I, chapter 6), which leads to great shock for the young Melanie, reads as a risible scene in the human comedy, not a satire of the pathetic groping of elderly folks past their prime, or even a lament for absent prowess. It is straight comedy. The same can be said of the forays by Aurora into Dr. Bruckner's bed, of the revelation that Pascal's penis has a unique bend in it, and of Rosie's accounts of sexual dissatisfaction with her lovers. At the same time, the comic is leavened with serious considerations. The children Aurora took to raise when her daughter, Emma, died of cancer are unaccountably disappointing: Tommy is serving a sentence for killing his lover; Melanie cannot be sure which wastrel has made her pregnant; Teddy survives after psychiatric confinement for attempted suicide by working alternate shifts in a 7-Eleven with Jane, the bisexual mother of their child, Jonathan (called Bump). As though to underline the waywardness of the process of growing up, Rosie's children have achieved respectable lives and Patsy envies Aurora her custody of Emma's offspring.

The comic without the serious in the novel would verge to emptiness, one more tired rendition of sexual folly. The serious without the comic would be simply another confirmation that life lacks inherent meaning. In combination, though, and by connection to the dominant character of Aurora, the seriocomic conjunction leads to the plot underlying *Evening*

Star. Aurora is at the end of a protracted struggle to give her life zing and quality. Her manipulation of suitors and dominance of conversations constitute an effort to control life, an effort mirrored by the construction of the novel around her presence. Beneath an exterior of unpredictable eccentricity, Aurora senses that life is as existentialist philosophers describe it, deeply absurd. What significance life may seem to have results from application of will within the limited arena left to us by the determining conditions of existence. From this perspective, the sprawl of the novel assumes function. The lengthy third-person narrative description and the conversations that often seem to do no more than fill space and time become the mundane context of life, the wash of events and talk that occupy our waking moments. Burrowed within the mundane context lies the plot seeking to dramatize the effort to give it some sense. Perhaps like Danny Deck, Aurora Greenway knows that one inhabits a mental landscape without landmarks, but unlike Danny, she sets out to chart a path across emptiness.

The Late Child again examines the psychology of contention with pain and loss. Where *Some Can Whistle* works to document the unrelieved condition of depression, and *Evening Star* relates the story of a woman struggling to resist depression in the face of meaninglessness, *The Late Child* traces the path of recovery from a grief that threatens to bring permanent depression in its train.

When last seen in *The Desert Rose*, the novel to which *The Late Child* is sequel, Harmony, once the most beautiful and celebrated showgirl in Las Vegas, had fallen victim to the demands of show business for younger, more perfect bodies. Her child, Pepper, who succeeded her on the casino stage, had left her for a temporary marriage and to pursue a dream of starring in New York. Because the focus of the first novel was attentive to Harmony, readers tended to know Pepper mostly through her mother's responses. Since Pepper has died of AIDS before the opening of *The Late Child*, she exists exclusively in the memory of those who knew her, her mother, and her lover, Laurie, which, naturally, makes her instrumental to the plot if not substantial in it. The report of her death in a letter to Harmony from Laurie sets events in motion.

The journey is an archetypal motif for McMurtry. In *Moving On, Cadillac Jack*, the series begun with *Lonesome Dove*, and other works, he uses journeys to underpin the progress of character and the emergence of theme, so in *The Late Child*, he resorts to the motif again to frame Harmony's passage through the stages of grief and to record her return to her family's home in Tarwater, Oklahoma. The journey works also to introduce a large cast of incidental characters who provide distraction from the misery of Harmony's loss, reassurance that the world contains hopeful personalities, and a comic complement to the serious matters at the heart of the story.

Speaking in terms of episodes, the journey covers physical and social territory, conveying the narrative from Las Vegas to New York City, to a small town in Oklahoma, and back to Las Vegas. The foundation of plot, though, is to be found in the phases of mind through which Harmony passes during the physical travel. She begins in a state of stunned inability to absorb the news conveyed in Laurie's letter announcing Pepper's death. Harmony pushes the letter aside, throws it out of her house, and never really accepts its message until her sisters have arrived to comfort her (*The Late Child*, 76). Aimless sightseeing and an overwhelming desire for numbness consume Harmony in the next phase of her grief, while the loss of her U-Haul trailer holding all of her worldly possessions at Canyon de Chelly, the breakdown of her borrowed car in Grants, New Mexico, and a bewildering arrival at La Guardia Airport after a flight from Albuquerque load the traveling party with practical burdens that provoke Harmony's sister, Neddie, to wonder aloud if God is testing them to see how much shit they can survive (166). At this point, Harmony experiences a sense of identity with Sheba, the homeless prostitute whom her son, Eddie, has invited to join their band, thinking that she had been but a step away from hooking herself during hard times in Vegas until friends gathered around (185). It is a time when acknowledgement of the fact of Pepper's death and her own limited resources— no special skills marketable for more than minimum wage employment, a string of rotten men who have used her and left her until she cannot imagine ever having a loving relationship—drives her to wish for a sort of death: " 'I wish I could be anywhere on earth but where I am,' she thought. 'I wish it could be another day. I wish I could be in a faraway place where I don't know anybody. I wish nobody at all was with me. I wish I could just be in bed alone, with my head under the covers' " (218). The staccato sentences gradually circumscribing her wishes symptomize the arrival of a deadening depression in Harmony. Subsequently described symptoms include a feeling of emotional helplessness. Her son's dog has jumped off the Statue of Liberty generating a lengthy comic run through the making of celebrity, but for Harmony "it was if the accident had occurred at a moment when her maternal emotions were unavailable" (230). Later, driving through the Holland Tunnel, she is seized with claustrophobia (230). When President Clinton telephones

Eddie about the wonderful survival of his dog, Iggy, Harmony cannot arouse interest in a possible visit to the White House (252).

In these low moments, Harmony can summon recognition that she and Laurie need further outlet for their grief, need to grieve together (*The Late Child*, 283), and that she needs to resist feelings of self-pity (320). When her physical travels take her home to Oklahoma, grief seems to level off at the same time as it extends to feelings about the hopeless lives of her family. Encountering her sister's children, she has a hard time imagining what good things might lie in the future for them (362). They are all so skinny, "but in ways that had nothing to do with their bodies. It was their experience that was skinny" (364).

The nadir of Harmony's descent is hit in a scene bearing the evidence of a mental crack-up. Assembled with the family for a meal at the Waffle House, Harmony feels her appetite go, then claustrophobia seizing her again; she feels displaced, no longer at home, "either in the past or in the present," without a clue "as to what to do next," but afraid. Shaking uncontrollably, she exhibits symptoms for all the world like a fit and has to retreat to a motel room (*The Late Child*, 383–90).

Ironically, engagement with the troubles of her family seems to begin to pull Harmony back from the pit of depression. Her sister, Neddie, enlists Harmony to tell her husband that she is leaving him to marry his brother. Her sister, Pat, who has confessed to being a drug addict, is arrested in possession of 17,000 illegal pills. Her father, enchanted by Eddie and fed up with his termagent wife, hints that he would like to return to Las Vegas with Harmony. And Laurie, who reveals to Harmony that her great love with Pepper was largely unrequited, decides it is time for her to return to New York City and get on with her life (*The Late Child*, 420). It ought to be enough to lock Harmony forever in depressive immobility. To the contrary, though, it lifts her at least to the point of being able to function in what appears to be a normal way. The dependence of others, it seems, challenges her to let memories go and, like Laurie, get on with life: "She had to let the memories go, and the regrets as well; she had to fold them away, as she had folded away her hopes for a man who would love her and care for her. Such a man wasn't going to come; but [her father and Eddie] were there, she had to quit being selfish, she had to be good; even if she didn't think she *could* be good, she had to try" (460). If there is not optimism evident in Harmony's completion of a plot of grieving, there is at least a manifest resilience. With that, McMurtry completes the third of his explorations of the varieties of mental depression.

CHARACTER DEVELOPMENT

As the teller of his own tale. Danny Deck has the excuse to describe his own character also. The result is an autobiographical exposition mixed with frank self-assessment. After drowning the manuscript of his second novel and balking at doing the same to himself, he walked out of the river, hitchhiked to the coast, and took the "first step on the ladder to screenwriting stardom" by writing cartoon dialogue. The ladder proved to be steep. Ten years later, in a "low, almost despairing state," he wrote the pilot for the television show that was "Number One in the ratings: six years straight, Number One, an unprecedented thing" (*Some Can Whistle*, 55–57). At the time he is speaking, Danny can recall every line of the dialogue in the 198 episodes he wrote of *Al and Sal* (84), but cannot draft the first sentence of the novel he has been trying to write over the years since his television show was cancelled and he sold his production company. Perhaps the problem is that the recent project does not tap into his imagination, for, as Danny characterizes *Al and Sal*, the show was the idea of a man who "had never enjoyed one day of normal domestic life" projecting from his "fantasies of what domestic life could be a sitcom that had held America in thrall for nine years" (56).

The title of his work-not-quite-in-progress, "My Girlfriends' Boyfriends," signifies the secondhand quality to his life in wealthy forced retirement and also some effort to make a narrative out of the life he actually is living. He has had girlfriends, and they all went on to other men. In his days of monetary success he had many women friends, none of them evidently material for a life's companionship, except maybe Jill Peel, but, then, his emotional preparation for permanency was also flawed. In Los Dolores, the mansion he had built on a hill in Hardtop County—the house where Jacy Farrow stayed when she returned in *Texasville*—Danny wanders about dressed in caftans (*Some Can Whistle*, 25); holding telephone conversations with his female friends, just as often with their answering machines (33); receives his daily mail of magazines, newspapers, and videos by the pickup truck load (45); idles away time with Godwin; grouses with Gladys; and fiddles with that opening sentence, which in its latest version reads, "True maturity is only reached when a man realizes he has become a father figure to his girlfriends' boyfriends—and he accepts it" (43).

Having climbed to TV success, Danny finds there are no more rungs upward on the ladder for him to climb. He spends his time not in going somewhere, but in reflecting on where he has been: "the thought that was making me gloomy was that the self-parodic not only was beginning to infest my life, it *was* my life. Day after day, month after month, everything that I did, said, or thought seemed to be a parody of something that I had once done, said, or thought more vigorously and better" (*Some Can Whistle*, 90).

The entrance of TR into his life sends Danny on a McMurtry journey, physically to Houston to bring TR home, mentally into the ruminative state that occupies most of *Some Can Whistle*. There is no lack of resources to hinder Danny from connecting with life. He has the money to buy therapy, time to do whatever he needs or wants to do, and access to friendships, but, as he explains to TR when analyzing why he could not marry Emma Horton (whom he loved in *All My Friends Are Going to Be Strangers*), he once wanted to live with Emma in her nice kitchen and be "proper," but after thinking it over for twenty years realizes that he "wouldn't have been able to live in that kitchen, even if [he'd] got to try . . . It's not a way [he] could live" (*Some Can Whistle*, 238–40). He is a congenital loner, one of the "sorrowing nomads" he mentions to readers when characterizing himself at the end of the novel (368).

There is an ancient convention of drama and fiction prescribing a change in characters. Because the experience of events is expected to have influence, characters should not be the same at the end of the story as they were at the beginning. But that is an ancient humanistic convention. In late twentieth-century literature, another convention runs counter. This one holds that some characters are irreparable. They ought to be malleable, because it is our belief that experience matters, but they are not. Danny Deck in *Some Can Whistle* is that sort of static character, drawn to illustrate a condition of isolating social disability. That condition results not from traumatic influences, certainly not from choice. Danny just is.

By contrast, TR is almost a super kid, one of those youngsters who baffle social scientists, because despite deprivation and mistreatment, their self-healing energy makes them successful in the world's terms. In her foreshortened lifetime, TR bounces back from the adversity of her upbringing to become an engaging, caring person. She goes through life being her natural self. She gives attention and reasonable advice to friends and her father, love and discipline to her children. At one point, she walks through a crowd at a water park with an aura of beauty leaving strangers smiling (296). How does one explain this Aphrodite, except as Danny is explained—she just is. For one small moment with TR and her friends at the Mr. Burger shop, Danny's affectless mien changes: "Life at the Dismuke Street Mr. Burger," he says, "had a balmy Neapolitan quality that I was beginning to like. One sat around dining al fresco on local delicacies while discussing the grand issues of life with optimistic, not to mention animated, young women. It was just the way I had always planned to live" (*Some Can Whistle*, 144). Still, it is a momentary feeling, a fantasy at that. Before long, TR will be dead and Danny will still be depressed, an entirely plausible outcome in a novel premised on resignation to the lack of chance for change.

Apart from Aurora Greenway herself, the most entertaining character in *Evening Star* is Jerry Bruckner, the stand-up comedian from Las Vegas who acquires the equipment to pose as a lay analyst through the accident of his mother's lover leaving him a library of psychiatric volumes. The description of Jerry's entry into the healing profession could not be less promising, but surprisingly his catch-as-catch-can psychotherapy (196) seems to help his patients, who are described as "ordinary people, many of them elderly, whose psyches had been mangled by life. They were not well informed about psychiatric concepts, or the structure of their own personalities. They just needed a little sympathy, a little company, and a little common-sense advice" (317). If Bruckner's success with his patients—when he tells them he lacks any academic authority for his therapy, they are "too depressed to care about his lack of formal credentials" (194)—seems far-fetched, it may be because everyone in *Evening Star* exists in distress. For example, Jerry seems to be trying to ratify his identity by pursuing vulnerable young women at the same time that he thoughtlessly sleeps with his patients, Aurora and Patsy. The project suffers utter failure for the simple reason that dalliance leads to his murder by a jealous boyfriend.

With Bruckner disqualified from any legitimate role as a mental health professional, Aurora must resort to her own wits for assistance in managing her life. McMurtry has gained a reputation for facility in the portraiture of women characters, with the development of Aurora Greenway among those receiving praise. In reviews of the novel in which she first appeared, *Terms of Endearment*, Roberta Sorenson found Aurora "the saving element in the novel" (Peavy 1968, 358), and Robert Mewshaw thought her a model for older women "striving to redefine their roles" (*Texas Monthly*, November 1975). Discussing the same novel in extended critical essays, Ernestine P. Sewell took Aurora to be McMurtry's symbol of Houston (in Reynolds 1989, 202), and Mark Busby interpreted her as a type of artist like Virginia Woolf's Mrs. Dalloway in the novel of that name (Busby 1995, 143). In her repeat appearance for *Evening Star*, however, the attenuated blab of her conversation and relentless insistence on her ideals of decorum become exhaustive and stereotypical. She is the sort of character who is significant in conception, but tedious in the execution of her story. Again, McMurtry has produced a static character, this time not by intention.

Harmony is another example evoked in evidence of McMurtry's way with women characters. Not only book jacket blurbs, but reviewers like Emily Benedek, writing in *The New Leader* (14 November 1983), found her to be a winning figure in *The Desert Rose*. On the other hand, Rod Davis's review of the novel in *Texas Monthly* (November 1983) said that she was created by McMurtry without a functioning brain and in caricature of "the honky-tonk angel," who is, in fact, "neither angel nor rose but eternal bimbo." And Busby, after noting that McMurtry wanted his characters to speak authentically in *The Desert Rose*, finds the result to be "vapid vocabulary and anemic thought" (Busby 1995, 173).

The serious business of *The Late Child* sets such assessments to the side. Here, the portrayal of Harmony experiencing grief achieves pathos unavailable to stereotypes or bimbos. The assembly of secondary figures surrounding Harmony on her journey across America and through loss of the mooring she felt she had in the role of mother to Pepper displays the tendency to excess found in a writer with the inventiveness of McMurtry, a writer said by a *New York Times* reviewer of *Evening Star* to have a "quick, eager sympathy for his characters" and "an uncanny ability to zip in and out of all their minds" (12 May 1992). Amidst all the clutter, though, Harmony alone among all the characters in the sequels discussed shows development in her character. The phases of her novel's plot each mark change and progress toward the sort of normal behavior that makes families possible. McMurtry does not have her reborn. That would be improbable and entirely out of place in a serious handling of depression. She does, however, experience recovery that leaves her different from the purposeless figure she was at the conclusion of *The Desert Rose* and before she entered the forced experience of mental breakdown.

This novel, too, has a lay therapist. He is five-year-old Eddie, the indomitable realist whose childish preoccupation with the immediate reminds the other characters that, first, you have to get through the day. "Do you ever get the feeling that you just don't know how to live?"

Harmony asks Laurie. Before she can answer, Eddie pipes up, "Yes, you do know how to live ... How to live is you fix my breakfast and help me get ready for school, and then you go to your job at the recycling plant and when your job is over I'll come home and we'll eat macaroni and cheese and we'll watch some TV shows and if Gary comes over we'll play cards and then I'll take my bath and you can read me a story and I'll go to sleep and that's how to live" (314). Of course Eddie's description is simple, and certainly it is childishly self-centered being all about "me," but it is also about companionship and unqualified love. It is about first things. Eddie's function is to demonstrate through enthusiasm and open affection that he is the model character in the narrative, the child whose need (as he gives his comments and expresses his demands) for caring adults is so evident and spontaneous that it can provide some guidance on the journey through the dark night of depression, provided that the depression is not organic. The differences Harmony exhibits in contrast to Danny Deck, however, confirm that she can recover. Probably it is a matter of opinion whether or not McMurtry stops short of sentimentality in the portrayal of Eddie, but without question, he works effectively as a necessary agent for the story about contending with depression that McMurtry intended to stand in opposition to the example of *Some Can Whistle*.

THEMATIC ISSUES

Given the fact that Danny Deck in *Some Can Whistle* is approximately the same age as Larry McMurtry himself, and seeing that by the time of the novel's appearance both Danny and Larry had achieved popular fame in television—Danny with the sitcom *Al and Sal*, Larry with the miniseries *Lonesome Dove* that ran in eight episodes in the same year as the novel's publication—it is hard not to think that Danny is Larry's fictional surrogate. John Gerlach (*Dictionary of Literary Biography*) takes just that view, and suggests that Danny's story "could be considered McMurtry's attempt to deal with the fact that a shy man has been granted his secret wish and his secret dread: fame. Elaborating the point, Gerlach indicates that the novel allows McMurtry to explore the dichotomies of his own career: "the opposition of art high (the novel) and low (the television series *Al and Sal*, which leads to wealth and fame) and with the nurturing and chaos of family versus the need for solitude."

Solitude, he goes on to say, is necessary for writing the novel, while family (and fame) both fulfill "one's wishes for the expression of self while threatening death to the self."

The interpretation sounds plausible, because it echoes the romantic idea that the artist must live in an ethereal reality in order to have the creative imagination run free, but for the reading actually to work with *Some Can Whistle* would require McMurtry to have written a different novel, one that omitted the realistic descriptions of depression's symptoms. Danny's withdrawal, his building of fences between himself and the world, his persistent migraines—these are not entered into the novel as metaphor, but as actual infirmities. The much more useful reading of the novel's primary theme, useful because it does not blink at the mental state of Danny, can be found in Mark Busby's declaration that the opening scene when TR enters Danny's life "indicates the primary thematic opposition . . . communication-connection-community instead of silence-disconnection-isolation" (1995, 215). In this account of theme, Danny tries to connect, to cross the past years of estrangement from his daughter, but cannot manage the trip and even if TR had lived would not have.

McMurtry reinforces this primary theme with another contrast that he states explicitly when he has Danny bring TR home to Los Dolores. When she meets Godwin for the first time, it is, Danny says, a "delicious Jamesian moment." The reference is to the international novels of Henry James, works like *The American* (1877) and *Daisy Miller* (1878), that place "innocent" Americans of the newly affluent middle class in contrast to the tired heirs of European aristocracy. Danny describes TR in the scene as "beautiful despite her terrible-taste new clothes, sailing up to the house with [her daughter] on her hip, the epitome of American youth, American good looks, American ignorance, American energy" and Godwin as "the ultimate Euro, drugged out, fucked out, arted out—nothing left but brain" (203). Danny might as well be speaking of himself, too, for although he is not European in his proclivities, he is as dragged out and overcivilized as Godwin.

Danny's recall of his career in television provides a second thematic line to *Some Can Whistle*. The irony in the creation of *Al and Sal* has been noted. Danny, the man without a day's experience with normal family life, wrote a show about "a normal middle-class family living in Reseda, California, with their three normal middle-class kids," who "experienced the normal strains, the normal delights, the normal tragedies of American life." Despite the unpromising origin of the show in what had to be fantasy for Danny, "eighty or ninety million Americans chose each week to experience these same strains, delights, and tragedies with Al and Sal and their children." Moreover, in syndicated reruns, the show continued to cause "people who actually *had* domestic lives in places as far flung as Pakistan, Finland, and Brazil to neglect their own perfectly normal domesticities to watch a series that had been born of my own despairing fantasies" (55–56). Television and its audience prefer fantasy to reality, but the significance of the seemingly obvious occurrence—and the twist upon the romantic idea of an artist needing his solitude to commune with a higher reality—lies in Danny's indication that though the popular taste is for fantasy, the populace thinks they have a taste for reality. The theme about art, therefore, links *Some Can Whistle* to such other Mc-Murtry works as *Anything for Billy* and *Buffalo Girls*, and to McMurtry's long-term concern with the popular preference for the West of myth.

In *Evening Star*, McMurtry uses another literary reference to draw attention to theme. Aurora Greenway, whom we recall is described by Mark Busby as an artist *manque* (Busby 1995, 143), conceives in her later years a memory project modeled it seems upon Marcel Proust's massive *Remembrance of Things Past* (1922–32). After Jerry Bruckner's death, she reads Proust "straight through." The effect is to make her weep "from a profound sense of wasted time." The narrative states: "Somehow she had let her life slip by, achieving nothing. She did not suppose, in her hours of regret, that she had ever had mind enough to achieve a great work, like Monsieur Proust. Perhaps she hadn't mind enough to achieve a work of even modest scope—yet it did seem to her that she had mind enough and sufficient individuality that she ought to have achieved more . . . She had, in the end, merely lived, partaking rather fully of the human experience, absorbing it, yet doing nothing with it" (*The Evening Star*, 538–39).

The reading of Proust, it must be noted, is also the prescription suggested by Dr. Honor Blackman for her patient, Duane Moore, in *Duane's Depressed*. In that novel, the reading is intended to prepare the patient to start therapy for depression. Interestingly, Aurora Greenway gives herself the same prescription in her novel published seven years before *Duane's Depressed*. The common reference suggests that McMurtry may well have intended us to recognize in Aurora Greenway symptoms of potential depression, but in her case, the feeling of despair and bafflement in the face of events has not yet progressed to the clinical state. As can be seen in her continuing efforts to control life by talk and will, she is still actively resisting despair and loss of self-esteem. The memory project, which might have been expected to accord Aurora control of her

past, fails, because memory is always faulty when one is not living in
Proustian solitude, but in the present of her life, Aurora survives.

Whether by deliberate intention or as a result of McMurtry's continuing interest in the requirements of domestic life, the presiding theme
of *The Late Child* comments upon and sums up the themes informing
Some Can Whistle and *Evening Star*. First, it makes the point that depression is endemic. When Sheba seems morose and Eddie attributes the
mood to low blood sugar, Neddie interposes, "No, I think Sheba's just
sad. I wake up feeling that way half the time myself. Them moods hit
me and I just feel, What's the point? Why feed the chickens?" The rhetorical questions go on and on, until she realizes everyone has fallen
silent. "Why even live?" she concludes (*The Late Child*, 199). Despite the
universality of depression, one can make do, the novel shows. Harmony,
the least advantaged of the protagonists in the three sequels, finds guidance through her journey of grief by intuition into the experience she is
living, not by imaginative fantasy or in the imaginary creations of art,
popular or high. However much she wants to, she does not complete
her attempted withdrawal from life, nor does she try to relieve her despair and calm her fears by dominance of others. Her remedy for incip-
ient depression therefore contrasts with the strategies of Danny and
Aurora. This is the commentary *The Late Child* offers for its companion
novels. The summary it gives is found in the general depiction of perceived reality. Disinterested chance rather than inherent purpose rules
Harmony's universe. What else can explain Pepper's death, or, for that
matter, the unexpected encounters with Sheba and Otis, Rosie, Omar,
Salah, Abdul, Laurie, and Sonny Le Song? Who could have predicted
that the children in Tarwater would be such wrecks? From the standpoint of the human creatures in these novels, the complexity of life is
beyond their understanding, and there is no indication that another vantage, say, a divine plan, exists. As Eddie says, "my teacher doesn't believe in an anthropomorphic God" (166). Given the theme of reality
pervading these novels, it is no wonder.

AN EPISTEMOLOGICAL READING

Epistemology is that branch of philosophy dedicated to investigation
of the nature and methods of human knowledge. Simply put, it addresses the question, How do we know reality? Common sense indicates
that we apprehend reality through the senses. We see, hear, smell, taste,

feel the world around us; and that is reality. Common sense also provides contrary evidence that we seem to know some things intuitively, values for instance, or that there seems to be a connection between events. The thinking brain thus becomes as much an object of study as the optic nerves. Complicating the matter further, there is the issue of language. The words of our native language and syntactic constructions mediate in some fashion between what we observe or intuit and the consequent expression we give to perception. In that regard, it might well be said that we know reality through previously constructed social codes that name the objects around us, or that have selected some experiences, say, warmth toward another person. Whatever warmth may be—heat in the body or an elevation of blood pressure metaphorically describable as heat—it is clear that other human beings before us have given special attention to it, and by repeated statements about it in speech, writing, and art have conditioned us to single out warmth in human interaction as a favorable occurrence.

Extended to the study of cultural forms, perhaps painting, epistemological analysis demonstrates the differences between eighteenth-century landscapes and impressionist studies resulting from learned ways of observing. Impressionist painting is informed by knowledge of optic science, which is why the brush strokes are applied to replicate particles of light, while the older landscapes derive from a differently conditioned way of seeing. When the investigative methods of epistemology are applied to forms of literature, they indicate that literary genres are selective renderings of reality. Their most common plots and their usual ways of portraying scene or character produce implied statements about the nature of reality and suggestive ways to see it. The novel with its usual attention to a singular featured character puts forth the view that an individual is privileged over a social collective or often may stand in opposition to society. The lyric poem proffers the notion that subjective feeling may be primary experience.

In this reckoning, all texts are propositions about reality. The selection of a genre amounts to a writer's initial choice of a way to see reality. In solving such technical problems as which narrative point of view to use, what traits of a protagonist ought to be emphatic and which minor, what gender should the protagonist be, what ethnicity, the author is drawing upon his or her conditioned sense of dominant reality. At some point, most authors also deal directly with the question, what sort of world am I portraying? This is why we find Danny Deck in *Some Can Whistle* relating that he was surprised by the success of *Al and Sal*. Serving as a mouthpiece for Larry McMurtry, Danny is introducing the epistemological question, what do audiences believe reality is? Is reality, after all, what fantasies like Danny's sitcom condition an audience to prefer?

Epistemologically based literary criticism can also offer an oblique or indirect insight into the construction and themes of novels. The mass of details making up *The Evening Star* and the nonstop talking that often seems to be about nothing convey an impression of an overwhelmingly pedestrian life. The explanation for the presence of the details and talk, as well as their pedestrian effect, according to an epistemologically informed criticism, lies not in Larry McMurtry's refusal to shut up, but in his proposition that such a welter constitutes the reality of life, at least in the world of that novel. Similarly, the mounting record of mishaps experienced by the characters of *The Late Child* signify the nature of reality without evident moral order.

The best critical practice admonishes us to avoid detaching themes from novels and to resist taking fiction as though it were documentation. Epistemological criticism provides the discipline to meet those proscriptions. Analysis with the purpose of uncovering the writer's proposition about reality demands attention to all of the representative techniques and devices; they all contribute to the composition of a fictional world in which every piece counts. Even when a text embodies references to a reality external to itself in history or biography, epistemological criticism contends that everything has become subject to the shaping hand of the author who borrows those references. The resultant work is his or her hypothesis that reality is nothing other than the way it appears to the careful reader of the book.

9

Collaborative Legends— Works Written with Diana Ossana
Pretty Boy Floyd (1994)
Zeke and Ned (1997)

Collaboration projects always raise the question of how the writers divide the labor. Luckily, Larry McMurtry and Diana Ossana in a note to *Pretty Boy Floyd* explain their way. Daily, he writes "a skeletal five pages," they say, and then she fleshes them out to ten. Apparently it works for them. Besides the novel about Floyd and *Zeke and Ned*, they coauthored the scripts for the miniseries based on *Streets of Laredo* and *Dead Man's Walk*, as well as a screenplay about Floyd that preceded their novel. In none of these do the seams show where one writer left off and the other began (a point stressed by Tom Danehy in his review of *Zeke and Ned* for *Tucson Weekly* [6–12 February 1997], which suggests that as McMurtry and Ossana talk over their projects, they come to be of one mind).

In the case of the two novels they have so far published together, the evident basic agreement was that they would return to a subject that has held McMurtry's interest from the start of his career—Western legends. McMurtry has alternately scoffed at the fabled stories of the West (as in some of the essays collected for *In a Narrow Grave* or the novel *Anything for Billy*), explored their appeal (also in *Anything for Billy*, along with *Buffalo Girls*), remarked upon their irrelevance to contemporary life (for example, in the Thalia and Houston novels), and attempted to supplant them with his own realistic histories (the *Lonesome Dove* series). The difference in *Pretty Boy Floyd* and *Zeke and Ned* lies in the decision by

McMurtry and Ossana to leave the legends standing, but to give them a human scale by treating the characters with sympathy, while their adventures are related as sometimes humorous and mostly accidental.

The leading characters in both novels are historical figures with their lives on record. A website and a biography by Michael Wallis, *Pretty Boy—The Life and Times of Charles Arthur Floyd* (1992), will lead any investigator to an outline and "facts" of Floyd's life (1904–34) that prove to be essentially the same as they appear in McMurtry and Ossana's novel. Other websites, some maintained by representatives of the Cherokee Nation, and a popular book for young readers by Phillip W. Steele called *The Last Cherokee Warriors: Zeke Proctor, Ned Christie* (1989) will make pretty much the same demonstration about the novelists' handling of Ezekiel Proctor (1831–1907) and Ned Christie (1852–92).

What makes legends, though, is interpretation and a retelling of stories so that they exceed their factual outlines. A contemporary magazine story about Charles Floyd shows some of the elements lending themselves to the creation of legend. In the story, he is described as "a murderously cool shot," a man "fond of flashy clothes," who "likes to show his bravado by returning to his home town ... for brief visits." In an encounter with the law in 1934, he showed, the magazine continues, "that he had lost none of his finesse. Jumping into a car ... he led police on a wild chase to an empty house at the dead end of a road. There he turned on them with a machine gun and automatic rifles, shot his way out and away" (*Time*, 22 October 1934). Add to this kind of journalistic treatment the plot given to Floyd's career in Woody Guthrie's lyrics to "The Ballad of Pretty Boy Floyd." Starving farmers, Guthrie wrote, tell how the outlaw paid their mortgages, while others say that he left a thousand dollars to pay for a meal given him. In Oklahoma City, he gave a carload of groceries for the families on relief. Completing his invention of a latter-day Robin Hood, Guthrie opines that, unlike those who will rob you with a fountain pen, an outlaw (like Pretty Boy Floyd) will never "drive a family from their home." Together, the journalism and the ballad created an appealing folk hero for the hard times of the Great Depression.

Ned Christie achieved his status as folk hero through dramatic actions that came to represent the cause of the Cherokee people. A "civilized" tribe who lived an agrarian life in the southeast United States and possessed a written language developed by the famous Sequoyah, the Cherokees were driven from their land in 1838, force-marched into the West on what became known as the Trail of Tears, and resettled in the Indian

Territory (later the state of Oklahoma). Ezekiel Proctor traveled the Trail of Tears as a child of seven; Ned Christie was born after the arrival in Indian Territory. Both men, however, were members of the Keetowah Society, a group devoted to maintenance of traditional Cherokee ways. At the time that Christie was accused of killing Marshal Dan Maples, a treaty between the Cherokees and the U.S. government assigned legal powers to the Cherokees and denied jurisdiction to the federal government. Pursuit of Christie by federal authorities was, thus, violation of Cherokee sovereign authority, Ned's resistance a potent political act. Living in a hilltop fortress and repulsing posses attempting to dislodge him, Ned Christie acquired the aura of a patriot.

With the devices of fiction, Larry McMurtry and Diana Ossana are able to add dimension to the facts and folk legends. Through the conventions of third-person narration, they gain entry into the minds and feelings of the characters with one result being that they are freed from the conventions of professional historical writing that require a sifting of evidence. When they believe Pretty Boy was blue, or Zeke's wife was probably furious at him when he wanted to take another woman into their home, they can just say so. Just as important, fiction accords them the authority to create the tone of description they wish, so a robbery in *Pretty Boy Floyd* and a courtroom shoot-out in *Zeke and Ned* can be made out to be slapstick comedy as easily as they can be shown to manifest startling violence. Finally, the significant result of McMurtry and Ossana's freedom to color in the historical outlines is a new kind of legend, fond and amusing, where the older legends were grave and reverent.

PLOT DEVELOPMENT

A comparison of the opening action sequence of *Pretty Boy Floyd* with the historical record and prior versions of the legend reveals the authors' design for their novel. When the narrative begins, Charley Floyd and Bill "The Killer" Miller sit in their "flivver" awaiting the arrival of an armored car carrying the payroll to the Kroger Baking Company of St. Louis. While they wait in the fog, the evidently inexperienced robbers idly but nervously converse about a waitress from the boarding house where they are staying. As the Tower Grove Bank vehicle draws up, Charley jumps out of their own car, announcing to the driver that it is a stickup. "What?" says the elderly guard, "it's so foggy I can't hear you son." Sure enough, it is so foggy that Charley loses sight of Bill, who has their only weapon, and cannot determine if he is covering Charley or has run off, but could the fog prevent the guard from hearing the dramatic announcement of the stickup? As Charley proceeds to tie up the guard, Bill reminds Charley that he is supposed to take the guard's gun first. The guard, however, has forgotten his gun. Well, then, best go ahead and finish tying him up, while Bill keeps his gun on him. Only the gun is pointed at Charley, not the guard. The bumbling continues throughout the escapade, the guard sardonically promising he won't move, because he never "interfere[s] with professionals" (6–8).

According to Michael Webb's reconstruction of the actual robbery (available on the Web) there were three bandits involved in the robbery on September 11, 1925, and they robbed the cashier's office on the second floor of the bakery offices, not an armored car. Moreover, a car chase followed the robbery. Two days after the robbery, Floyd was arrested in Oklahoma in the company of a man named Fred Hilderbrand (no Bill Miller present), with conclusive evidence of their guilt being currency wrappers from the Tower Grove Bank in their possession. McMurtry and Ossana use the same evidence, but otherwise have altered the readily available "facts" to create their own version of events.

That sort of license, though, is the least of the liberties the writers take with the life story of Pretty Boy Floyd. Apparently, they have also invented the series of missteps committed by the novice bandits in order to give the episode a comic tone that the recorded "facts" alone would not convey. And yet, even more important than that, they have begun Floyd's story not when he is a child on a poor farm, but when he is already twenty-one, married, and a father. Leaving out all of his earlier life from their narrative, except as it is recalled in dialogue with other characters, McMurtry and Ossana have also omitted the sort of information that conventionally serves to suggest the sources of character and the influences from youth that might be thought to have shaped the adult.

These selections, omissions, and adjustments of the record signal the writers' purpose in constructing a narrative of the famous bank robber. They do not intend their novel to substitute for a biography. Instead, they confine their attention to the public career of Charles Arthur Floyd, the time when he was the figure of legend. That is the reason they start the story with the St. Louis robbery, and leave Floyd's actual first robbery of $350 in pennies from the post office when he was eighteen to later passing mention. Nor does it seem that they intend to give an environmental justification for Floyd's life of crime—poverty drove him to become a robber. Even less do they want to elevate him to the level of a purposeful Robin Hood, as Woody Guthrie's lyrics would have us understand Pretty Boy. The comic tone of the Kroger robbery and most of the subsequent bank robberies in the narrative defy veneration of Floyd. On the other hand, the telling of Pretty Boy's criminal career in the novel also runs counter to the view that McMurtry and Ossana say J. Edgar Hoover encouraged in his Public Enemy campaign, because the comic tone equally well resists reduction of Floyd to a vicious and brutal man. If the criminal career of Pretty Boy Floyd permits generalization and explanation at all in this novel, it allows only that vainglory and vanity led him to his occupation and confused affections kept him on the move as much as did the law.

Typically, the plot of a legend follows an upward movement through conflicts, until the protagonist arrives to a representative champion's role, at which point powerful forces set out to cut down the champion, but only partially succeed, for memory of the hero's life continues to give moral instruction for all who care to hear about the hero. That is the implicit plot of Woody Guthrie's "Ballad of Pretty Boy Floyd" and dozens of other treatments where the outlaw hero stands for the interests of ordinary people. In *Pretty Boy Floyd*, that typical plot is replaced by one that severs the connection between the protagonist and the growing legend. From other sources, readers of the novel will be aware that the exploits of Pretty Boy reported in newspapers and magazines entertained his contemporaries and contributed to a view that he was, in some way, their champion when robbing banks and eluding capture, but within the novel, Floyd is curiously detached from all of that. He decries the false attribution of robberies and killings that he did not commit in some reports, as though unaware why he gains his reputation, and reads other articles with more wonder than satisfaction.

Instead of mimicking the plot of conventional legend, then, the plot of the novel proceeds in uninterrupted linear order, no event rising much more prominently than another. Many of the robberies are not even described, only counted up, while the focus of narration stays upon characters before or after the crimes. Legend is being constructed elsewhere, it would seem, while the novel shows Pretty Boy living out his brief life in a prosaic way. Except for the fact that Floyd is a bank robber instead of a traveling salesman, the plot of his story, devoted as it is to his trying to reconcile his attachments to different women and to figuring out how best to work with partners, would seem mundane. What the plot of the novel achieves, then, is not to make a critique of legend as McMurtry has done in other works, but instead to present a career that is, so to speak, within the legend.

Except that *Zeke and Ned* concerns itself with more serious thematic issues, this second collaboration shows similarities to *Pretty Boy Floyd* in construction. In the second novel, as in the first, McMurtry and Ossana foreshorten the relating of the lives of their protagonists to concentrate attention on the dramatic period of their maturity and fame, and they employ the antiheroic tone of comedy in relating violent events, such as the melee at Zeke's trial (131–47), and in describing officers of the court like the bailiff Chilly Stufflebean and Judge Parker. Again like *Pretty Boy Floyd*, *Zeke and Ned* expends more time on the invention of the personal lives of the characters—material that cannot be fully known from historical sources—than on events taken from recorded history. Finally, *Zeke and Ned* is equally linear in narration.

Where the second novel departs from the first is in giving the plot the complexity of reversal and a shift of focus. The two lead characters are associated from the start of the book and become even more closely tied when Ned gets Zeke's daughter Jewel as his promised wife. The original focus, however, rests upon the foolish attempt by Zeke to take a second, additional wife, who is already married. This leads to the accidental killing of his beloved and Zeke's becoming the object of revenge for her husband's siblings. While Zeke is, as the saying puts it, "on the scout" (a fugitive on the run), a marshall sent to apprehend him is killed and the blame put on Ned. With that, the plot becomes largely Ned's, as he is lifted to the first position of the narrative. The tone of the narrative also alters, becoming serious rather than comic in the ensuing conflict between Cherokee and "White" law in the Territory.

Ned's flight and resistance to illicit authority might have made a story separate from Zeke's, especially since the outcome of the two stories differs—Zeke gets an amnesty, while the falsely accused Ned becomes the object of a relentless siege. McMurtry and Ossana, however, join the two, suggesting that because the protagonists are close friends, the plots of their experiences intertwine. It is a narrative choice that risks incongruity and disunion. What saves the twin plots from failure and assures their connection is that they are set in late nineteenth-century Cherokee country, where Zeke and Ned are both prominent leaders united in their advocacy of the "old ways." From this common position underlined by their friendship and family tie, they diverge, first, in the distinct plots of their troubles and, then, as Ned gains the fame of an uncompromising champion of the Cherokee, they also grow apart personally. Ned's zeal puts him in an Olympian role (literally on a mountain top) that burnishes his legend, but also isolates him from the ongoing life of his friend, who becomes himself a sheriff and in the last portions of the novel a historian who preserves the record of "Ned's War." The irony that Zeke goes on to a life of service to the Cherokee Nation while Ned dies the isolated hero thus gains effect, because Ned's story and Zeke's story have been made inseparable in the novel.

CHARACTER DEVELOPMENT

Pretty Boy Floyd treats us to varying estimates of Charley's character. J. Edgar Hoover is so convinced that he is the public enemy Hoover has made him out to be, that he threatens the author of a favorable newspaper article about Floyd. Viv Brown, the journalist, responds that because bankers are no friends of tenant farmers, folks look up to Charley Floyd down in Oklahoma (285–86). Bill Miller thinks Charley is a "big hick" (3). Beulah Baird, the waitress in Ma Ash's boarding house, takes a fancy to him and calls him "pretty boy" (5). Lulu Ash figures him to be a sexual object for her lusts, but also a cute fellow worth some advice, if he is going to follow crime (29). Big Carl Bevo, an inmate in the Jefferson City state prison, thinks him callow, but because Lulu wants him to, he gives Charley practical instructions in robbery (97). Charley's wife, Ruby, leaves him when he is in jail, but is swept off her feet when he comes to make love with her and take her away from her new husband (200). His son, Dempsey, idolizes him. George Birdwell thinks him a swell partner for bank robbing, while his wife, Bob, at one point says bandits like him should leave nice women alone (363). The epilogue that completes the novel adds to the variety. A sheriff says he became real friendly with Charley. The woman who gave him a meal just before he was killed thought he looked doomed. Bob Birdwell says he was fundamentally dishonest. Dempsey holds in mind a memory of his parents sleeping in bed, looking like kids. If perceptions are reality, then Charley is all of these things.

Also, Charley is the character whose feelings are related in the third-person narration. Sometimes he is blue and lonely, other times homesick. He misses his wife and child when he is away from them, but loves Beulah when he is with her. He cannot resist spending his money on showy cars and clothes for himself, and on presents to make people love him. He is generous, but just as often thoughtless of others, especially

the women in his life. None of the behaviors attributed to him by the
narrative voice, any more than the estimates of him by other characters,
portray Charley Floyd as heroic. Described in the narrative conducting
a bank robbery, he seems like a character in a slapstick comedy (*Pretty
Boy Floyd*, 131–33). Which is the real Pretty Boy Floyd? Instead of what
the hero legend would make him, he seems to be all the things people
say he is, because his personality development was arrested in adolescence. Not surprisingly, he is inconsistent, self-centered, and seemingly
powerless to control his life. Once started in crime, this big boy just went
with it. Yet, he became a legend. How to figure it? McMurtry and Ossana
do not answer this question raised by their characterization of Charley
Floyd, they just ask it.

In contrast to many of the other characters in Larry McMurtry's later
books, Zeke Proctor and Ned Christie exhibit change during the course
of their stories. While Zeke at the beginning of the novel can rationalize
his lust for Polly Beck as a way of living traditionally, by the middle of
the book he begins to feel his wife, Becca, deserves loyalty, and when
he turns to writing the history of "Ned's War," he expresses genuine
concern for her (*Zeke and Ned*, 416). Significantly, this is well after the
novel has ceased to describe events in a comic way and after information
about his formation of an informal Keetoowah militia makes it clear that
he has found purpose for his life outside of his personal impulses.

Ned's display of character change evidently results from the pressure
of events upon him. This pressure he ascribes first to all the women
around him and their demands (313–14). In time, though, the attack upon
his house by a posse of White outlaws fixes the source of his troubles as
the Anglo society that appears bent upon extermination of the Cherokee
Nation. He resolves to build a fortress and, to complete his withdrawal
from the larger society, never to speak English again. Zeke's account of
a visit to the fort emphasizes the alteration in his friend's character. The
structure sits in a spot cleared of all trees for 150 yards around. Because
of its windowless design, natural light cannot enter it. Unlike earlier
houses, this one is not made for enjoyment, "unless what you enjoy is
killing and dying" (418). An attack that blinded Ned in one eye has left
his mental vision equally impaired. He lives besieged. Rejecting Zeke's
suggestion that he plead to the White judge that he was wrongly accused
of the Maples killing, because the judge does not speak Cherokee, Ned
displays an increasing rigidity of character. He cannot any longer really
be a friend to Zeke. While the plot development of *Zeke and Ned* has wed

the two stories of the protagonists into one, character development shows that their reactions to events have driven the men apart.

THEMATIC ISSUES

All of the narrative elements of *Pretty Boy Floyd* work together to make its primary theme the making of legend. Quite apart from Charley's intentions or motives, and very much in contrast to what would be expected from the way his crimes are depicted, he becomes a favorite subject for journalists who give their readers information in a way that strikes a responsive chord. To illustrate this process is the function of the interview by Viv Brown and the crowd of people, including Charley's grandfather, who gather to witness the holdup of the bank in his hometown (268) and the report by Bessie Floyd that 20,000 people came to Charley's funeral and only two hundred to the governor's (442). To give the theme an added punch, the narrative introduces J. Edgar Hoover's public relations campaign. While journalists are developing a populist legend of Pretty Boy, the champion of common people mistreated by the banks, Hoover in his desire to gain support for his agency creates an alternate, but nevertheless complementary legend of Charley Floyd, the dangerous enemy of public order. As the third-person narration relates the story of the man and actions on which the legends are based, the disparity between reality and legend grows greater. Still and all, everyone colludes in choosing the legend over reality. In light of McMurtry's treatment of legends in his other works, this novel about the legend of Pretty Boy Floyd requires no further comment except to note that in this stage of his writing career, McMurtry withholds his ire and remains content to show that legends are an appealing phenomenon of the popular culture, no matter how inaccurate they are.

While *Zeke and Ned* is also a novel about a legend, this novel goes beyond entering the contrast between presumed reality and the legend to investigate the relationship between the causes and content of the legend. The history of injustice toward the Cherokee people, beginning with their eviction from land in Georgia so that White settlers could take its mineral wealth, and continuing through the involuntary transportation of the Cherokees to alien territory, followed by the intrusion of federal authority and White settlers on the new area that had been designated by treaty as theirs, forever forms the backdrop of the legend of resistance. Against that backdrop, McMurtry and Ossana draw their account of the outlaws deputized by order of President Grant to pacify the territory and arrest Ned Christie. Where they enrich a theme that might have been too familiar or hackneyed if it had been left as one more tale of callous mistreatment of Indians, is in the addition of the "inside story" of the resultant legend of resistance.

One part of the enrichment results from the novel's examination of the protocols governing relations between men and women. The Cherokee Zeke Proctor and the White T. Spade Beck and Dan Maples all view wives and likely wives as their property to control. Similarly, Ned's affection for Jewel reflects the practice of treating women as chattel. Fancying Jewel, Ned consults her father, Zeke, but not her, about taking her as a mate, and Zeke gives her over, again without consulting Jewel. All of the subsequent disputes between Zeke and Becca, as well as the stressed feelings of Ned, are traceable to this manner of treating women. And the incident that initiates the plot of armed conflict and flight arises from it also, in the sense that Zeke's accidental shooting of Polly directly results from his conviction that he can take her for a wife with the same impunity with which he took her as a sex partner.

The introduction of a theme of male dominance must not be taken as anachronism or simply documentation. The subject does not come into the novel because the writers are applying today's ideas to yesterday's events. Of course, they think gender equality should be a universal value, but they are also seeking the causes of conflict in history and have made the plausible assumption that cultural practices of dominance infused into personal lives are a cause of contention. If the attempt to force dominance bears truth in the depiction of relations between Cherokees and Whites, why should it not bear upon relations between men and women? Older history may have failed to record it, but new historical understanding has taught us that sexual conflict has underlain most cultures. Therefore, by the implication of the issue in this novel of the nineteenth century, McMurtry and Ossana reveal a likely site of contention within the warring cultures of the Indian Territory.

The other important way the authors elaborate an "inside story" of the legend is in their description of the personal consequences of heroism for Ned Christie. The account of Zeke's visit to Ned's fortress in the history of "Ned's War" is a powerful use of literary narrative techniques. The sparely written first-person sketch conveys through selection of details of darkness and insulation a powerful image of a man cut off from the sources of his life, doomed to eventual destruction at the same time that his legend flourishes. The irony of it all makes an affecting addition to the theme of disparity between reality and the imaginings of romantic story.

A MODERNIST READING

The consideration of gender relations in the discussion of thematic issues suggests the possibility that a feminist reading of *Zeke and Ned* could be fruitful. Adding to that general topic the insights developed by feminist critics about ways that women are conditioned to play prescribed gender roles would give a feminist reading applicability to the treatment of Beulah and Ruby in *Pretty Boy Floyd*. Other alternate readings that could further open the novels are: New Historicism, which could be applied to the whole issue of determining what history is in the two novels; or Epistemological Criticism, which could be used in contrasting the reality of legend with the reality of the novels. In the interests of expanding the collection of methods for analysis, however, this section will be an outline of a way to think about *Pretty Boy Floyd* and *Zeke and Ned* in terms of Modernist literature.

Modernism is the name given to a body of writing in the early twentieth century, most often literature written between the two world wars. Artists and other thinkers of that period experienced a cognitive break with past thinking. Noting the change in literature following World War I, literary historians often say that the change resulted from the First World War casting doubt on received values of patriotism and rational social order. The ferociously devastating war that upon reflection seemed to have no purpose other than the advancement of poisonous ideas of nationalism, threw into crisis the notion that Europe was a place of humane civilization. One result was to undermine confidence that established canons of belief were rational and to stimulate wonder about how one discerns at all what is real and true. This line encouraged new concern with epistemology—how it is that we can secure some surety about ways to describe experience.

Another cause advanced for the marked change in literature during the 1920s is a debasement of culture in the wake of the arrival of a consumer age. This is a view held by critics made uncomfortable by the explosive growth of the reading public as a consequence of universal literacy. When practically everyone can read, the market for junk writing naturally becomes enormous. Moreover, when new technology, notably the technology of motion pictures, makes image and story available at little cost to masses of people, the traditions of high literature are marginalized to an elite. Some writers of the period decried what they saw as a general loss of faith, not just in reason, but loss of religious faith or faith in more than immediate experiences, those too often hedonistic.

While some of the respondents to the cognitive crisis were very conservative and expressed yearning for the pre-war past, which in retrospect seemed a version of some greener pastures, other more liberal or radical thinkers took the disorientation about values as a sign of the breakup of an old order that should in time be replaced by better ways of thinking and new arrangements of social life. However much the analyses differed from one critic to the next, one point of agreement seemed to be that the contemporary world had lost coherence. Such presumed lack of cultural coherence forms a background for McMurtry and Ossana's handling of the problem of the real Pretty Boy Floyd. The impossibility of drawing a consistent sketch of the man results, a Modernist reading would say, from the replacement of a consensual view of right and wrong that would generate broad agreement that Floyd was either a grubby outlaw or a justified rebel. Lacking agreed-upon standards for judging behavior, Pretty Boy's identity becomes a matter of personal opinion. If you're Ruby, you think one thing. If you're Hoover, you think another. This Modernist interpretation shows that McMurtry and Ossana believe no dependable standard of judgment exists. Their effort to contrast the varying personal opinions of Charley Floyd with the mundane reality of the way he lives his daily life works to indicate that there really are not grounds for consensus about him. Actuality and perceived reality diverge so greatly that experience defies conclusive definition.

A less elaborated sense of lost standards is conveyed by *Zeke and Ned*, but still the striking irony that the lawmen sent to apprehend Ned are themselves confirmed outlaws presents an irony that may be termed Modernist. So, too, can it be called Modernist irony when Ned becomes both an inspiring Cherokee hero and an embittered, increasingly powerless old man, because, again, McMurtry and Ossana are demonstrating a vast gap between presumed or perceived reality and actuality. The gap can never be bridged. The interests of the Whites will allow them to overlook the brutality of the agents who secured control of Cherokee lands for them, and Cherokee resisters will never fully appreciate that Ned has sacrificed a large part of his humanity in his resistance to White power. If one takes a distanced view, like the novel does, allowing observation of all sides of a difficult issue, no coherence can be found.

A further Modernist quality to these collaborative novels can be seen in regard to the interest displayed by some early Modernists in resurrecting frameworks of past times when society seemed to have desirable coherence. One such framework is, or seemed to be, myth. Myth, it can be reasoned, is a product of a culture's deepest values, and expresses its comprehension of moral order. Myth would seem, therefore, impossible in contemporary culture. Impossible, but not unusable. Suppose a writer were to take a well- known myth to use as a narrative framework and deploy within the framework the story of people living in the faithless present. The result would be a neat contrast. Of course, that strategy is precisely that of James Joyce's masterpiece *Ulysses* (1922), the work that uses the plot of the Homeric poem in telling of a day in the life of Leopold Bloom, contemporary Dubliner and a far cry from a culture hero. It is also the strategy that T. S. Eliot thought a brilliant solution to the problem of writing a modern work of literature and that he adopted in part for his long poem *The Waste Land* (1922).

This use of myth was not the only strategy of Modernist writers. It was not even the dominant strategy. It did, however, serve to make the Modernist point that mankind had been diminished in the reality of the present. In that way, it makes an interesting but not exact parallel to McMurtry's view of myth and legend. McMurtry and Ossana make themselves heir to this Modernist strategy by setting up legend as a reference for *Pretty Boy Floyd* and *Zeke and Ned*. They improvise on the strategy by using legends from the near present, but nonetheless they put those legends to the purpose of establishing contrast between the fabular and the real, just as did Joyce and Eliot. And is it the point of McMurtry and Ossana that reality diminishes alongside myth? Again they improvise on the strategy, preferring to show instead that legend and reality are different kinds of truths, not equally valuable kinds, but nevertheless for practical purposes both truths. As the two novels show, some people are as convinced of the validity of legend as other people are convinced that the legends are untrue. In the final analysis, what the Modernist legacy of McMurtry and Ossana leads them to do is state that discovery of reality is no simple matter.

Bibliography

Citations in text refer to later paperback editions of McMurtry's works.

NOVELS

Horseman, Pass By. New York: Harper, 1961; Touchstone Books, 1992.
Leaving Cheyenne. New York: Harper, 1963; Pocket Books, 1992.
The Last Picture Show. New York: Dial, 1966; Touchstone Books, 1992.
Moving On. New York: Simon and Schuster, 1970; Pocket Books, 1988.
All My Friends Are Going to Be Strangers. New York: Simon and Schuster, 1972; Pocket Books, 1992.
Terms of Endearment. New York: Simon and Schuster, 1975; Touchstone Books, 1989.
Somebody's Darling. New York: Simon and Schuster, 1978; Pocket Books, 1988.
Cadillac Jack. New York: Simon and Schuster, 1982; Pocket Books, 1988.
The Desert Rose. New York: Simon and Schuster, 1983; Pocket Books, 1988.
Lonesome Dove. New York: Simon and Schuster, 1985; Pocket Books, 1986.
Texasville. New York: Simon and Schuster, 1987; Pocket Books, 1988.
Anything for Billy. New York: Simon and Schuster, 1988; Pocket Books, 1989.
Some Can Whistle. New York: Simon and Schuster, 1989; Pocket Books, 1990.
Buffalo Girls. New York: Simon and Schuster, 1990; Pocket Books, 1991.
The Evening Star. New York: Simon and Schuster, 1992; Pocket Books, 1993.
Streets of Laredo. New York: Simon and Schuster, 1993; Pocket Books, 1994.
The Late Child. New York: Simon and Schuster, 1995.

Dead Man's Walk. New York: Simon and Schuster, 1995; Pocket Books, 1996.
Comanche Moon. New York: Simon and Schuster, 1997; Pocket Books, 1998.
Duane's Depressed. New York: Simon and Schuster, 1999.

COLLABORATIONS WITH DIANA OSSANA

Pretty Boy Floyd. New York: Simon and Schuster, 1994; Pocket Books, 1995.
Zeke and Ned. New York: Simon and Schuster, 1997.

NONFICTION

"Ever a Bridegroom: Reflections on the Failure of Texas Literature." *Texas Observer* (13 October 1981): 1, 8–19.
In a Narrow Grave: Essays on Texas. Austin: Encino Press, 1968; Touchstone Books, 1989.
It's Always We Rambled: An Essay on Rodeo. New York: Hallman, 1974.
Film Flam: Essays on Hollywood. New York: Simon and Schuster, 1987; Touchstone Books, 1988.
Rodeo: Photographs and Text, Louise L. Serpa. New York: Aperture Foundation, 1994. Notes by Larry McMurtry.
Walter Benjamin at the Dairy Queen: Reflections at Sixty and Beyond. New York: Simon and Schuster, 1999.
Crazy Horse. New York: Viking Penguin, 1999.

SCREENPLAYS

Falling from Grace. Columbia Pictures, 1992.
The Last Picture Show, with Peter Bogdanovich. Columbia Pictures, 1971.
Memphis, with Cybill Shepherd (based on a novel by Shelby Foote). Turner Home Entertainment, 1992.
Montana. Turner Network Television, 1990.
Texasville. Columbia Pictures, 1990.

WORKS ABOUT LARRY MCMURTRY

Bibliography

Ahearn, Kerry. "Larry McMurtry." *Fifty Western Writers: A Bio-Bibliographical Sourcebook*, ed. Fred Erisman and Richard W. Etulain. Westport, CT: Greenwood Publishing Group, 1982, 280–90.
Busby, Mark. *Larry McMurtry and the West: An Ambivalent Relationship*. Denton: University of North Texas, 1995, 311–27.
Huber, Dwight. "Larry McMurtry: A Selected Bibliography." *Larry McMurtry:*

Unredeemed Dreams, ed. Dorey Schmidt. Edinburg: Pan American University, 1978, 52–61.

Landess, Thomas. "Larry McMurtry." *Southwestern American Literature: A Bibliography*, ed. John Q. Anderson, Edwin W. Gaston, Jr., and James W. Lee. Chicago: Swallow, 1980, 352.

Major, Mabel, and T. M. Pearce. *Southwest Heritage: A Literary History with Bibliographies*. 3rd rev. ed. Albuquerque: University of New Mexico Press, 1972.

Metzger, Linda, ed. *Contemporary Authors: A Bio-Bibliographical Guide to Current Writers in Fiction, General Nonfiction, Poetry, Journalism, Drama, Motion Pictures, Television, and Other Fields*. New revision. Vol. 19. Detroit: Gale, 1987, 329–34.

Peavy, Charles D. "A Larry McMurtry Bibliography." *Western American Literature* 3 (1968): 235–48.

Biographical Sources

Anderson, Patrick. "Lone Star: Washington's Best Texas Novelist Doesn't Live Here Anymore." *Washingtonian* (June 1992): 27–30.

Anon. "A Novelist of Characters and Place." *Humanities Interview* (Summer 1989): 1–6.

Authors in the News. Vol. 2. Detroit: Gale, 1976.

Bennett, Patrick. "Larry McMurtry: Thalia, Houston, and Hollywood." *Talking with Texas Writers*. College Station: Texas A&M University Press, 1980, 15–36.

———. "Larry McMurtry." *Encyclopedia of Frontier and Western Fiction*, ed. Vicki Piekarski and Jon Tuska. New York: McGraw, 1983, 230–31.

Brown, Norman D. "Larry McMurtry." *Southern Writers: A Biographical Dictionary*, ed. Robert Bain, Joseph M. Flora, and Louis D. Rubin, Jr. Baton Rouge: Louisiana State University Press, 1979, 293–94.

Cleveland, Ceil. "Memories of McMurtry." *Houston Post* (2 January 1991): D1.

Deen, Sue McMurtry. "The McMurtry Family." *Archer County, Texas 1880–1980 Centennial Family History and Program June 29–July 6, 1980*. Archer City: McCrain, 1980.

Dictionary of Literary Biography Yearbook. Detroit: Gale, 1980, 1981, 1987, 1988.

Dunn, Si. "Ex-Native Son McMurtry." *Texas Observer* (16 January 1976): 13.

English, Sarah. "Larry McMurtry." *Dictionary of Literary Biography Yearbook: 1987*, ed. J. M. Brook. Detroit: Gale, 1988, 265–74.

Horowitz, Mark. "Larry McMurtry's Dream Job." *New York Times* (30 November 1997): magazine 110.

Jones, Kathryn. "Larry McMurtry's Next Career." *Biblio* (August 1999): 50.

Jones, Malcolm. "The Ghost Writer at Home on the Range." *Newsweek* (2 August 1993): 52–53.

———. "The Poet Lariat." *Newsweek* (11 January 1999): 62.

Landon, Brooks. "Larry McMurtry." *Dictionary of Literary Biography Yearbook 1980*, ed. Karen L. Rood, Jean W. Ross, and Richard Ziegfield. Detroit: Gale, 1981.

Lanham, Fritz. "Rice University Buys McMurtry Collection." *http://www.chron. com/content/chronicle/ae/books/9899/12/06/1210mcmurtry.html* (13 January 1999).

Moritz, Charles. *Current Biography Yearbook 1984*. New York: H. W. Wilson, 1984, 276–79.

O'Keefe, Ruth Jones. *Archer County Pioneers: A History of Archer County Texas*. Hereford, TX: Pioneer Book Publishers, 1969.

Pellecchia, Michael. "Larry McMurtry Expands His Book Country." *Publishers Weekly* (21 December 1998): 19.

Rothstein, Mervyn. "A Texan Who Likes to Deflate the Legends of the Golden West." *New York Times* (1 November 1988): C17.

Streitfeld, David. "The Yellowed Prose of Texas; For Larry McMurtry Happiness Means Having the Best Used Bookstore in the Lone Star State." *Washington Post* (6 April 1999): C1.

Watson, Bruce. "Racing to Round Up Readers." *Smithsonian* (March 1999): 78.

GENERAL CRITICISM

Abernethy, Francis E. "Strange and Unnatural History in *Lonesome Dove*." *Texas Books in Review* 8.2 (1988): 1–2.

Adams, Robert M. "The Bard of Wichita Falls." *New York Review of Books* (13 August 1987): 39–41.

Birchfield, D. L. "Lonesome Duck: The Blueing of a Texas-American Myth." *Studies in American Indian Literatures* 7.2 (1995): 45–64.

Bold, Christine. "Anti-Western Westerns." *Selling the Wild West: Popular Western Fiction, 1860–1960*. Bloomington: Indiana University Press, 1987, 155–65.

Burke, John Gordon, ed. *Regional Perspectives: An Examination of America's Literary Heritage*. Chicago: American Library Association, 1971.

Busby, Mark. "Larry McMurtry." *Twentieth Century Western Writers*, ed. James Vinson. Detroit: Gale, 1982, 534–36.

———. *Larry McMurtry and the West: An Ambivalent Relationship*. Texas Writers Series. Denton: University of North Texas Press, 1995.

Byrd, James W., Scott Downing, and Art Hendrix. "McMurtry Circles His Wagons: An East Texas Roundup." *Southwestern American Literature* 14.2 (1989): 4–19.

Clark, L. D. "Texas Historical Writing: A Sample of the Myth at Age 150." *American West* (January/February 1986): 80–81.

Clifford, Craig Edward. *In the Deep Heart's Core: Reflections on Life, Letters, and Texas*. College Station: Texas A&M University Press, 1985.

Clifford, Craig Edward, and Tom Pilkington, eds. *Range Wars: Heated Debates, Sober Reflections, and Other Assessments of Texas Writing.* Dallas: Southern Methodist University Press, 1989.

Contemporary Authors. http://galenet.gale.com/m/mcp/netacgi. 4 June 1997.

Cox, Diana. "*Anything for Billy*: A Fiction Stranger Than Truth." *Journal of American Culture* (Summer 1991): 75–81.

Crawford, Ian. "Intertextuality in Larry McMurtry's *The Last Picture Show.*" *Journal of Popular Culture* (Summer 1993): 43–54.

Davis, Kenneth W. "The Themes of Initiation in the Works of Larry McMurtry and Tom Mayer." *Arlington Quarterly* 2.3 (1970): 29–43.

———. "Innocent No More: Folk Speech and Realism in McMurtry's *The Last Picture Show* and Michael Adams' *Blind Man's Bluff.*" *McNeese Review* 32 (1986–1989): 58–63.

Dean, Patricia E. "Names in Larry McMurtry's 'Thalia Trilogy.' " *The Dangerous, Secret Name of God: Fartley's Compressed Gas Company; The Barf 'n' Choke; and Other Matters Onomastic.* Sugar Grove, IL: Papers of North Central Names Institution, Series 2: 71–76.

Degenfelder, E. Pauline. "McMurtry and the Movies: *Hud* and *The Last Picture Show.*" *Western Humanities Review* 29 (1975): 81–91.

Dugger, Ronnie. "Fallow Fields." *Texas Observer* (5 November 1971): 21–24.

England, D. Gene. "Rites of Passage in Larry McMurtry's *The Last Picture Show.*" *Heritage of Kansas* 12.1 (1979): 37–48.

Folsom, James K. "*Shane* and *Hud*: Two Stories in Search of a Medium." *Western Humanities Review* (Autumn 1970): 359–72.

Gerlach, John. "Larry McMurtry." *Dictionary of Literary Biography: American Novelists Since World War II*, ed. Jeffrey Helterman and Richard Layman Detroit: Gale, 1978, 328–31.

———. "*The Last Picture Show* and One More Adaptation." *Literature/Film Quarterly* 1 (1973): 161–66.

Giesen, Tom. "Novels by Larry McMurtry." *Northwest Review* 9.1 (1967): 120–21.

Giles, James R. "Larry McMurtry's *Leaving Cheyenne* and the Novels of John Rechy: Four Trips Along 'the Mythical Pecos.' " *Forum* 10.2 (1972): 34–40.

Goodwyn, Larry. "The Frontier Myth and Southwestern Literature." *American Libraries* (February 1971): 161–67; (April 1971): 359–66.

Graham, Don. "Is Dallas Burning? Notes on Recent Texas Fiction." *Southwestern American Literature* 4 (1974): 68–73.

———. *Texas: A Literary Portrait.* San Antonio: Corona, 1985.

———. "Regionalism on the Ramparts." *USA Today* (July 1986): 74–76.

Graham, Don, James W. Lee, and William T. Pilkington, eds. *The Texas Literary Tradition: Fiction, Folklore, History.* Austin: Texas State Historical Association, 1983.

Graves, Frank. *The American Southwest: Cradle of Literary Art.* Ed. Robert W. Walts. San Marcos: Southwest Texas University Press, 1981.

Greene, A. C. *The Fifty Best Books on Texas.* Dallas: Pressworks, 1981.

———. "The Texas Literati: Whose Home Is This Range Anyhow?" *New York Times Book Review* (15 September 1985): 3.

Harrigan, Stephen. "The Making of *Lonesome Dove*." *Texas Monthly* (June 1988): 82–86, 156–59.

Hulbert, Ann. "Rural Chic: Fiction and Films Are Living Off the Fad of the Land." *New Republic* (2 September 1985): 25–30.

Jones, Roger Walton. *Larry McMurtry and the Victorian Novel*. College Station: Texas A&M University Press, 1994.

Kehl, D. G. "Thalia's 'Sock' and the Cowhide Boot: Humor of the New Southwest in the Fiction of Larry McMurtry." *Southwestern American Literature* 14.2 (1989): 20–33.

Landess, Thomas. *Larry McMurtry*. Southwest Writers Series. Austin: Steck-Vaughn, 1969.

Lee, James Ward. *Classics of Texas Fiction*. Dallas: E-Heart, 1987, 102–104.

Lich, Lera Patrick Tyler. *Larry McMurtry's Texas: Evolution of a Myth*. Austin: Eakin Press, 1987.

Limon, Jose E. "A 'Southern Renaissance' for Texas Letters: A Literary Flowering in South Texas." *Texas Observer* (28 October 1983): 20–23.

Linck, Ernestine Sewell. "Larry McMurtry." *Updating the Literary West*. Fort Worth: Texas Christian University Press, 1997, 628–32.

Lindstrom, Naomi. "The Novel in Texas: How Big a Patrimony?" *Texas Quarterly* 21.2 (1978): 73–83.

Miller, L. "Is There Life in Texas after McMurtry?" *Balcones* 1.2 (1987): 88.

Mogen, David. "Sex and True West in McMurtry's Fiction: From *Teddy Blue* to *Lonesome Dove* to *Texasville*." *Southwestern American Literature* 14.2 (1989): 34–45.

Morrow, Patrick D. "Larry McMurtry: The First Phase." *Seasoned Authors for a New Season: The Search for Standards in Popular Writing*, ed. Louis Filler. Bowling Green, OH: Bowling Green University Popular Press, 1980, 70–82.

Neinstein, Raymond L. *The Ghost Country: A Study of the Novels of Larry Mc-Murtry*. Berkeley, CA: Creative Arts, 1976.

Nelson, Jane. "Larry McMurtry." *A Literary History of the American West*, ed. J. Golden Taylor, et al. Fort Worth: Texas Christian University Press, 1987, 612–21.

Pages: The World of Books, Writers, and Writing. Detroit: Gale, 1976.

Peavy, Charles D. "Larry McMurtry and Black Humor: A Note on *The Last Picture Show*." *Western American Literature* (1967): 223–27.

———. "Coming of Age in Texas: The Novels of Larry McMurtry." *Western American Literature* 4 (1969): 171–88.

———. *Larry McMurtry*. Twayne's United States Author Series 291. Boston: G. K. Hall, 1977.

Pilkington, Tom. "The Recent Southwestern Novel." *Southwestern American Literature* 1 (1971): 12–15.

———. *My Blood's Country: Studies in Southwestern Literature*. Fort Worth: Texas Christian University Press, 1973, 163–82.

———. "Contemporary Texas Writers and the Concept of Regionalism." *Texas Humanist* (April 1980): 1.

Reid, Jan. "Return of the Native Son." *Texas Monthly* (February 1993): 202, 228–31.

Reynolds, Clay. "Come Home, Larry, All is Forgiven: A Native Son's Search for Identity." *Cross Timbers Review* (May 1985): 65.

Reynolds, Clay, ed. *Taking Stock: A Larry McMurtry Casebook*. Dallas: Southern Methodist University Press, 1989.

Ronald, Ann. "Company for a Lonesome Dove." *History and Humanities: Essays In Honor of Wilbur S. Shepperson*. Reno: University of Nevada Press, 1989, 299–309.

Sanderson, Jim. "Old Corrals: Texas According to 80s Films and TV and Texas According to Larry McMurtry." *Journal of American Culture* (Summer 1990): 63–73.

Sarll, Pauline. "Boundaries, Borders, and Frontiers: A Revisionary Reading of Larry McMurtry's *Horseman, Pass By*." *Journal of Popular Culture* (Summer 1994): 97–110.

Schmidt, Dorey, ed. *Larry McMurtry: Unredeemed Dreams*. Edinburg, TX: Pan American University, 1978.

Sonnichsen, C. L. "The New Style Western." *South Dakota Review* 4 (1966): 22–28.

———. "Sex on the Lone Prairee." *Western American Literature* 13 (1978): 15–33.

Speidel, Constance. "Whose *Terms of Endearment*?" *Literature Fiction Quarterly* 12.4 (1984): 271–73.

Stegner, Wallace. "History, Myth, and the Western Writer." *American West* 4.2 (1967): 61–62.

Stout, Janis P. "Cadillac Larry Rides Again: McMurtry and the Song of the Open Road." *Western American Literature* (November 1989): 243–51.

Summerlin, Tim. "Late McMurtry." *Lamar Journal of the Humanities* 2.1 (1975): 54–56.

Tangum, Marion. "Larry McMurtry's *Lonesome Dove*: "This Is What We Call Home." *Rocky Mountain Review of Language and Literature* 45.1–2 (1991): 61–73.

Thurn, Thora. "McMurtry's Settlers: Molly and Emma." *CCTE Studies* 47 (1982): 51–56.

Underwood, June O. "Western Women and True Womanhood: Culture and Symbol in History and Literature." *Great Plains Quarterly* 5 (1985): 93–106.

Willson, Robert. "Which Is the Real *Last Picture Show*?" *Literature Fiction Quarterly* 1.2 (1973): 167–69.

Woodward, Daniel. "Larry McMurtry's *Texasville*: A Comic Pastoral of the Oil-patch." *Huntington Library Quarterly* (Spring 1993): 167–80.
Wylder, Delbert E. "Recent Western Fiction." *Journal of the West* (January 1980): 62–70.

REVIEWS

Horseman, Pass By

Dallas Morning News, 28 May 1961, sec. 5: 9.
Library Journal, 1 February 1961, 603.
Library Journal, 1 September 1961, 2818.
Los Angeles Times Book Review, 15 September 1985, 8.
New York Review of Books, 13 August 1987, 39.
New York Times, 10 June 1961, 21.
New York Times, 18 June 1961, 27.
Southwest Review, Summer 1961, viii+.
Texas Observer, 15 September 1961, 6.

Leaving Cheyenne

Best Sellers, June 1986, 86.
Dallas Morning News, 13 October 1963, sec. 1: 24.
English Journal, December 1986, 49.
Kliatt, Winter 1980, 12.
Library Journal, 1 October 1963, 3644.
New York Times Book Review, 6 October 1963, 39.
San Francisco Sunday Chronicle, 6 October 1963, 31.
Saturday Review, 26 June 1976, 41.

The Last Picture Show

Chicago Tribune, 30 July 1967, 8.
Dallas Morning News, 26 February 1967, 2G.
English Journal, December 1986, 49.
Houston Post, 30 October 1966, 26.
Kirkus Reviews, 1 August 1966, 783.
Library Journal, 15 May 1989, 94.
New York Herald Tribune, 23 October 1966, 16.
New York Review of Books, 13 August 1987, 39.
New York Times Book Review, 13 November 1966, 68–69.
New York Times, 3 December 1966, 37.
Publishers Weekly, 18 July 1966, 74–75.

Publishers Weekly, 15 May 1967, 42.
Saturday Review, 22 January 1972, 70.
Texas Observer, 20 January 1967, 14–18.
Washington Post, 23 October 1966, 16.
Western American Literature, 2 (1967), 223–27.

Moving On

Best Sellers, 1 July 1970, 129–30.
Dallas Morning News, 31 May 1970, 7C.
English Journal, December 1986, 50.
Kirkus Reviews, 15 March 1970, 346.
Library Journal, July 1970, 2517.
National Observer, 13 July 1970, 19.
New Statesman, 9 April 1971, 503.
New York Times, 10 June 1970, 49.
New York Times Book Review, 26 July 1970, 16.
New York Times Book Review, 15 August 1971, 39.
New York Times Book Review, 3 May 1987, 40.
Observer, 27 June 1971, 27.
Publishers Weekly, 6 April 1970, 53.
Publishers Weekly, 28 June 1971, 64.
Saturday Review, 17 October 1970, 36.
Saturday Review, 23 October 1971, 86.
Saturday Review, 27 November 1971, 48.
Southwest Review, Autumn 1970, 427.
Southwestern American Literature, I (1971), 38–39.
Texas Observer, 8 January 1970, 22–24.
Washington Post, 21 June 1970, 6.
Western American Literature, Summer 1972, 151.

All My Friends Are Going to Be Strangers

America, 15 April 1972, 410–11.
Best Sellers, 1 May 1972, 55–56.
Best Sellers, 1 February 1973, 503.
Booklist, 15 May 1972, 796.
Books and Bookmen, November 1973, 101–102.
Commonweal, 20 October 1972, 70–71.
Dallas Morning News, 19 March 1972, 10e.
English Journal, December 1986, 50.
Kirkus Reviews, 1 January 1972, 21.
Library Journal, 15 February 1972, 699–700.

Massachusetts Review, Winter 1973, 190.
National Observer, 15 April 1972, 23.
New Republic, 1 April 1972, 28–29.
New Statesman, 2 March 1973, 314.
Newsweek, 20 March 1972, 110.
New York Times, 24 March 1972, 43.
New York Times Book Review, 19 March 1972, 5.
New York Times Book Review, 4 June 1972, 22.
New York Times Book Review, 3 December 1972, 72.
New York Times Book Review, 30 April 1989, 41.
New Yorker, 1 April 1972, 106.
Publishers Weekly, 7 February 1972, 91.
Publishers Weekly, 18 December 1972, 41.
Southwest Review, 57 (1972), 340–42.
Southwestern American Literature, 2 (1972), 54–55.
Texas Observer, 25 August 1972, 14–15.
Time, 3 April 1972, 64.
Time, 1 January 1973, 61.
Times Literary Supplement, 23 March 1973, 313.
Wall Street Journal, 6 June 1972, 26.
Western American Literature, Summer 1972, 151.

Terms of Endearment

Atlantic Monthly, November 1975, 126.
Best Sellers, January 1976, 302.
Booklist, 1 October 1975, 220.
Commonweal, 11 May 1979, 266.
Dallas Morning News, 2 November 1975, 11f.
English Journal, December 1986, 50.
New Leader, 15 March 1976, 19–20.
Kirkus Reviews, 15 August 1975, 935–36.
Kliatt, Winter 1977, 6.
Library Journal, 15 December 1975, 2343.
New Leader, 15 March 1976, 19.
New Republic, 29 November 1975, 37–38.
New York Times, 22 October 1975, 43.
New York Times Book Review, 19 October 1975, 4.
New Yorker, 27 October 1975, 166.
Publishers Weekly, 8 September 1975, 50.
Publishers Weekly, 16 August 1976, 122.
Saturday Review, 10 January 1976, 57.
Southwest Review, Winter 1976, 5.

Texas Monthly, November 1975, 44.
Time, 20 October 1975, 86.
Times Educational Supplement, 23 December 1994, 19.
Washington Post, 31 August 1975, 1.
Washingtonian, November 1975, 255–56.
Western American Literature, 11 (1977), 356–58.

Somebody's Darling

America, 5 May 1979, 379.
Booklist, 15 October 1978, 354–55.
Dallas Morning News, 5 November 1978, 7g.
Dictionary of Literary Biography Yearbook, 1980.
English Journal, December 1986, 50.
Houston Chronicle, 14 January 1979, *Zest Magazine* 35.
Houston Post, 12 November 1978, 12aa.
Kirkus Reviews, 1 September 1978, 966–67.
Library Journal, 15 October 1978, 2134.
Maclean's, 25 December 1978, 45–46.
Nation, 3 February 1979, 121–23.
New York, 25 December 1978, 99.
New York Times, 20 December 1978, C25.
New York Times Book Review, 19 November 1978, 15.
New York Times Book Review, 16 December 1979, 31.
New York Times Book Review, 3 May 1987, 40.
People Weekly, 6 November 1978, 14.
Prairie Schooner, 2 (1979), 181.
Publishers Weekly, 18 September 1978, 162.
Publishers Weekly, 29 October 1979, 81.
Texas Monthly, December 1978, 220.
Texas Review, 4 (1979), 79.
Time, 13 November 1978, 121.
Washington Post, 19 November 1978, E5.
West Coast Review of Books, January 1979, 26.

Cadillac Jack

America, 5 March 1983, 179–80.
Best Sellers, January 1983, 370.
Booklist, 1 September 1982, 2.
Bookwatch, December 1986, 50.
Chicago Tribune Book World, 17 October 1982, 3.
Cross Timbers Review, May 1985, 65.

Dallas Morning News, 17 October 1982, 4g.
Houston Post, 10 October 1982, 21aa.
Kirkus Review, 1 August 1982, 894.
Lamar Journal of the Humanities, 9.2 (1983), 53–55.
Library Journal, 1 October 1982, 1896.
Los Angeles Times Book Review, 14 November 1982, 1.
Nation, 20 November 1982, 536.
National Review, 26 November 1982, 1492–93.
New York Times, 13 November 1982, 13.
New York Times Book Review, 21 November 1982, 13.
New York Times Book Review, 3 May 1987, 40.
New Yorker, 13 December 1982, 184.
Penthouse, December 1982, 74–75.
People Weekly, 15 November 1982, 18.
Publishers Weekly, 30 July 1982, 63.
San Antonio Express-News, 21 November 1982, 7h.
Texas Books in Review, 5 (1983), 31–32.
Texas Monthly, October 1982, 177.
Texas Observer, 10 December 1982, 26–27.
Texas Weekly Magazine, Brazoport Facts, 12 December 1982, 11.
USA Today, 1 May 1987, 4d.
Village Voice Literary Supplement, October 1982, 5.
Washington Monthly, March 1983, 25.
Washington Post, 13 October 1982, B1.
West Coast Review of Books, January 1983, 27.
Western American Literature 19 (1984), 146–47.

The Desert Rose

Armchair Detective, Spring 1986, 176.
Best Sellers, October 1983, 239.
Booklist, August 1983, 1422.
Books, November 1995, 25.
The Bryan College Station Eagle, 8 October 1983, 1bb.
Chicago Tribune Book World, 25 December 1983, 30.
Dallas Morning News, 25 September 1983, 4g.
Houston Post, 4 September 1983, 13f.
Kirkus Reviews, 1 July 1983, 723.
Library Journal, 1 September 1983, 1721.
Los Angeles Times Book Review, 4 September 1983, 7.
National Review, 25 November 1983, 1495–96.
The New Leader, November 1983, 18–19.
New Yorker, 24 October 1983, 162.

New York Times Book Review, 23 October 1983, 12.
People Weekly, 10 October 1983, 14.
Playboy, November 1983, 32.
Publishers Weekly, 24 June 1983, 53.
Saturday Review, September/October 1983, 46.
Texas Books in Review, 6 (1984), 30.
Texas Humanist, March/April 1984, 51.
Texas Monthly, November 1983, 192.
USA Today, 1 May 1987, 4d.
Washington Post Book World, 28 August 1983, 3.
West Coast Review of Books, November/December 1983, 35.
Western American Literature, Summer 1985, 167–68.
Western American Literature, Fall 1989, 243.

Lonesome Dove

American Spectator, December 1987, 47.
American Spectator, January 1992, 16.
Atlanta, October 1985, 24.
Best Sellers, August 1985, 169.
Bloomsbury Review, January 1990, 17.
Booklist, 15 May 1985, 1274.
Chicago, October 1985, 128–29.
Chicago Tribune Book World, 9 June 1985, 33.
Dallas Morning News, 5 February 1989, 1c.
Dallas Morning News, 30 June 1985, 12c.
Houston Chronicle Magazine, 29 January 1989, 4.
Houston Post, 23 June 1985, 12f.
Kirkus Reviews, 15 April 1985, 341–42.
Library Journal, July 1985, 94.
Library Journal, May 1989, 46.
Los Angeles Times Book Review, 9 June 1985, 2.
New Republic, 2 September 1985, 26.
Newsweek, 3 June 1985, 74.
New York Review of Books, 13 August 1985, 39.
New York Times, 3 June 1985, 20c.
New York Times Book Review, 9 June 1985, 7.
New York Times Book Review, 27 July 1986, 28.
New York Times Book Review, 7 December 1986, 84.
New Yorker, 11 November 1985, 153–54.
People Weekly, 8 July 1985, 12.
Playboy, August 1985, 30–31.
Publishers Weekly, 19 April 1985, 71.

Publishers Weekly, 4 July 1986, 65.
Quill & Quire, November 1985, 29.
Rocky Mountain Review, July 1991, 61.
San Antonio Express-News, 21 July 1985, 2h.
Southern Living, November 1986, 132.
Texas Books in Review, 2 (1988), 1–2.
Texas Humanist, July/August 1985, 39–40.
Texas Monthly, June 1985, 160.
Texas Observer, 2 August 1985, 15–16.
Texas Review, 8 (1987), 22–29.
Time, 10 June 1985, 79.
Times Educational Supplement, 27 December 1991, 6.
USA Today, 21 June 1985, 9d.
Wall Street Journal, 15 August 1985, 25.
Washington Post Book World, 9 June 1985, 1.
Washington Post Book World, 3 August 1986, 12.
Western American Literature, Fall 1986, 219.
Western American Literature, Summer 1986, 165.
Western American Literature, Fall 1989, 243.

Texasville

Abilene Reporter-News, 3 May 1987, 7e.
Books, September 1987, 10–11.
Books, December 1987, 27.
Booklist, 15 February 1987, 857.
Bryan College Station Eagle, 15 August 1987, 14.
Chicago Tribune Books, 5 April 1987, 1.
Dallas Morning News, 26 April 1987, 8c.
Dallas Times Herald, 12 April 1987, 5c.
Denton Record-Chronicle, 26 April 1987, 5c.
Fort Worth Star-Telegram, 26 April 1987, 6d.
Houston Post, 19 April 1987, 12f.
Kirkus Reviews, 15 January 1987, 87.
Library Journal, 1 April 1987, 163–64.
Los Angeles Times Book Review, 12 April 1987, 1.
Modern Maturity, April/May 1987, 113.
New York Review of Books, 13 August 1987, 39.
New York Times, 8 April 1987, C24.
New York Times Book Review, 28 February 1988, 34.
New York Times Book Review, 19 April 1987, 7.
New Yorker, 15 June 1987, 91–94.
Publishers Weekly, 6 February 1987, 87.

San Antonio Express-News, 12 April 1987, 6h.
Southern Humanities Review, Winter 1989, 92–94.
Southwestern American Literature, 13.2 (1988), 37.
Texas Books in Review, 7.1 (1987), 15–16.
Texas Monthly, April 1987, 152.
Texas Observer, 17 July 1987, 14–15.
Time, 20 April 1987, 71.
Times Literary Supplement, September 1987, 978.
USA Today, 17 April 1987, 4d.
Wall Street Journal, 1 June 1987, 28.
Washington Post Book World, 12 April 1987, 3.
Western American Literature, 22 (1988), 373–74.

Anything for Billy

Booklist, 1 September 1988, 4.
Chicago Tribune Books, 9 October 1988, 1.
Christian Science Monitor, 27 December 1988, 18.
Dallas Morning News, 16 October 1988, 10c.
Dallas Times Herald, 11 September 1988, 10c.
Denton Record-Chronicle, 4 December 1988, 8c.
Fort Worth Star-Telegram, 16 October 1988, sec. 6: 7.
Glamour, November 1988, 188.
Kirkus Reviews, 1 August 1988, 1088.
Kliatt, January 1990, 14.
Library Journal, 15 October 1988, 104.
Los Angeles Times Book Review, 30 October 1988, 1.
New Mexico Historical Review, January 1990, 79–90.
New York, 3 October 1988, 70.
New York Times Book Review, 16 October 1988, 3.
New Yorker, 23 January 1989, 118.
Newsweek, 16 September 1988, 76.
Playboy, December 1988, 37.
Publishers Weekly, 19 August 1988, 59.
Publishers Weekly, 13 October 1989, 50.
Review of Texas Books, 3.2 (1988), 2.
Roundup, Spring 1990, 50
San Antonio Express-News, 9 October 1988, 6h.
Southern Living, April 1989, 120.
Southwestern American Literature, 14.2 (1989), 46–48.
Texas Books in Review, Spring 1989, 1.
Texas Monthly, October 1988, 146.
Time, 24 October 1988, 92–93.

Time, 7 November 1988, 11.
Times Literary Supplement, 9 November 1989, 1217.
Village Voice, 27 December 1988, 63.
Wall Street Journal, 6 October 1988, A16.
Washington Post Book World, 9 October 1988, 1.
Western American Literature, May 1989, 65–66.
World & I, January 1989, 333–42.

Some Can Whistle

Booklist, 15 September 1989, 114.
Books, March 1991, 7.
Chicago Tribune Books, 15 October 1989, 4.
Kirkus Reviews, 1 September 1989, 1274.
Los Angeles Times Book Review, 22 October 1989, 2.
Los Angeles Times Book Review, 2 September 1990, 14.
New York Times, 16 October 1989, C19.
New York Times Book Review, 22 October 1989, 8.
New Yorker, 4 December 1989, 187.
Observer, 11 March 1990, 68.
Publishers Weekly, 8 September 1989, 54.
Publishers Weekly, 10 August 1990, 440.
Texas Monthly, October 1989, 163.
Time, 16 October 1989, 89.
Virginia Quarterly Review, Summer 1990, 94.
Washington Post Book World, 22 October 1989, 5.
West Coast Review of Books, 2, 1989, 26.
Western American Literature, Fall 1990, 258.

Buffalo Girls

Booklist, 1 September 1990, 5.
Chicago Tribune Books, 15 July 1990, 4.
Chicago Tribune Books, 21 October 1990, 6.
Kirkus Reviews, 1 August 1990, 1033.
Library Journal, 1 October 1990, 118.
Los Angeles Times Book Review, 21 October 1990, 2.
New Statesman, 25 January 1991, 36.
New York Times, 16 October 1990, C17.
New York Times Book Review, 7 October 1990, 3.
New York Times Book Review, 6 October 1991, 32.
Observer, 27 January 1991, 58.
Publishers Weekly, 24 August 1990, 54.

Publishers Weekly, 6 September 1991, 101.
Roundup, Spring 1992.
Texas Monthly, December 1990, 64.
Time, 29 October 1990, 103.
Times Literary Supplement, 15 February 1991, 18.
Washington Post Book World, 7 October 1990, 6.
West Coast Review of Books, July 1991, 32.
Western American Literature, Summer 1991, 181.

The Evening Star

Booklist, 15 April 1992, 1483.
Chicago Tribune Books, 17 May 1992, 1.
Chicago Tribune Books, 16 May 1993, 8.
Kirkus Reviews, 1 April 1992, 420.
Los Angeles Times Book Review, 7 June 1992, 4.
Library Journal, 1 June 1992, 177.
New York Review of Books, 13 August 1992, 54–56.
New York Times, 12 May 1992, C17.
New York Times Book Review, 21 June 1992, 12.
New York Times Book Review, 11 July 1993, 32.
Newsweek, 8 June 1991, 58.
Observer, 20 September 1992, 54.
Publishers Weekly, 6 April 1992, 50.
Publishers Weekly, 15 March 1993, 84.
Southwestern American Literature, 18.1 (1992), 100–101.
Time, 25 May 1992, 73.
Times Literary Supplement, 30 October 1992, 20.
Washington Post Book World, 7 June 1992, 3.
Western American Literature, Spring 1993, 92.

Streets of Laredo

America, 28 August 1993, 23.
Atlantic Monthly, September 1993, 111.
Austin Chronicle, 13 August 1993, 20–22.
Booklist, 1 June 1993, 1734.
Booklist, 15 January 1994, 865.
Chicago Tribune Books, 15 August 1993, 1.
Christian Science Monitor, 31 August 1993, 15.
Entertainment Weekly, 26 August 1994, 105.
Entertainment Weekly, 15 April 1995, 55.
Kirkus Reviews, 1 June 1993, 680.

Kliatt, July 1994, 10.
Library Journal, July 1993, 120.
Los Angeles Times Book Review, 8 August 1993, 1.
New York Times Book Review, 25 July 1993, 9.
New York, 16 August 1993, 28.
New York Times, 30 July 1993, C27.
New York Times Book Review, 25 July 1993, 9.
New York Times Book Review, 5 December 1993, 65.
New York Times Book Review, 27 March 1994.
Newsweek, 2 August 1993, 52.
Publishers Weekly, 31 May 1993, 40.
Southwestern American Literature, 19.2 (1993), 93–94.
Texas Monthly, August 1993, 40.
Time, 9 August 1993, 59.
Times Literary Supplement, 26 November 1993, 22.
Virginia Quarterly Review, Spring 1994, 60.
Wall Street Journal, 1 September 1993, A13.
Washington Post Book World, 1 August 1993, 4.
Western American Literature, Spring 1995, 117.

The Late Child

America, 18 November 1995, 28.
Antioch Review, Fall 1995, 495.
Booklist, 1 April 1995, 1355.
Chicago Tribune Books, 18 June 1995, 5.
Entertainment Weekly, 19 May 1995, 56.
Kirkus Reviews, 1 April 1995, 417.
Library Journal, 15 May 1995, 96.
Los Angeles Times Book Review, 23 April 1995, 14.
Los Angeles Times Book Review, 4 June 1995, 3.
New York Times, 28 June 1995, C19.
New York Times Book Review, 21 May 1995, 12.
Newsweek, 22 May 1995, 61.
Publishers Weekly, 17 April 1995, 39.
Publishers Weekly, 4 November 1996, 71.
Southern Living, December 1995, 88.

Pretty Boy Floyd

America, 29 April 1995, 32.
Armchair Detective, Winter 1995, 109.
Booklist, August 1994, 1989, 1993.

Books, February 1996, 25.
Chicago Tribune Books, 4 September 1994, 3.
Entertainment Weekly, 26 August 1994, 105.
Entertainment Weekly, 14 July 1995, 50.
Kirkus Reviews, 1 July 1994, 874.
Los Angeles Times Book Review, 21 August 1994, 13.
New York Times, 26 August 1994, C28.
New York Times Book Review, 16 October 1994, 31.
Publishers Weekly, 1 August 1994, 70.
Publishers Weekly, 10 July 1995, 55.
Time, 19 September 1994, 84.
Washington Post Book World, 4 September 1994, 9.

Dead Man's Walk

Booklist, August 1995, 1910.
Chicago Tribune Books, 10 September 1995, 6.
Entertainment Weekly, 8 September 1995, 76.
Kirkus Reviews, 15 July 1995, 975.
Library Journal, 1 September 1995, 208.
Los Angeles Times Book Review, 1 October 1995, 1.
New York Times Book Review, 10 September 1995, 33.
New York Times Book Review, 3 December 1995, 76.
Publishers Weekly, 31 July 1995, 70.
Publishers Weekly, 6 May 1996, 76.
Time, 4 September 1995, 65.
Times Literary Supplement, 29 December 1995, 19.
Washington Post Book World, 27 August 1995, 3.
Western American Literature, Spring 1996, 86.

Comanche Moon

Booklist, 15 September 1997, 181.
Entertainment Weekly, 21 November 1997, 181.
Kirkus Reviews, 15 September 1997, 1408.
Library Journal, 15 October 1997, 93.
New York Times Book Review, 7 December 1997, 44.
People Weekly, 8 December 1997, 39.
Portland Oregonian, 3 November 1997.
Publishers Weekly, 27 October 1997, 54.
Time, 24 November 1997, 106.
Washington Post Book World, 4 January 1998, 3.

Zeke and Ned

Booklist, 15 November 1996, 549.
Entertainment Weekly, 24 January 1997, 52.
Kirkus Reviews, 15 November 1996, 1625.
Library Journal, January 1997, 148.
Library Journal, 1 March 1998, 144.
Los Angeles Times Book Review, 19 January 1997, 6.
New York Times Book Review, 19 January 1997, 18.
Publishers Weekly, 2 December 1996, 40.
Time, 10 February 1997, 82.
Washington Post Book World, 5 January 1997, 5.

Duane's Depressed

Christian Science Monitor, 14 January 1999, 18.
Library Journal, January 1999, 154.
New York Times, 7 January 1999, E9.
New York Times Book Review, 21 February 1999, 14.
Publishers Weekly, 7 December 1998, 51.
Time, 11 January 1999, 106.
Times Literary Supplement, 23 April 1999, 21.
Wall Street Journal, 8 January 1999, W10.
Wall Street Journal, 19 March 1999, W13.
Washington Post Book World, 17 January 1999, 1.

OTHER SECONDARY SOURCES

Abbott, E. C., and Helena Huntington Smith. *We Pointed Them North: Recollections of a Cowpuncher*. Norman: University of Oklahoma Press, 1955.

Allmendinger, Blake. *The Cowboy: Representations of Labor in an American Work Culture*. New York: Oxford University Press, 1992.

Atherarn, Robert G. *The Mythic West in Twentieth Century America*. Lawrence: University of Kansas Press, 1986.

Bucco, Martin. *Western American Literary Criticism*. Boise: Idaho State University Press, 1984.

Carr, Nick. *The Western Pulp Hero: An Investigation into the Psyche of an American Legend*. Mercer Island, WA: Starmont House, 1989.

Cawelti, John G. *Six-Gun Mystique*. 2nd edition. Bowling Green, OH: Bowling Green University Popular Press, 1984.

Cuddon, J. A., ed. *The Penguin Dictionary of Literary Terms and Literary Theory*, 3rd ed. London: 1992.

Davis, David Brion. "Ten-Gallon Hero." *The American Experience*, ed. Hennig Cohen. Boston: Houghton-Mifflin, 1968, 30ff.

Dinan, John A. *The Pulp Western: A Popular History of the Western Fiction Magazine in America*. San Bernardino, CA: Borgo Press, 1983.

Drew, Bernard A. *Western Series and Sequels*. New York: Garland, 1993.

Etulain, Richard W., and N. Jill Howard, eds. *A Bibliographical Guide to the Study of Western American Literature*. Albuquerque: University of New Mexico Press, 1995.

Foner, Eric, and John A. Garraty, eds. *The Reader's Companion to American History*. Boston: Houghton Mifflin, 1991.

Haley, J. Evetts. *Charles Goodnight: Cowman and Plainsman*. Norman: University of Oklahoma Press, 1949.

Hamilton, Cynthia S. *Western and Hard-Boiled Detective Fiction in America: From High Noon to Midnight*. Iowa City: University of Iowa Press, 1987.

Keating, Bern. *An Illustrated History of the Texas Rangers*. Chicago: Rand McNally, 1975.

Lukacs, Georg. *The Historical Novel*. Boston: Beacon Press, 1962; rpt. Lincoln: University of Nebraska Press, 1983. Trans. from German.

Manzoni, Alessandro. *On the Historical Novel*. Lincoln: University of Nebraska Press, 1984. Trans. from Italian.

Mason, Julian. "Owen Wister." *Dictionary of Literary Biography: American Novelists 1910–1945*. Vol. 9, ed. James J. Martine. Detroit: Gale, 1981, 166–72.

Milton, John R. *The Novel of the American West*. Lincoln: University of Nebraska Press, 1980.

Mitchell, Lee Clark. *Westerns: Making the Man in Fiction and Film*. Chicago: University of Chicago Press, 1996.

Sadler, Geoff. *Twentieth Century Western Writers*. 2nd ed. Chicago: St. James, 1991.

Slotkin, Richard. *Gunfighter Nation: The Myth of the Frontier in Twentieth Century America*. New York: Atheneum, 1992.

Sonnichsen, C. L. *From Hopalong to Hud: Thoughts on Western Fiction*. College Station: Texas A&M University Press, 1978.

Steele, Phillip W. *The Last Cherokee Warriors: Zeke Proctor, Ned Christie*. Grutna, LA: Pelican, 1989.

Taylor, J. Golden, ed. *A Literary History of the American West*. Fort Worth: Texas Christian University Press, 1987.

Tompkins, Jane P. *West of Everything: The Inner Life of Westerns*. New York: Oxford University Press, 1992.

Utley, Robert Marshall. *Billy the Kid: A Short and Violent Life*. Lincoln: University of Nebraska Press, 1989.

Veeser, H. Aram, ed. *The New Historicism*. London: Routledge, 1989.

Wallis Michael. *Pretty Boy—The Life and Times of Charles Arthur Floyd*. New York: St. Martin's Press, 1992.

———. *The New Historicism Reader*. London: Routledge, 1989.

Webb, Walter Prescott. *The Texas Rangers: A Century of Frontier Defense*. New
    York: Houghton Mifflin, 1935; rpt. University of Texas Press, 1935; 2nd
    edition, 1965.
Western Literature Association. *A Literary History of the American West*. Fort
    Worth: Texas Christian University Press, 1987.

Websites

Bywater, Roger. "The Death(s) of Billy the Kid." Kamloops Art Gallery. *http://
    www.galleries.bc.ca/kamloops/bywater.html* (22 May 1999).
Charles "Pretty Boy" Floyd. *http://www.geocities.com/capitolhill/lobby/3935* (9 June
    1999).
Contemporary Authors. http://www.galenet.gale.com/m/mcp/metacgi (4 June 1997).
Goldman, Steve. "Billy the Kid." *http://www.invsn.com/lhaney/refkid.htm* (22 May
    1999).
Lanham, Fritz. "Rice University Buys McMurtry Collection." *http://www.chron.
    com/content/chronicle/ae/books/9899/12/06/1210mcmurtry.html* (13 January
    1999).
"Myths and Facts About Billy the Kid." *http://www.nmia.com/~btkog/myths.htm* (22
    May 1999).
"Old West Gravesites-Ned Christie." *http://www.dimensional.com/~sgrimm/
    christie.htm* (10 June 1999).
"People in the West: William Frederick Cody, Buffalo Bill." The West Film Project
    and WETA. *http://www.3.pbs.org/weta/thewest/wpages/wpgs400/w403__cod.htm*
    (22 May 1999).
"Pretty Boy Floyd." *Time* (22 October 1934). *http://www.geocities.com/nashville/
    3448/pretty.html* (9 June 1999).
Webb, Michael. "Pretty Boy Floyd's Visit to the Gateway City." *http://www.
    qns.com/~dcordry/floyd.html* (9 June 1999).
West, Jared. "Virtual Photo Album: Portrait of Ned Christie." *http://www.
    ripon.edu/faculty/nicoletti/west.html* (9 June 1999).

Index

About the Author

JOHN M. REILLY is Professor of English and Director of the Graduate Program at Howard University. He is the author of *Tony Hillerman: A Critical Companion* (Greenwood, 1996) and an editor of *The Oxford Companion to Crime and Mystery Writing* (1999). His work on Popular Culture has earned him the George Dove Award from the Popular Culture Association, and his numerous publications on African American Writers have been recognized with a citation from the Society for the Study of the Multi-Ethnic Literature of the U.S. (MELUS) for distinguished scholarship in ethnic literature.

Critical Companions to Popular Contemporary Writers
Second Series

Rudolfo A. Anaya *by Margarite Fernandez Olmos*

Maya Angelou *by Mary Jane Lupton*

Louise Erdrich *by Lorena L. Stookey*

Ernest J. Gaines *by Karen Carmean*

John Irving *by Josie P. Campbell*

Jamaica Kincaid *by Lizabeth Paravisini-Gebert*

Barbara Kingsolver *by Mary Jean DeMarr*

Terry McMillan *by Paulette Richards*

Toni Morrison *by Missy Dehn Kubitschek*

Amy Tan *by E. D. Huntley*

Anne Tyler *by Paul Bail*

Leon Uris *by Kathleen Shine Cain*

Critical Companions to Popular Contemporary Writers
First Series—*also available on CD-ROM*

V. C. Andrews
by E. D. Huntley

Tom Clancy
by Helen S. Garson

Mary Higgins Clark
by Linda C. Pelzer

Arthur C. Clarke
by Robin Anne Reid

James Clavell
by Gina Macdonald

Pat Conroy
by Landon C. Burns

Robin Cook
by Lorena Laura Stookey

Michael Crichton
by Elizabeth A. Trembley

Howard Fast
by Andrew Macdonald

Ken Follett
by Richard C. Turner

John Grisham
by Mary Beth Pringle

James Herriot
by Michael J. Rossi

Tony Hillerman
by John M. Reilly

John Jakes
by Mary Ellen Jones

Stephen King
by Sharon A. Russell

Dean Koontz
by Joan G. Kotker

Robert Ludlum
by Gina Macdonald

Anne McCaffrey
by Robin Roberts

Colleen McCullough
by Mary Jean DeMarr

James A. Michener
by Marilyn S. Severson

Anne Rice
by Jennifer Smith

Tom Robbins
*by Catherine E. Hoyser and Lorena
Laura Stookey*

John Saul
by Paul Bail

Erich Segal
by Linda C. Pelzer

Gore Vidal
by Susan Baker and Curtis S. Gibson